The New Americans
Recent Immigration and American Society

Edited by
Carola Suárez-Orozco and Marcelo Suárez-Orozco

A Series from LFB Scholarly

Responding to Immigration
Perceptions of Promise and Threat

Brian N. Fry

LFB Scholarly Publishing LLC
New York 2001

Copyright © 2001 by LFB Scholarly Publishing LLC

Library of Congress Cataloging-in-Publication Data

Fry, Brian N.
 Responding to immigration : perceptions of promise and threat / Brian N. Fry.
  p. cm. -- (The new Americans)
 Includes bibliographical references (p.   ) and index.
 ISBN 1-931202-14-1
 1. United States--Emigration and immigration--Government policy. 2. Immigrants--Government policy--United States. 3. Nativism. I. Title. II. New Americans (LFB Scholarly Publishing LLC)
 JV6483 .F79 2001
  325.73--dc21
                              2001002027

ISBN 1-931202-14-1

Printed on acid-free 250-year-life paper.

Manufactured in the United States of America.

Table of Contents

v

List of Tables

List of Figures

Acknowledgements

I wish to thank Rubén Rumbaut, my advisor, for sharing his knowledge, imagination, and time with me. Few advisors call their advisees during Christmas break to assist them with their first grant proposal or leave their office three hours late because one of their students had a "quick question" about immigration. His sociological rigor and keen insights greatly improved the design and presentation of this research. I am sincerely grateful on all accounts. Steve Gold directed me to important sources and pressed me to write more clearly. He helped me to ask the right questions and develop a research design to answer them. Maxine Baca Zinn led me to specify the structural basis for contemporary nativism and steered me through a dizzying maze of race research. Marilyn Aronoff introduced me to the art and science of interviewing and taught me, by way of example, to appreciate (and utilize) the richness of interview data.

Special thanks go to Tom Kuecker. He read and reread every chapter I sent him, and listened patiently to my ideas and discoveries. Thanks to Tom, I usually reminisce about graduate school with a smile. His friendship is priceless. Thanks also to Sok Be and Jody Fry for helping me transcribe some of the interviews. The Department of Sociology and Graduate School also deserve mention, as they provided me with some seed money to attend three conferences.

My parents—Harvey and Barb Fry and Dave and Gayle Deur—supported me from beginning to end, but only my wife Jody knows about all of the stuff in the middle. On some days, her patience and love were the only things brightening up our apartment. Few spouses are as understanding as she, and I thank her for it.

CHAPTER 1
Introduction

Does international migration undermine the well-being and progress of host countries, as some people argue, or is the problem the reactions of those who express such views? Should waves of workers, family members, and refugees be regarded with alarm or are migration flows a benign outcome of economic interdependence, emerging markets, foreign policies, risk management strategies, and transnational communities (e.g., see Gold 1997; Massey 1998; Sassen 1996; Weiner 1997)? Conflicting answers to these questions occasion little surprise because they originate on different planes of consideration and travel through divergent worldviews. But these arguments are predicated on the assumption that international migration is a public matter, an issue demanding government intervention (LeMay 1994).

For some, the problem is borders and their guardians. They reason that international migration is only international because humans have erected national boundaries. If people were only more tolerant and less xenophobic, and governments not so preoccupied with jurisdiction, borders could be swept into the dustbin of history. For others, the problem is international migration. They argue that immigration endangers the culture, economy, environment, polity, and/or national security of receiving countries. Is the problem a matter of perception and unwarranted apprehension or is international migration a destabilizing element in national and international relations? Is immigration a crisis or a management problem (e.g., see Sassen 1996; Weiner 1995)?

Dichotomizing the complexity of international migration returns simplistic answers, but this contrast captures the polarized character of the debate over immigration. The purpose of this book is not to assess the myriad of empirical and moral arguments presented for and against the continuation of current U.S. immigration and immigrant policies, but to examine immigration reform—*intentional actions designed to*

1

produce or prevent change in immigration realities. In many instances, these efforts are regarded as "nativist," illegitimate native reactions to immigrants. The decision to lodge the *process* of immigration reform, and the *perception* of these actions, under one analytical roof is grounded in this reality.

Arguments about immigration reform are often arguments about legitimacy (Bosniak 1997). Is it "right" to restrict noncitizens from federal and state means-tested programs? Should the needs of the host country or the needs of migrants be the primary criterion for admission? Is migration selectivity discriminatory? Can national borders be justified? (e.g., Carens 1997; Gibney 1997; Massey 1998; U.S. Commission on Immigration Reform 1997; Weiner 1997)? Wrangling over the effectiveness of public policy and the national interest repeatedly raises questions of legitimacy: Are these policies constitutional? Do they contradict international protocol? Are they "un-American," "nativist," humane, or just? Observing this phenomena in the past and present, and interviewing individuals involved in immigration reform, highlights the core of this controversy and deepens our understanding of the people who contribute, directly and indirectly, to American immigration and immigrant policies.

Research Issues

Contemporary analyses of American nativism are primarily guided by three "orientations." These orientations are not analytical models (which are discussed in the next chapter) but are "analytical threads" woven into more comprehensive and more complex interpretations of nativist phenomena. Each perspective explains the emergence of immigration reform, or more specifically, nativism, in a different manner.

The first "thread," or orientation, basically equates nativism with immigration restriction and/or the reduction of immigrant "rights." In many cases, this assumption clears the way for analyses brimming with motive imputation and moral indictments instead of empirical research. The second orientation focuses on the interaction of economic, social, and political contexts for purposes of comprehending nativist initiatives. In the final analysis, however, this perspective generally ignores the variety of individual perceptions and decisions made within these contexts. The third orientation is the exact opposite of the second approach insofar as it considers the discernment of individual motivations, or more generally, *personal* perceptions and actions, as the key to understanding *social* action. At some point, though, nativism becomes larger than the sum of its parts and develops into a "climate" or collective initiative. The summation of individual attitudes and behaviors cannot fully explain the content, timing, or force of social movements. Elaborating briefly on the content of each orientation is necessary because the model of American nativism developed in the next chapter is designed to hurdle these pitfalls.

Self-evident Nativism

Immigration scholars frequently use the term "nativism" to describe attempts to reduce the number of legal entries and/or redefine state-noncitizen relations in the direction of less rights and benefits for noncitizens. For some researchers, the concept is synonymous with immigration restriction, regardless of the explanation(s) offered in its defense. Other scholars apply the term to restrictionist attitudes and efforts *if* the motives and concerns underlying the preferences and behavior are considered illegitimate in some normative sense (e.g., restricting immigration for racist reasons). For a number of scholars, though, the concept not only refers to restrictionist attitudes and/or behaviors, but also imputes motives to proponents of immigration restriction (e.g., see Sánchez 1997: 1025).

Analyses informed by these perspectives tend to cloud, rather than clarify, our understanding of American nativism, immigrant adaptation, and immigration reform—and the relationship between all three processes—inasmuch as these perspectives tend to rely on one or more of the following assumptions or arguments:

1. Although "nativism" is laden with normative significance and associated with a variety of beliefs and behaviors, the concept is used as if its meaning and importance were self-evident (Bosniak 1997: 279-284). For example, what makes a sentiment "antiforeign" or constitutes a "fear of 'foreignness'" (e.g., see Sánchez 1997: 1018-1020)?

2. It is assumed that reducing immigration levels is nativistic. For example, is the entry of 915,900 legal immigrants in 1996 legitimate, but an annual ceiling of 650,000 legal admission per year illegitimate? On what basis are such designations made?

3. Motives are routinely imputed to "nativists," but rarely, if ever, backed by data. One prevalent assumption is that environmental and economic arguments are surrogates for other, less acceptable rationales, such as racial concerns (e.g. see Johnson 1997: 174).

Establishing the origin of these premises is a complicated undertaking, but they are based upon different worldviews and experiences. Perspectives like these are examined in Chapters 5-7.

Contextual Nativism

The second perspective attributes the occurrence of nativism primarily to demographic and economic contexts, such as increases in immigration and worsening economic conditions (e.g., see Bennett 1995; Calavita 1996; Muller 1997; Perea 1997). In this respect, this perspective is the exact opposite of the third insofar as it examines the contexts in which nativism occurs, but almost completely ignores the perceptions and beliefs of individuals within these contexts—particularly those which diverge from the context(s) being emphasized. Of course, understanding a certain phenomenon requires a thorough understanding of the contexts in which it occurs, but there are at least two potential problems with this line of analysis:

1. Precipitating factors are often treated as causal factors. For example, Calavita contends that California's passage of Proposition 187 was not "simply an instrumental response to economic conditions" or a "purely symbolic measure," but can "best be understood as a particular type of symbolic statement, *the content of which and the motivation for which are grounded in prevailing economic conditions*" (1996: 285, italics added). While economic conditions certainly

precipitated Proposition 187, to what extent did these conditions actually shape and kindle nativist notions or provide people with nativist motives? Even a cursory review of the interviews conducted by journalists reveals a number of concerns which seemingly have little to do with economic conditions (e.g., see Kadetsky 1994). A precipitating factor often gives generalized beliefs immediate substance, but in and of itself, is not the cause of anything. "It must occur in the context of...other determinants" (Smelser 1965: 17). Context is certainly critical to understanding the variety and intensity of nativism at a given locale and time, but overemphasizing its importance can obscure the different motivations people bring to a nativist initiative. Terms like "economic nativism" and "racial nativism" highlight the contextual character of nativism, but at times, this terminology implies cause and effect, and tacitly imputes motives to nativists (e.g., see Bennett 1995). The ironic consequence is that nativistic contexts are often better understood than the very nativists who construct meaning and act within them.

2. By focusing on fairly dramatic circumstances, this orientation seemingly precludes analyses of nativism in less noticeable contexts. Higham recognized this tendency three years after the publication of his now classic, *Strangers in the Land* (1955): "What bothers me most...is that the concept of nativism has proved serviceable only for understanding the extreme and fanatical manifestations of ethnic discord...Nativism owes its significance to this intensity of feeling: and historians, fascinated by the men of passion and moods of alarm, have neglected the less spectacular but more steadily sustained contentions imbedded in the fabric of our social organization" (1958: 151). The social and legal foundations of American nativism (primarily citizenship and immigration and immigrant policies) are often neglected when researchers examine nativism as overt behavior. For example, Bonilla-Silva (1997) notes that subtle expressions of racism, and the rational foundations upon which racial practices commonly rest, are frequently forgotten by scholars who examine racism as an overt, irrational behavior.

To what extent have social scientists resorted to motive imputation and identity politics because they have not been examining the institutional foundations upon which the ideas of race and nation rest?

The challenge is to analyze social phenomena without losing sight of the people who manufacture meaning and act upon ideas in different contexts—a difficult undertaking when the broader social context is only considered.

Attitudinal Nativism

The third orientation pinpoints the attitudes, perceptions, prejudices, and stereotypes of the American populace as a way of understanding American nativism. There is little doubt that perceptions of threat (e.g., economic anxiety or "the browning of America") and intergroup attitudes are linked to a broad range of behaviors (e.g., the recurring push to exclude legal and illegal immigrants from social welfare programs). However, there are at least two problems with this kind of analysis:

1. The attitudes and perceptions related to nativist attitudes and behaviors are usually assumed. By specifying the relevant variables beforehand, the explanations offered by such projects are limited to the researchers' assumptions about relevant attitudes and perceptions. The informal hypotheses are rarely, if ever, based on interviews with "nativists," but are presuppositions about the values, beliefs, and perceptions of "nativists."

2. Collective actions (e.g., the passage of Proposition 187) are, at times, almost entirely analyzed in terms of individual attitudes and beliefs (e.g., see Johnson, Farrell, and Guinn 1997). Even when American attitudes toward U.S. immigration levels and immigrant populations are correlated with micro-level *and* *aggregate* factors (e.g., economic conditions), the implicit assumption is that restrictionist sentiments can be understood by examining *individual* perceptions (e.g. see Espenshade and

Hempstead 1996). Not withstanding the long-standing attitude-behavior consistency debate, the sum total of individual attitudes and perceptions cannot always account for the prevalence of ideas, perceptions, or behaviors. Consideration of the broader social context is imperative.

For example, the legislation proposed by Representative Lamar Smith and Senator Alan Simpson to simultaneously crackdown on illegals and cut *legal* immigration by approximately 40 percent seemed assured in early 1996. But six months later, legal immigration was left basically untouched, largely because a coalition of expansionist organizations convinced journalists and public officials that illegal immigration should be distinguished from legal immigration. The idea to "split the bill" originated in a strategy meeting[1] and was successfully promoted by a powerful coalition—even though public opinion polls indicated that U.S. citizens desired reductions in legal and illegal immigration (Heilemann 1996; Johnson, Farrell, and Guinn 1997). A plethora of advocacy organizations, lobbyists, and politicians shape—and at times, generate and implement—ideas that are not necessarily embraced by the body politic.

Each orientation contributes to our understanding of American nativism. However, these orientations belong to more comprehensive models of American nativism. These analytical frameworks organize the social traffic converging at the intersection of social structure, values, beliefs, and behaviors. The relationship between ideas and the material world is unclear and no model of human behavior enjoys unquestioned acceptance, but the review of analytical models in Chapter 2 is designed to clarify the connection between ideas and

---

[1] This analysis is informed by Heilemann's (1996) study of the political coalitions and elected officials active in the 1996 immigration debates and based upon interviews I conducted with immigration activists in the spring and summer of 1997. A prominent expansionist recalled the strategy meeting where he and other expansionists decided to try splitting the bill: "[We] said 'No...let's distinguish legal from illegal immigration as a way to thwart the momentum of the restrictionists as a way of clarifying the debate and then we're in a stronger position both to defend legal immigration and to debate the right ways to deal with illegal immigration.'"

structural arrangements. Before reviewing the contents of this and other chapters, however, it is important to examine some of the ambiguous and controversial concepts used in immigration research and the immigration debate.

Choosing Sides by Choosing Terms

In partisan issues "a choice of words is a choice of sides" (Luker 1985: 2). The vocabularies of government officials, immigration activists, journalists, and researchers routinely disclose their opinions of immigration and the United States' management of it. The entry of *illegal* aliens should presumably be *impeded*, but the status of *undocumented* aliens, who also entered the United States surreptitiously, should apparently be *regularized* (Weiner 1995). Should immigrants be accommodated, assimilated, incorporated, or integrated? And the people who use these terms—are they immigration enthusiasts or immigration critics, xenophiles or xenophobes, pro-immigrant or anti-immigrant, "open borders" supporters or nativists (e.g., Brimelow 1996; Perea 1997)? When used indiscriminately, this terminology obscures an already complex set of phenomena.

Expansionists and Restrictionists

In this book, individuals and organizations proposing lower immigration levels are referred to as restrictionists whereas those seeking to maintain or increase immigration levels are referred to as expansionists.[2] The terms are used literally and figuratively. In comparison to replacement-level immigration or net emigration, current immigration levels are expansive. The continuation of today's policies expands the U.S. population and rate of population growth. Comparatively, the restriction of present policies reduces the U.S.

---

[2] These signifiers were suggested to me an interviewee, and are discussed in Chapters 5-7.

population and growth rate (e.g., see Beck 1994; Edmonston and Passel 1994).[3]

Expansionists contend that current immigration levels, relative to the U.S. population, are not high by U.S. historical standards. Restrictionists argue that current immigration levels, in absolute numbers, are historically high. Both sides are correct. It is not the disagreement, however, that unsettles restrictionists and expansionists, but the conclusions drawn from the data, which disturb them. Proponents of restriction are persuaded that "absolute numbers matter—absolutely" (Brimelow 1996: 37) and expansionists are convinced that immigrant arrivals, as a percentage of the U.S. population, is "the most relevant measure of the impact of immigrants on our culture, infrastructure, and labor markets..." (*Cato Handbook For Congress* 1997: 315). While neither side is likely to agree with the other's assessment, the immigration levels for which they advocate are, if nothing else, higher and lower, respectively, than that of their counterpart.

There is also the issue of *immigrant* reform. Legal distinctions between citizens and non-citizens is probably the most obvious example. In general, most expansionists disapprove of recent attempts to further restrict the number of programs and benefits available to noncitizens. Most restrictionists seemingly approve of these measures, although some argue that such initiatives are inappropriate and ignore the real issues of immigration and population control.

In a figurative sense, expansionists and restrictionists also view the impact of immigrants on the economy, population and culture of the United States in terms of expansion and restriction. For example, restrictionists generally see the economy in zero-sum terms. Immigrants entering the labor force compete with native-born workers for a fixed number of jobs, thereby restricting the opportunities of American citizens and residents. Expansionists, on the other hand, visualize an expanding economy. American opportunities are expanded by immigrants: jobs that would have otherwise been lost are retained and new jobs are created. These representations are not

---

[3] For a systematic analysis of assumptions (e.g., fertility, mortality, immigration, emigration, etc.) employed in population projections, see Edmonston and Passel (1994).

flawless, but less ideological than conventional depictions: anti-immigrant, pro-immigrant, nativist, and pro-open borders (e.g., see Brimelow 1996: 11-15; Muller 1997). Generalizations pertaining to the economy, culture, and population are explored in greater detail in Chapters 5-7.

Nativism

The word "nativism" was selected for reasons of consistency and relative neutrality. First, an entire body of work exists under the subject heading of nativism. The literature is replete with untested assumptions and unanswered questions which ultimately served as the impetus for this research project. Secondly, I have found the term "nativism," as a matter of inquiry, to be rather inoffensive. Restrictionists interviewed for this study generally did not object to its negative connotation or my use of the term. This may be surprising, but when restrictionists learned of my interest in nativism, they often recommended books on the subject and, at times, expressed their interest in, and concern with, the issue. In fact, restrictionists often argue that their policies will help neutralize nativist backlash (Bosniak 1997: 280).

A number of restrictionists view American nativism as a brief blip on America's radar screen, an overzealous movement to bridle the behavior of immigrants and Catholics in the mid-1800s (see Chapter 4 for details). Because nativism is something that *happened*, some restrictionists seemingly think it is impossible to be guilty of something which no longer *happens*. Expansionists, of course, may question this, but the important point is this: restrictionists do not see themselves as nativists and therefore do not conclude that a study of American nativism necessarily includes them.

The term "immigration reform" is not substituted for "nativism" because the process of immigration reform connotes a wider array of actions and attitudes. As explained in Chapter 2, "nativism" is a better descriptor of illegitimate behavior. The first half of this book primarily focuses on nativism and the second half on immigration reform. The two processes separate at the point of legitimacy—immigration reform is deemed legitimate and nativism considered illegitimate—but they are similar to the extent that each process leaves an indelible mark on immigration and immigrant policies.

The Importance of Immigration Reform

Concerns pertaining to international migration reemerged in the early 1970s. Since then, the unease has only grown. Developed and developing countries regularly expel guest workers, redirect refugee flows, curb legal and illegal entries, and delimit citizenship (Papademetriou and Hamilton 1996; Weiner 1995). The apprehension is not universally experienced or executed, as the global dimensions of the migratory processes are uneven and changing, but remains a transformative force in national and international relations.

National Dimensions

One critical dimension of the incorporation process is established by national governments as they influence migration decisions and look to diverse membership models (from assimilation to multiculturalism) to integrate immigrants and their children. While immigration laws and membership rights are only two dimensions of a multidimensional process, they constitute one of the most critical contexts of reception influencing the incorporation of immigrants and their descendants into the United States (Portes and Rumbaut 1996: 84-92; Soysal 1994).

The policies designed to manage immigration often engender unforeseeable consequences. For example, the unprecedented rush toward citizenship in the last few years has been attributed to restrictive measures, particularly California's Proposition 187, the 1996 *Personal Responsibility And Work Opportunity Reconciliation Act and Illegal Immigration Reform and Immigrant Responsibility Act*. Restrictionist in intent, these strategies have backfired. In trying to reduce the presumed lure of social benefits, Congress unintentionally created more immigration by widening the gap between citizens and noncitizens, thereby encouraging naturalization. Unlike family members of legal noncitizen immigrants, the spouses and minor children of naturalized immigrants can immediately enter the United States outside of established quotas. "Thus, each new person that becomes a U.S. citizen creates more people entitled to immigrate to the United States without numerical restriction and new classes of people entitled to come in under numerically limited categories" (Massey 1998). These actions have also been associated with the political right and apparently persuaded many of the newly naturalized to affiliate with the Democratic party (Booth 1996; McDonnell 1996). Notwithstanding these outcomes, one wonders what other kinds of consequences might follow. When immigrants are "coerced" into becoming citizens, how will they view their newfound status—as an invitation to participate in the civic culture or as an insurance policy against future measures?

International Dimensions

In settling questions of admittance, enforcement, and incorporation, government practices are a potential item in international relations. When governments violate the human rights of their citizens, fail to quell civil unrest, or generally create conditions conducive to emigration, people are apt to cross national boundaries. When they do so, receiving countries generally conclude they have the right to intervene in the affairs of the sending country. In 1994, the U.S. occupation of Haiti and negotiations with Cuba were both provoked, in part, by migration flows. What were once regarded as national affairs are now considered international issues (Mitchell 1992; Rumbaut 1996: 28; Sassen 1996; Weiner 1995: 14-15; 1997: 188-90).

Even larger in scope, the immigration policies formulated in highly developed countries like the United States regularly conflict with other major policy frameworks and human rights regimes and codes (Sassen 1996). The North American Free Trade Agreement (NAFTA) attempts to create border-free economic spaces, but does not foresee a proportional opening of labor markets. Much like colonial and neo-colonial bonds, economic links simultaneously invite the movement of capital *and* people. Formulating immigration policy as if it were a strictly national matter can, and does, lead to detrimental consequences for citizens and migrants alike (Massey 1998: 22-27; Sassen 1996: 74-88). Women are especially susceptible to changes in immigration policy because legal immigration to the U.S. has—for much of the past 50 years—been predominantly female (Fitzpatrick 1997).

National states are also increasingly accountable to international agreements and human rights codes. The tight linkage between citizenship and human rights has been expanded as national governments are increasingly expected to observe international instruments and conventions which confer rights on *persons* instead of citizens (Kerber 1997; Sassen 1996).[4] By disregarding international codes, this "ecumenism of human rights" (Berger 1997), nation-states undermine their own legitimacy and jeopardize relations with other states (Sassen 1996; Weiner 1997).

National and international processes must be understood relationally. The formulation and reformulation of immigration policy is a strategic research site for examining the tension between notions of state sovereignty and human rights, the preservation of national sovereignty and safeguarding of human lives and prerogatives (Sassen 1996: 60-63). A comprehensive understanding of immigration reform (intentional actions designed to produce or prevent change in current immigration realities) requires that current efforts be clearly defined and historically situated. It also requires an understanding of the worldviews (constructed from interviews and publications) which fundamentally incite and interpret today's contexts and changes. Knowing why people become involved in immigration reform and understanding the meanings they attach to immigration is of practical and theoretical significance. Ultimately, this book redefines nativism by examining the historical record and reconstructing the worldviews of immigration activists.

Book Plan and Approach

As noted earlier, immigration scholars and journalists often use the term "nativism" to describe and analyze events they deem "anti-immigrant," but the concept is often used as if its meaning is obvious (Bosniak 1997). Efforts to reduce immigration flows and/or the advantages of permanent residency are often characterized as "nativist" or "nativistic" by those who oppose such initiatives, but on what basis? The answer to this question is explored in Chapters 2 and 3 by

---

[4] Examples include the 1950 European Convention on Human Rights, 1969 American Convention on Human Rights, 1975 Helsinki Accords, and 1990 UN International Convention on the Protection of the Rights of All Migrant Workers and Members of Their Families.

uncovering the constitutive properties of the process, examining their historical and social underpinnings, and arranging their interrelations into a plausible definition. Designed to demystify the phenomena of American nativism, the proposed definition integrates empirical and evaluative observations into one coherent process.

Chapter 3 identifies the constitutive properties of nativism by comparing the multifarious reactions confronted by immigrants and their descendants throughout the history of American nativism. These observations are incorporated into the definition of nativism introduced in Chapter 2, but the conditions associated with nativist initiatives are primarily examined at this juncture. This investigation does not systematically analyze every occurrence of American nativism, but places some of the more infamous events into one of three nativist eras: religious nativism (1600-1859), racial and radical nativism (1860-1929), and wartime nativism and emerging anxieties (1930-1998). These phases are not discrete, but organize events according to the prevailing interests and concerns typically sighted during these times.

In Chapter 4, the central questions of this study are reiterated. They are: What is American nativism?, Under what conditions does heightened nativist activity occur? and What does immigration mean to people involved in immigration reform? The multiple research methods used to explore these questions are delineated, as are the assumptions and perspectives that contributed to the overall design of this investigation. The specifics of historical-comparative and field research methods are fully described, particularly the semi-structured interviews and analysis of written and visual records. This overview will explain the methodological and theoretical rationale behind the interviews and describe the interview settings, recruitment procedures, format, and respondent pool.

In terms of methodological technique this research is a mixture of grounded theory (Strauss 1991) and the extended case method (Burawoy et al. 1991). My analysis of American nativism is largely built upon (or *grounded* in) the data I have collected. Because theory develops during the process of data collection (Strauss 1991: 23), this approach provided the kind of flexibility needed for exploratory research. However, unlike the grounded theory approach, I do not seek generalizations across diverse social situations (see Burawoy et al. 1991: 275-76), nor do I develop an analysis of American nativism by relying exclusively on micro-level observations. Rather, I contrast phenomena, organizations, and interview data for the purpose of better understanding nativistic contexts and the people promoting and opposing these circumstances. I use these observations to *build* theory and *reconstruct* existing analyses in the final chapter. In line with the extended case method, I have tried to uncover the "macro foundations of a microsociology" (Burawoy 1991: 282) without ignoring the micro-level interactions that ultimately contribute, in ways rarely specified, to social structures.

Chapters 5 and 6 examine the people and organizations involved in immigration reform. Interviews with expansionists and restrictionists, along with a content analysis of immigration reform agency documents and archives, illuminates the major issues dividing immigration reform activists. Interviews with immigration advocates furthers our understanding of what immigration means to them and the roles they play in shaping public policy and opinion. These chapters, along with Chapter 3, deepen our understanding of immigrant reception and immigration reform, which revolve on an axis of politics where there is no clear liberal or conservative position. Rather, the worldviews of advocates are distinguished by, among other factors, their different visions of immigrants, natural resources, human nature, the nation-state and globalism.

In light of the historical and interview data, the definition of American nativism proposed in Chapter 2 will be critically examined in Chapter 7. The interplay between meaning systems, social context, and social structures is explored. Consulting expansionists and restrictionists, and grounding their perspectives in various institutions (e.g., citizenship and national sovereignty), social locations, and unique experiences, provides a nuanced analysis of nativism relatively free of the grand abstractions where people are objectified and social structures reified. A preliminary attempt to explain nativism is suggested and compared to explanations offered by other scholars.

In sum, the proposed research aims to reconceptualize the concept of nativism for the purpose of *exploring* and *explaining* how and why nativism occurs in the United States. Multiple research methods are used to examine the conditions under which heightened nativist activity occurs and understand why some people become collectively involved in organized efforts to reform current immigration and immigrant policies. Using historical-comparative methods, the basic elements of nativist reactions are identified and developed into a set of criteria for comparing varied cases of immigrant reception. Interviews with individuals who promote and oppose immigration restriction in the United States, along with a provisional content analysis of immigration reform agency documents and archives, furthers our understanding of what immigration means to immigration activists and the roles they play in shaping public policy and opinion. The collected data are analyzed in order to develop a conceptual scheme for examining the different discourses, beliefs, and behaviors of immigration activists, and will be compared to dominant perspectives on nativism and intergroup hostility.

CHAPTER 2
The Discourse and Social Organization of Nativism

The term "nativism" simultaneously signifies what behavior is and what it should be. It is used to designate certain attitudes and actions as undeserving of consideration (Bosniak 1997). But it also describes a process. The normative assumptions underpinning this classification process are incorporated into a sociological definition of American nativism. Using social expectations to delimit the basic parameters of nativism promotes an interpretation relatively free of personal judgments by emphasizing social, rather than personal, standards.

To this end, four analytical models (nationalism, resource competition, prejudice, and group position) of American nativism will be reviewed. Each model envisions different motivational systems and circumstances in explaining the emergence of nativist phenomena. To varying degrees, all four perspectives combine ideological and structural points of view. However, the group position model supplies the most satisfactory micro-macro linkage by placing national identities and perceptions of threat within the legal and social contexts of native advantage.[5]

Parts of this framework are used to connect the discourse and social organization of American nativism. The legal basis of nativism is established by national constitutions and treaty law (Habermas 1996; Sassen 1996: 64-67), which in turn secure their legitimacy by extending de facto recognition to national sovereignty. While international law and transnational realities increasingly circumscribe the exercise of sovereign power (Appadurai 1996; Soysal 1994; Sassen 1996; Weiner 1997), the principles of national sovereignty and national interest

---

[5] Analyses of racial phenomena, especially by Blumer (1958), Bonilla-Silva (1997), Collins (1991), Cornell (1996), Omi and Winant (1994), Wellman (1994), and Winant (1994; 1997) have informed my analysis of native phenomena and been adapted to the exigencies of American nativism.

currently serve as the final arbiters of appropriate and inappropriate conduct with respect to immigration reform. In addition to other values and beliefs, these principles inform our conventional understandings of where immigration reform ends and nativism begins, and generally serve to structure the discourse over immigration reform (Bosniak 1997: 285).

Examining Nativism

Because nativism is associated with a variety of beliefs and behaviors, its meaning is imprecise. Scholars have used the term to denote, among other things, hostility towards immigrants and aspiring immigrants, the aversion to "foreign" religions and "foreign" peoples, the defense of cultural values, and efforts to protect America from "foreigners" residing in the U.S. (e.g., see Beck 1992; Bennett 1995; Bergquist 1986; Billington 1963; Bosniak 1997; Higham 1992; Leonard and Parmet 1971). One *variety* of nativism, that based on considerations of race and ethnicity, is "unquestionably the most common" today, in both the scholarly literature and everyday usage (Bosniak 1997: 282).

Nativism is generally associated with immigration and immigrants, but has also been used to analyze events in which native-born Americans were perceived and/or treated as "aliens" in some sense. The word "alien," which generally suggests that someone is "not of one's own," incorporates all of these connotations and is used here to underscore this perception. As Sartre points out, contrastive identities are more than simple categories. They are also *passions* because they tells us who we are by telling us who we are not. "Others" are a "pretext" for our identities. "By adhering to antisemitism, he is not only adopting an opinion, he is choosing himself as a person" (1947: 177-78). Using the example of an antisemite, Sartre explains: "The Jews existence simply allows the antisemite to nip his anxieties in the bud by persuading himself that his place has always been cut out in the world, that it was waiting for him and that by virtue of tradition he has the right to occupy it" (1947: 178).

The descriptions and illustrations used in this chapter generally refer to immigrants because the foreign-born usually bear the brunt of nativist initiatives. This decision rests on the assumption that nativism suggests a posture towards immigration and immigrants, towards resident immigrants and those seeking permanent residence. The original meaning of nativism may or may not conform to this connotation (e.g., see Beck 1992; 1994: 131-32), but this is inconsequential compared to the inferences developed by individuals (Beck 1992: 147-48).

Developing a definition of nativism, and assessing its historical and contemporary "fit," is manageable when one is familiar with the perspective(s) from which it originated. The following review examines some of these explanations and lays the groundwork for the definition of nativism proposed later in the chapter. Each approach leads to a different understanding and evaluation of the people and actions being characterized as "nativist."

Four Models

Analyses of nativism often resemble those applied to ethnic processes and interethnic relations. For instance, scholars interpret nativism as a response to perceived group threat or locate nativist hostility in individual prejudices and stereotypes (Bobo and Hutchings 1996). Because nativist activities are usually interpreted after their occurrence, the models and theories used to examine them seem plausible, if not perfect. These interpretations are not mutually exclusive. In fact, scholars of nativism often use more than one model to analyze nativist phenomena. They frequently explain the occurrence of nativism by relying on one or more of the following analytical frameworks: (1) nationalism, (2) resource competition, (3) prejudice, and/or (4) group position. This restricted survey of theories inevitably overlooks other perspectives, such as world systems theory (Balibar and Wallerstein 1991), colonialism theories (Blauner 1972), and split-labor market theories (Bonacich 1980), but includes some of the more common approaches.

Before delving into the specifics of each model, three caveats are in order. First, there are a number of variants for each model. Consequently, to speak of a "nationalism model" is misleading to the extent that there is no single nationalism model used by scholars to examine nativism. Other scholars have, and would, most likely identify other approaches and take issue with the content of the models I have outlined here (e.g., see Bergquist 1986). Second, each scholar's work is pigeonholed to some extent. Nativism scholars tend to draw on multiple models throughout their analyses, but in order to simplify the discussion, I have tried to fix upon each scholar's *primary* interpretation. Third, the perspectives of each researcher were undoubtedly shaped by the events they examined and the historical circumstances surrounding them. If they had examined other events, they may have used or developed different models to examine and explain their occurrence. With these qualifications in mind, it is best to first review the two most popular approaches—the nationalism and resource competition models.

Nationalism

Nativism is routinely represented as a variant of American nationalism or as competition for scarce resources. Two factors can partially account for the prevalence of these interpretations. First, the discourse on immigration reform is decidedly *national* and *economic* in content, often referring to cultural and fiscal "costs." The "rhetoric of exclusion" frequently contains arguments about limited resources and national sovereignty (e.g., Chavez 1997; Kawanabe 1996; Knapp 1996). Second, both of these perspectives are utilized in the preeminent work on American nativism, John Higham's *Strangers in the Land* (1992). Although Higham integrated both national ideas and resource competition into his analysis (e.g., see 1992: 53) he generally interpreted nativism as a defensive type of nationalism: "Specific nativistic antagonisms may, and do, vary widely in response to the changing character of minority irritants and the shifting conditions of the day; but through each separate hostility runs the connecting, energizing force of modern nationalism" (Higham 1992: 4; Higham 1958: 150). This perspective, and the definition which fosters it, has been adopted by numerous scholars (e.g., see Friedman 1967; Lane 1987: 21; Perea 1997: 1).

This has been especially true of historians, who often apply Higham's approach by connecting nativism to the nationalist pendulum of American interests and fears. For example, the increasing political strength of immigrant groups and job competition were partly responsible for the rise of the Know Nothings in the 1850s, but, according to Michael Holt, largely because they were "*regarded as dangerously un-American*" (1973: 327, italics added). In *American Nativism, 1830-1860* (1971), Leonard and Parmet define nativism as an attempt to "safeguard America" from certain perceived threats, and conclude that: "All nativists...regardless of geography or social position, had one thing in common. They were able to identify with a primary belief in 'Americanism'" (pp. 6, 108). In perhaps the most inclusive survey of American nativism, *The Party of Fear: From Nativist Movements to the Far Right in American History* (1995), David Bennett stresses the importance of "un-American" ideas, but like Higham, also attributes the emergence of nativism to "objective" conditions, such as economic competition (1995: xii, 3-12). Bennett concludes, however, that the "nativist tradition passed into history" after World War II, largely because "*un-American*" *ideas* were no longer imputed exclusively to "alien peoples," as illustrated by the anti-communist crusades of the 1940s and 1950s (1995: 278, italics added). By reasoning that the historic break between "un-American" ideas and "foreign" people marked the end of "traditional" nativism, Bennett (1995) seemingly chose to interpret nativism, first and foremost, as a process intensified and sustained by some type of protective nationalism.

This defensive kind of nationalism is the cornerstone of Higham's analysis. His discriminating analysis in *Strangers in the Land* can largely be attributed to a painstaking effort to delimit the concept of nativism. He stressed that ethnocentric reactions to immigrants are not intrinsically nativistic, but "become so only when integrated with a hostile and fearful nationalism" (1992: 24). In an effort to avoid labeling every type of unfriendliness toward immigrants as nativist (1958: 150), Higham defined nativism as "an intense opposition to an internal minority on the ground of its foreign (i.e., 'un-American') connections" (1992: 4). While drawing on ethnocentric and, sometimes, racist ideas, "nativism translates them into a zeal to destroy the enemies of a distinctively American way of life" (1992: 4). He used this approach to identify three nativist themes—anti-Catholic, anti-radical, and racial nativism.

Higham's (1992) analysis of American nativist thought in *Strangers* has seemingly become the standard by which related works are measured (Dinnerstein and Reimers 1986). His definition of nativism, and its continued relevance, has been assessed on numerous occasions, most notably in *The Catholic Historical Review* in 1958, *American Jewish History* in 1986, and at the 1996 Social Science Research Council's Conference on International Migration to the United States. On each occasion, Higham and others re-examined his original formulation, and to all appearances, came to agree on its strengths and weaknesses. In particular, Higham questioned the prominence he assigned to nationalism in conceptualizing nativism (1958: 154; 1992: 342) and considered his treatment of ethnocentrism, and its relationship to nativism, to be the principal shortcoming of his work (1996: 5-6). Whether or not scholars are aware of these reflections, some of their interpretations approximate Higham's original analysis in *Strangers*.

Wimmer interprets nativism and racism as "ways of reassuring the national self and its boundaries, as attempts at making sense of the world in times of crisis" (1997: 27). He argues that certain populations (e.g., immigrants) are regarded as a threat to the national community, particularly by "downwardly mobile groups," because they seemingly interfere with the nation-state's primary responsibility—"namely to look after the well-being of its 'owners'" (pp. 17, 30). Like Bennett (1995) and Higham (1992), Wimmer interprets nativism as a mixture of nationalism and resource competition, but in the end, concludes that aliens are viewed as illegitimate competitors for the state's resources and protection because they do not belong—in the eyes of natives—to the national community (1997: 32).

In his examination of contemporary immigration reform proposals, Chavez interprets nativism as a "nationalist response" to the "transnationalist challenge," sparked by the newest wave of immigration (1997: 73). Chavez argues that natives are not only troubled by the fiscal impacts of immigrants, but by their "races" and cultures as well. Immigrants "undermine the notion of a singular American identity...as the transnational movements of people across borders—both political and cultural—underscore the disorder inherent in the order implied by the fiction of a singular cultural heritage" (1997: 66, 73).

By focusing on *nationalist ideas*, Higham avoided labeling as nativist every reaction against immigrants or immigration, but admittedly slighted underlying *social processes*, such as ethnic integration and resource competition (1958: 150-55). This pitfall was usually avoided by his successors who viewed nativism as an attitude arising from interethnic tensions rather than as an intellectual phenomenon (Bergquist 1986: 128). But Higham's decision to place nationalism at the center of his analysis deserves serious consideration.

Because the touchstone of restrictionist (and expansionist) initiatives are justified as being in the nation's best interest (Light 1996: 59), a certain type of nationalism propels them, or at the very least, is used to legitimate them. This distinction between nationalism as an *impetus* and nationalism as a *vocabulary* is necessary if we are to keep the *influence* of ideas and *usage* of ideas analytically separate. In so doing, one avoids the assumption that people's explanations for their behaviors are the causes of it. Clearly, the forces "behind" an action and the ensuing explanations that are used to justify it are not always the same (Mills 1940). Distinguishing between the *influence* and *usage* of nationalism can be rather complicated, but discerning the *kind* of nationalism underlying a given nativist movement is not as difficult to discern. For example, both restrictionists and expansionists contend that their suggestions for reform are in the national interest. Expansionists, however, define this interest largely in terms of the economy whereas restrictionists generally define it in terms of the environment.

Calhoun makes it clear that nationalism "is not an intrinsically 'bad' ideology," especially when it affirms differences instead of promoting the "pseudo-democracy of sameness" (1994: 25). Light makes a similar point when he contends that the self-interest of the nation-state often requires "it to ignore, dampen, or even suppress popular ethno-chauvinism and racism rather than intensify them" (1996: 59). Just as low immigration initiatives can be nationalistic in that they accentuate the interests of the nation-state, so too can high immigration initiatives be nationalistic when maintaining or increasing "high" immigration levels is seen as being in the nation's best interest (pp. 59-60). Obviously, as Higham made clear in *Strangers*, it is the *kind* of nationalism at work that is decisive.

These observations prompt three critical questions. First, how does one explain the emergence of an exclusive, instead of an inclusive, nationalism (e.g., see Higham 1992: 27)? Second, why do "nativist" arguments *not* "appeal equally to all members of a society" (Wimmer

1997: 31; also see Blumer 1958)? And thirdly, when making distinctions between "they" and "we," why do nativists bank on a national identity rather than one based upon class, religion, gender, age, etc. (Wimmer 1997: 27; also see Basch, Glick Schiller, and Szanton Blanc 1995: 35-45)? The answers to these questions are debated and very complex, but Wimmer's phenomenological approach to interpreting nativism and racism (1997: 27-33)—which is very similar to the nationalism framework outlined here—ventures an explanation characteristic of other nationalism models.

In general, the nationalism model attributes the emergence of nationalist feelings to societal crises. But societal crises do not always provoke an exclusive nationalism, so where does this arrangement of ideas and interests come from? The answer to this question directs us to the third question: why do nativists rely on a nationalistic self-image? Or even more fundamentally, how do people come to see themselves as "natives"? Wimmer (1997), following Benedict Anderson (1994), suggests that certain events in the late 1800s accounted for the emergence of what Anderson calls an "imagined community"— a sovereign, limited, *imagined* political community (1994: 5-7). The national community is imagined "because the members of even the smallest nation will never know most of their fellow-members, meet them, or even hear of them, yet in the minds of each lives the image of their communion" (Anderson 1994: 6). Within this imagined community the "rights of participation and solidarity appear as collective goods of a nation with the state as its guardian" (Wimmer 1997: 28). Over time, access to state power and services were restricted to members of the nation-state, which had the "combined effect of state, culture and territory seeming to belong to members of the nation" (1997: 29). Thus, the state is "owned by the people who have been united into a nation" (p. 29). In the case of the United States, political and social membership has been, and is, circumscribed by considerations of gender, race, nativity, religion, and sexuality (e.g., see Chapter 4).

As indicated above, scholars working within a nationalism framework (with respect to nativism) tend to rely on historical interpretations and discourse analyses to demonstrate the plausibility of their perspectives. Espenshade and Hempstead (1996), however, used quantitative methods to uncover a strong correlation between restrictionist immigration sentiments and isolationist attitudes. While there is no shortage of illustrations, there is admittedly little empirical support for some of the explanations proposed by scholars using a nationalism perspective to interpret nativism, especially as it relates to the *process* of nativism (Wimmer 1997).

Three years after the publication of *Strangers*, Higham published an essay entitled "Another Look at Nativism" and suggested that nativism be viewed as an attitude arising from ethnic integration where competition for resources and prestige arose from interethnic conflict, rather than from irrational myths (1958: 147-52). He observed that the concept of nativism had "proved serviceable only for understanding the extreme and fanatical manifestations of ethnic discord" and thereby neglected the "less spectacular but more steadily sustained contentions imbedded in the fabric of our social organization" (1958: 151). This insight—that *nativism is maintained by a more regular and less striking set of exclusionary ideas and practices*—has been incorporated into other interpretations. Specifically, resource competition models tend to emphasize exclusionary *practices*, while the nationalism, prejudice and symbolic interactionism models regularly focus on exclusionary *ideas*.

Resource Competition

Theories of native-alien competition are comparable to competition theories of ethnicity. From this perspective, competition for scarce resources thickens ethnic boundaries, contributes to the formation of new ethnic groups (ethnogenesis), and fuels ethnic conflicts and movements (Nagel 1995; Roosens 1989). Similarly, hostility between natives and aliens originates in contexts where the supply of certain resources (economic, political, etc.) is exceeded by the demand for them.

The assumptions of rational choice theory underpin many of the generalizations advanced in resource competition theories (Banton 1995: 489). Perhaps the most prevalent assumption is that there is an *objective* basis for intergroup conflict. In describing what they call the "simple self-interest model," Bobo and Hutchings (1996) conclude: "Objective personal vulnerability to economic or political deprivation provides the direct basis for intergroup hostility" (p. 953). Resource competition models often adopt Max Weber's concept of social closure to explain nativist phenomena. Social closure occurs when one social group takes "some externally identifiable characteristic of another group of (actual or potential) competitors—race, language...residence, etc." as a pretext for attempting to close certain social and economic opportunities to them (Weber 1922/1968, cited in Stone 1995: 397). The concept of social closure has been used to juxtapose different models of citizenship (Brubaker 1992) and compare American and Canadian nativist activities (McCauley 1990).

Scholars frequently look to unemployment rates, wage scales, and immigration levels to gauge job market competition. Much of the quantitative research on American attitudes toward U.S. immigration levels and immigrant populations correlates this kind of aggregate data (and micro-level factors) with receptivity to U.S. immigration (e.g., see Espenshade and Hempstead 1996). Correlations between job market competition and receptivity to immigration frequently demonstrate that proxies for job competition do not reliably predict immigration attitudes (Wimmer 1997: 20-21, 34-35). One could argue that such aggregate data cannot predict *individual* responses and has little relevancy to competition in *specific* industries (Banton 1995: 487; Wimmer 1997: 20). However, even when these qualifying factors are taken into account, as they are by Susan Olzak (1986: 24-42; 1993), Wimmer illustrates that it is not *real* competition, but the *perception* of competition, which provokes racist and nativist reactions. The resource competition model is not annulled by this qualification, "but rather the thesis of conflict turning on *individual* goods such as jobs or housing. It seems more probable that ethnic conflicts as well as xenophobic movements are waged over *collective* goods" (Wimmer 1997: 21, italics in original). Researchers stressing the importance of perception and collective definition in fueling nativist acts often interpret nativistic processes as the outcome of group positions, a perspective which will be discussed shortly.

Historical analyses of nativism are replete with references to job competition and economic envy. Leonard Pitt concludes that "[s]heer economic jealousy...brought on the first xenophobia" in nineteenth-century California (1961: 24), and according to David Hellwig, much of the "black response" to immigrants between 1830 and 1930 can be described as "nativistic." "Black dislike of the foreign-born, unlike that

of most whites, was rooted in envy and resentment" (1982: 90).
However, even though blacks frequently viewed the Chinese and
Japanese as job competitors in the late 1800s, the majority of blacks
consistently rejected measures proposing the exclusion or curbing of
Asian immigration (1982: 91; also see Rubin 1978). Hellwig interprets
this decision as a *rational* response to *objective* conditions:

> Like many whites they [blacks] often feared the impact of
> aliens on traditional American values and institutions and not
> infrequently were quite vociferous in expressing their
> concerns. But some features of American society that
> they—as blacks—sought to protect and extend, white nativists
> rejected; namely, the image of the United States as a free,
> open and dynamic society, a nation in which diversity was
> affirmed rather than feared. As an oppressed minority
> incapable of large-scale passing, *self-interest dictated that they*
> *support a fluid social structure* in which people would be
> treated on their merits rather than on the basis of ascribed
> status (1982: 91-92, italics added).

By connecting patterns of black nativism to economic and political
interests, Hellwig depicts black nativism as a response to competition
with immigrants for political and economic resources. Whereas job
competition is more objective, and "economic jealousy" more
subjective, Hellwig tends to privilege the role of objective conditions in
accounting for the occurrence of nativism among African Americans
(e.g., see 1982: 88-90).

In *Solidarity or Survival?*, A.T. Lane (1987) examines the
reception afforded immigrants from southern and eastern Europe by
American labor between 1830 and 1924. Sensitive to a variety of
interpretations, Lane appreciates the complex mixture of motives and
circumstances surrounding nativist phenomena. The features of
immigrant communities (e.g., the scope of their skills and occupations,
degree of geographical concentration, and political participation), the
destabilizing effects of technological innovation, and prevailing
prejudices of the day—to name only a few factors—can, and did,
influence the ways in which American workers responded to
immigration (1987: 20-23). Lane nevertheless concludes that the

varied responses of American labor were clearly rooted in an effort to protect themselves from the political influence and economic competition posed by foreign-born labor (pp. 22-32). To describe Lane's interpretation as "resource competition" is not to ignore the other determinants that he so carefully weighed, but to conclude that this was his *primary* interpretation.

On the contemporary front, researchers studying the economic and demographic impacts of immigrants on American society probably garner more headlines and journal space than researchers investigating other immigration-related issues. While increasing the United State's economic productivity is only one of "five principal goals of U.S. immigration policy" (Fix and Passel 1994: 13), researchers understand that economic considerations are usually paramount to policy analysts and legislators (Light 1996: 61). When researchers conclude that immigrants are an economic asset (or at least a benign influence) to a certain economy or population, calls for restriction are thought nativistic, but if immigrants are judged to be an economic liability, calls for restriction are considered reasonable.

While numerous scholars and journalists explain nativism as some form of competition for resources, their assumptions and foci vary. For instance, George Borjas, a Harvard professor and Cuban émigré, and William Frey, a University of Michigan researcher, both utilize the resource competition model to analyze immigration, but in different ways. For Borjas, the underlying assumption is that immigration "changes how the economic pie is sliced up," with some natives gaining and other natives losing (Borjas 1996: 4-6). He reasons that the most appropriate model for assessing the economic impact of immigrants on the United States is one attentive to resource competition.

William Frey (1995a; 1996), on the other hand, applies the resource competition model to the out-migration of native whites from high immigration states. Unlike Borjas, however, Frey uses the resource competition approach to not only examine the domestic migration of native-born whites, but also to explain why native whites are leaving California, New York, Texas, and other high immigration states. Relying on regression coefficients and anecdotal evidence, Frey makes various assumptions about the multiple motivations (e.g., job competition, rising taxes) behind the migration patterns of native whites in high immigration states (1995b). The resource competition model, then, has been used to examine nativism-related issues and speculate about the various motivations influencing individual-level decisions. Much of the same can be said about each of the models being reviewed here, but this is perhaps especially true of the prejudice model.

Prejudice

According to the sociocultural model of prejudice, a *psychological* and largely *irrational* calculus underlies racial conflict. Unlike resource competition models, which interpret racist and nativist behavior as a *rational* response to *objective* conditions, contemporary theories of prejudice generally assume there is a *subjective* and *irrational* basis for nativist and racist hostility (Bobo and Hutchings 1996: 953-54). Typifying this perspective is one of the earliest works on nativism, Ray Billington's *The Protestant Crusade 1800-1860* (1963). In Billington's analysis there is little difference between what he calls "antipapal prejudice" and nativism (1963: 4). Because anti-Catholicism "played so large a part in pre-Civil War nativist thinking...historians have sometimes regarded nativism and anti-Catholicism as more or less synonymous" (Higham 1992: 5). However, some scholars continue to examine nativism as a process directed by prejudiced individuals (not necessarily against Catholics) or individuals given to conspiracy theories.

Two popular works emphasizing the psychological and irrational qualities of "antialien" activity, but which focus more on the "conspiratorial" aspects of nativism than on prejudice per se, are Richard Hofstadter's essay (1996) "The Paranoid Style in American Politics" (originally published in 1952) and *The Politics of Unreason* (Lipset and Raab 1978). Both of these works argue that conspiracy theories play a central role in nativist activities (e.g., Hofstadter 1996: 4, 29, 39; Lipset and Raab 1978: 490). According to Hofstadter, a "paranoid mentality" or "paranoid disposition" is "mobilized into action chiefly by social conflicts that involve ultimate schemes of values and...bring fundamental fears and hatreds, rather than negotiable interests, into political action" (1996: 39). Similar to the authoritarian personality model (Adorno, Frenkel-Brunswick,

Levinson, and Stanford 1950; Brown 1995), the personalities of certain nativists render them susceptible to conspiracy theories describing how their national, or cultural, way of life is threatened by powerful, yet subtle, forces (Hofstadter 1996: 4, 29). Similarly, Lipset and Raab define nativism as a "strong attachment to a reference group to which one has, so to speak, 'been born'" and contend that conspiracy theories are a critical element in "nativist bigotry" (1978: 488, 490).

There is nothing inherently prejudicial about conspiracy theories. However, both approaches assume that the inability of certain individuals to cope with profound changes in society (particularly in terms of their own social status) manifests itself in various forms of prejudice (i.e., the "paranoid style" and "nativist bigotry"). While these works at various points do emphasize objective conditions (e.g., see Hofstadter 1996: 39; Lipset and Raab 1978: 268-69), their orientations toward the irrational and psychological, as captured in the concept of conspiracy theories, is comparable to other approaches associated with the prejudice approach.

Contemporary research has largely moved away from this type of analysis to one that regards various prejudices, or the ethnocentric beliefs that support such attitudes, as the foundation upon which nativist activities are built. Rogers Smith defines nativism as an extreme form of "ethnocultural Americanism" (1988: 228) and Juan Perea contends that nativists try to reinforce America's "core culture" by labeling those traits and cultures at odds with this core as "un-American" or "foreign" (1992: 278). After surveying 458 adult residents in a Wisconsin community, Ruefle, Ross, and Mandell (1993) found that ethnocentrism accounted for most of the variance in attitudes toward Southeast Asian refugees when controlling for various economic and demographic factors.

Compared to nationalism and resource competition models, the sociocultural model of prejudice has few adherents. That prejudice and ethnocentrism contribute to many nativist initiatives is an unquestioned assumption among students of nativism. For scholars, however, the critical question is not whether or not prejudice or ethnocentrism contributes to nativism, but rather to what *extent* these attitudes influence nativist outcomes. According to Higham, ethnocentrism provides the "cultural subsoil" in which nativism grows:

An ethnocentrism that applied largely to "mere habits of life," that raised no question of the newcomers patriotism or his ultimate assimilation, could survive side by side with a generally tolerant and receptive outlook. Yet we cannot afford to ignore the simpler ethnocentric judgments that persist beneath the ebb and flow of nativism. Although those judgments often exist where nativism does not, they provide the cultural subsoil in which it grows (1992: 24).

For Higham, then, the relationship between ethnocentrism and nativism is straightforward—ethnocentrism can, and often does, contribute to nativism by arousing certain concerns or justifying various actions, but in the final analysis, its presence is not imperative. What makes one event "nativistic" and another event not, will be discussed in the second half of this chapter, but before one can outline any kind of nativist criteria, it is necessary to review and assess the group position framework.

Group Position

From a group position perspective, comprehending an individual's "definition of the situation" (Thomas and Thomas 1928) is the key to understanding collective processes like nativism. In this sense, the group position approach is very similar to symbolic interactionism. For this reason, it is necessary to interject brief descriptions of symbolic interactionism when delineating the group position approach.

By utilizing an individual's point of view to understand collective action, symbolic interactionism is first and foremost a subjectivist sociology. Instead of *social structure*, the imagery of *social process* is used to understand how people come to interpret, and act toward, "social objects," such as immigrants or immigration policy (Lal 1995: 421-23). Focus is placed on an individual's perceptions and decisions, but this emphasis is tempered by the understanding that one's personal abilities and choices are profoundly influenced by their historical circumstances and relative power.[6]

---

[6] "From the actor's point of view, the world consists of social objects—that is, anything that the actor can name...The meaning of an object is conferred on it

To varying degrees, the perspectives presented thus far—nationalism, resource competition, and prejudice—have considered, to varying degrees, the *perceptions* of natives. What separates the group position model from these models—with respect to nativism—is its attempt to simultaneously interpret the symbolic and material interests affecting these perceptions. Nationalism and prejudice models accentuate the role of symbolic identities (e.g., "American," "foreigner," or any other relevant contrastive identity) in triggering nativist initiatives, whereas resource competition models tend to focus on the material interests of nativists. Even though Blumer's original formulation was not intended for such purposes, his group position model integrates all three perspectives into a single, sociological framework.

Blumer (1958) argued that racial discrimination results from a collective process of racial identification where racial groups form conceptions of themselves and others. By characterizing each other, they define their positions relationally, thereby contributing to what Blumer calls a "sense of group position." This sense of group position is a product of history and everyday experience, in which the dominant group develops the view that they are entitled to privileged (or prior) rights in certain spheres of importance—a sense of group position in other words. When the dominant group senses a challenge to its exclusive claims, racial discrimination is likely (Blumer 1958:3-5; Quillian 1995: 588).

Scholars have recently begun to use Blumer's group position model to examine nativism and racism as responses to perceived threat. Quillian found that the average degree of prejudice toward immigrants and racial minorities in each of the twelve countries comprising the

---

on the basis of the ways in which people are prepared to act toward the object. This in turn, reflects past socialization and social interaction. Old meanings may be reinforced or emergent meanings may arise on the basis of current and future interaction or on the basis of imagination. The meanings of objects are considered through a process of interpretation during which the actor takes into account the relevant objects in the situation he or she confronts, including the activities of others, the anticipated activities of others, conventional definitions of the situation, past experience, goals, interests, values, and so on" (Lal 1995: 423).

EEC (European Economic Community) was "strongly related to the threat perceived by the dominant group resident there" (1995: 605). In his study, different levels of prejudice between EEC countries could not be explained by individual characteristics.

> The economic conditions in a country and the size of the racial or immigrant group influence people's views of group relations, and in so doing influence prejudicial attitudes. Threat is perceived by individuals, but its relationship to prejudice *depends on a comparison of the relations between dominant and subordinate social groups*" (1995: 606, italics added).

It is the *positional relation* of the dominant and subordinate groups which contributes to intergroup hostility (Blumer 1958). "The core factor in Blumer's model is the subjective image of where the in-group *ought* to stand vis-à-vis the out-group" (Bobo and Hutchings 1996: 955, italics in original).

Blumer's framework has been used to examine other race-related phenomena (e.g., see Bobo and Hutchings 1996; Bobo and Zubrinsky 1996; Smith 1981) but is particularly attractive to scholars analyzing intergroup hostility because it bridges micro- and macro-level processes. However, some of these works overlook Blumer's emphasis on the defining and redefining of subordinate groups and the role of one's reference group in shaping this ongoing process.

Blumer's concept of group position resembles the concept of reference group. A reference group is "that group whose outlook is used by the actor as the frame of reference in the organization of his [or her] perceptual field" (Shibutani 1955: 565). A sense of group position supplies the dominant group with a certain perspective. Likewise, a reference group is a perspective, "an ordered view of one's world...an order of things remembered and expected as well as things actually perceived, an organized conception of what is plausible and what is possible; it constitutes the matrix through which one perceives his [or her] environment" (Shibutani 1955: 564).

The concept of reference group can account for choices that seemingly contradict an individual's best interests by focusing on the communication channels available to him or her. People in different social, economic, or legal positions develop different worldviews, not because there is anything intrinsic to these positions, but because their similarity of position disposes them to a limited number of communication channels. By participating in a restricted set of communication channels an individual can be oblivious to alternatives (1955: 562-66).

Leaders and interest groups attempt to challenge or maintain the meaning of certain social objects (e.g., "American") through various forms of communication. Given that every social world has some type of communication system and special symbols (e.g., the English language) leaders can narrow or widen the social distance between groups by controlling various communication systems to which they have access (Shibutani and Kwan 1965: 227-28). Shaping people's perspectives, of course, requires power. The group position perspective is not only attentive to the material and symbolic interests of groups, but also to the relative power of each.

Of course, the social world is much more complex because people simultaneously participate in a number of social worlds:

> Because of the ease with which the individual may expose himself to a number of communication channels, he may lead a segmentalized life, participating successively in a number of unrelated activities. Furthermore, the particular combination of social worlds differs from person to person; this is what led Simmel to declare that each stands at that point at which a unique combination of circles intersects (Shibutani 1955: 567).

In order to understand the worldviews of individuals one must access their unique perspectives and learn about the social worlds in which they participate (Shibutani 1955: 567). This is the rationale behind the interviews conducted for this study (see Chapters 5-7). However, before these interviews can be fruitfully examined, it is necessary explain my perspective, which incorporates, to varying degrees, the four approaches just outlined.

Reviewing the Four Models

All four perspectives identify the perception of threat as the mainspring of nativism, but they begin to separate at the specification of this threat. The nationalism model assumes natives are threatened by "un-American" ideas and practices, but the resource competition model understands nativism as an outgrowth of competition between natives and aliens. The prejudice model presumes nativists cope with societal change by embracing certain prejudices and conspiracy theories, and the group position model locates nativist hostility in a population's sense of group position. It is argued that the group position model incorporates the above interpretations into a coherent framework which can account for the motivational systems underlying nativist attitudes and behavior. Before elaborating on this approach, however, it is important to grasp how each model pictures the genesis of nativism.

In each model, the process of nativism is initiated by people who see themselves (in some sense) as natives, or by organizations contending that their proposals advance the interests of the country at large. Although their goals and procedures vary, their efforts are always directed towards "aliens." This term is to be understood in its etymological sense. "Alien" comes from the Latin word "alienus"—"of or belonging to another person or place." It generally refers to something or someone who is "not of one's own" (Oxford English Dictionary 1989: 314-15). Those who belong to another family, race, or nation, are strangers or foreigners, and cannot, as far as "natives" are concerned, be "of one's own." "Native" and "alien" are socially constructed and always subject to revision.

Natives are threatened by an intrusion, which is—at its most basic level—a perception of alien presence or behavior. This perception, however, is partly shaped by the attendant expectations attached to the status of "native." This status position is lodged within the context of national sovereignty and the institution of citizenship. Even though this legal and social foundation is implicitly recognized by nationalism, resource competition, and prejudice models, they primarily focus on the ideology of nativism rather than the structure of native advantage. It is argued that both components need to be integrated and that the group position approach is ideally suited for combining nation-related ideas (like national sovereignty and "native") to the institutions which reflect and enforce these ideas (like citizenship and immigration policies).

Placing these components under one conceptual roof necessitates a discussion of legitimacy. The term "nativism" suggests that certain attitudes and actions are illegitimate, and because the legitimacy of a given political practice is rooted in values and their formal codification, it is necessary to examine the normative assumptions underpinning the debates over immigration reform and the system of native advantage in which these deliberations take place.

The Discourse and Social Organization of Nativism

When racism is considered a purely ideological phenomenon, the social hierarchies influencing relations between racial groups are generally disregarded. This idealist conception of racism tends to use social-psychological terms (e.g., belief, irrational thinking, prejudice, and overt behavior) to analyze racial discrimination. This perspective, however, tends to regard racial phenomena as "abnormal," overlooks subtle expressions of racism and ignores the rational foundations upon which racism rests (Bonilla-Silva 1997; Wellman 1994). I use Bonilla-Silva's distinction between racism (racial ideology) and racialized social systems (the structural foundations of racism) to analyze the social organization of American nativism. Specifically, nativist processes are maintained by a legal system of native advantage and legitimated by ideas of national sovereignty and national interest. Configuring the relationship between the ideology and social organization of nativism is best accomplished by situating these processes within the larger debate over immigration reform, for it is here where the notion of national sovereignty collides with the international right of emigration, and where the "normative status" of each principle is tentatively settled.

Linda Bosniak (1997) argues that the concept of nativism simultaneously describes and evaluates behavior and that the examination of nativist phenomena is encumbered by their confounding:

> The meaning of "nativism" is in important respects indeterminate to us, and we will find ourselves unable to agree

on whether any particular set of conditions in the world can appropriately be described in these terms. But when we argue about whether the current wave of immigration restrictionism should or should not be characterized as "nativist," we are not merely engaged in a dispute over social classification. For quite beyond the empirical "correctness" of the label (even if we could determine such a thing) in any given situation, the designation of a statement or policy as "nativist" is laden with enormous normative significance...*When we ask, therefore, what it is that we are arguing about when we argue about nativism, perhaps the best answer is that we are arguing about legitimacy* (Bosniak 1997: 282-84, italics added).

Bosniak explains that the meaning of nativism is difficult to establish because—with respect to immigration restriction—differing evaluations of the appropriateness or inappropriateness of a given attitude or behavior form the foundation upon which empirical criteria rest. However, she goes on to analyze nativism, and in particular, the discourse over immigration reform, by focusing on the legitimacy and illegitimacy of arguments advanced by immigration advocates. Her focus on legitimacy is the proper starting point for a study of contemporary nativism but, as will be emphasized later, can be reified if the wider social fabric is examined without referring to individual perceptions and choices.

Debating Immigration Reform: Legitimacy and Perceptions of Nativism

When individuals argue about nativism they are often arguing about legitimacy, about the normative status of their disagreements over immigration and other related issues. It is the normative backdrop behind these debates that gives content to "our conventional understandings of what nativism is" (Bosniak 1997: 284, 291). Bosniak suggests that arguments for restricting immigration, if placed on a hypothetical legitimacy continuum, "broadly frame our conventional understandings of where nativism begins and ends" and "serve to structure the way we argue about immigration more generally" (1997: 285).

Today, she asserts, exclusionary arguments based on race fall on the *illegitimate* end of the continuum, the "nativist" end. Although Peter Brimelow's (1996) unrepentant use of race-based arguments in *Alien Nation* may have may have opened the front door for similar expressions, most restrictionists who agree with his assessment probably still prefer the back door approach. At the *legitimate* end of the continuum we find disagreements over the material costs of immigration. Expansionists rarely label such arguments as "nativist," although they do at times question the motives of those using them to advance their appeals for restriction (Bosniak 1997: 284-88; Crawford 1992: 148-53).

We have, then, two "legitimacy benchmarks" structuring the way Americans think and argue about immigration. They give us a general sense of what is socially permissible with respect to the discourse on immigration. In the middle fall various arguments about American culture. These arguments begin to slide toward the illegitimate end of the spectrum if they are suspected of being proxies for race-based arguments. A modification of Bosniak's analysis (1997: 284-291) might look something like this:

FIGURE 1
Contemporary Legitimacy Spectrum of
Arguments for Restricting Immigration

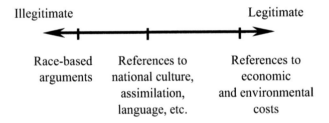

Aside from the question of motives, however, what makes an argument legitimate or illegitimate in the first place? Why are material arguments permissible? Bosniak's suggestion is worth quoting at length:

What I wish to emphasize about the debate over costs is its unspoken normative backdrop: it presumes that determining who is right in empirical terms on the cost question is dispositive of the immigration policy issue. It presumes, in other words, that if immigrants could somehow be definitely determined to cost more than they contribute, then restrictionists' efforts to curtail immigration would be basically unassailable on normative grounds. One is unlikely to hear the argument (except in the refugee context, where the structure of normative argument is different) that it is illegitimate to cut back on immigration if immigration is, in fact, shown to materially disadvantage the nation. But why should this be? Why isn't this assumption, like so many others, up for normative debate? The reason is that we live in a world in which it is ordinarily presumed that "compatriots take priority," in philosopher Henry Shue's phrase; it is presumed that national immigration policy should promote the welfare, first and foremost, of the national society's members. This is, after all, the normative heart of the principle of national sovereignty: the sovereignty principle "affirms the priority of particular peoples—the citizens of particular states—over any universalizing claims to humanity as such"...One might well respond that the "national priority thesis" runs counter to a powerful tradition in American political consciousness—the tradition of American identity as "a nation of immigrants"...Yet even this "cosmopolitan" strain in American national thought, as John Higham has called it, presumes that American openness to immigrants serves American material interests. The point is that cost arguments for immigration restriction presume that what counts in determining immigration policy is the health and well-being of Americans. And as such, they are unlikely to be regarded as illegitimate—or "nativist"—forms of argument, since their underlying premise is treated as almost beyond question in our political culture. Cost arguments may be wrong on the facts—and I think they often are—but they are certainly not intrinsically "bad" (1997: 288-89).

Bosniak argues that the general acceptance of cost arguments is grounded in the notion that the material interests of natives supercede those of aliens, or more abstractly, that the legitimacy of material arguments are grounded in the notion of national sovereignty and its correlate, the "national priority thesis."

Her analysis, however, raises two questions that need to be addressed if the normative assumptions underpinning nativism are to be incorporated into a plausible definition of American nativism. With respect to immigration reform: (1) What is legitimacy and on what bases does it rest? and (2) How has the concept of legitimacy changed over time? A historically usable definition of nativism can be developed by focusing on the legitimation and delegitimation of "immigration ideas."

What is Legitimacy and What Are Its Bases?

Legitimacy is a desired quality. Political authorities and principles enjoy legitimacy when their directives are regarded as "right" on some grounds, when constituents consider a given authority structure or idea as binding on their actions (Albrow 1990: 161-63; **Weber** 1968: 31). "It was this binding nature on...participants which Weber terms 'legitimacy'" (Albrow 1990: 162).

Weber used the concept of legitimacy to reveal how social action (i.e., actions directed toward other people) can be "guided by the belief in the existence of a legitimate order" (Weber 1968: 31). Aside from the belief that a social order ought to exist, social order does not solely depend upon the presence of common ideas or common values, but frequently arises out of different and conflicting individual motivations (Albrow 1990: 162-165). For example, two controversial, immigrant-related bills proposed in 1996—the *Personal Responsibility and Work Opportunity Reconciliation Act* and the *Illegal Immigration Reform and Responsibility Act*—were passed despite considerable opposition. The citizens, advocacy groups, and national representatives who objected to their provisions considered the bills, once they were enacted into law, as legitimate—that is, as binding on their future actions. Why? Because the legitimacy of legal authority, the predominant form of power (*Herrschaft*) exercised in the United States, "rests upon rational grounds, themselves contingent upon the propensity of people to believe in the validity of enacted rules and the right of those elevated to authority under such rules to issue commands" (Friedman 1981: 37; Weber 1968: 53, 215). In other words, legislation (or more generally, political rule) is seen as binding if its enactment is realized according to procedures the public considers legitimate (Mommsen 1989: 47). There is, however, an exception to this argument. The legitimacy of a given law rests upon its formal rationalization (i.e., "the successive tightening of its logical structure as a system of ideas") *and* its substantive rationalization (i.e., "the successive elaboration of the law's objectives"). When these two processes do not coincide, its legitimacy, or its "binding nature," is undermined (Friedman 1981: 54-56).

A diverse literature on legitimacy implies that the phenomenon of legitimacy is most commonly analyzed as a relationship between political theory and political practice. Legitimacy inheres in the relationship between these two caches of political conceptions. Specifically, "the degree of legitimacy enjoyed by a regime rests upon a congruous relationship between (1) political principles and practices, and (2) the rulers and the ruled. Definitiveness regarding the concept 'legitimacy' has not been achieved, yet the phenomenon is most commonly analyzed in terms of these two broad sets of variables" (Friedman 1981: 16). For instance, a discrepancy between political principles (e.g., equality under the law) and political practices (e.g., racial discrimination) produces "a sense of inappropriateness that undermines the image of the legitimate use of authority in a regime" (1981: 16).

Weber's discussion of "formal rationality" and "substantive rationality" helps clarify the interdependent relationship between political theory and political practice and the "origins" of legitimacy. Because the law has a logical structure, it can undergo formal rationalization and because it has a substantive content, it can undergo substantive rationalization. "Formal rationalization of law refers to the successive tightening...of the law's logical structure as a system of ideas," and the substantive rationalization of the law "refers to the successive elaboration of the law's objectives" (Friedman 1981: 54). A law's meaning is derived from its purpose. The purpose of a law can be ethical, ideological, religious, expediential, and so forth, but aside from its particular objectives, its content explains why, apart from the power of the state, it merits obedience.

The purpose(s) toward which the law is oriented give the law its legitimacy, over and above the fact that it is the law...The substance of the law refers to the rationale that underlies the socially constructed relationships that are the order...It is the formal character of the law's rationalization that attaches legal consequences—and therefore the coercion of the state—to...these relationships. But the decision as to which of all possible social relationships to "legalize" requires a guiding substantive rationale (such as the paramount importance of freedom of contract, individual rights, social justice, or the like). Therefore, the law's legitimacy ultimately derives from its substance. Weber treats the continuing quest for the law's "spirit," "kernel," "real intent," or ultimate "meaning" in terms of the notion of the law's "logical sublimation"...Logical sublimation, as Weber uses the term, is essentially equivalent to the law's substantive rationalization. Both refer to the elaboration of the law's ultimate objectives. It is clear that if the law's guarantee is to be effective—to reach those whom it is intended to reach—the law needs to be formally rationalized...Correlatively, if the law is to be legitimate—in line with the values of the body politic—elaboration of the reasons behind the law (substantive rationalization) is necessary. In sum, formal and substantive rationalization are complementary and parallel processes. Unless they are synchronized so that they occur parallel to one another, their complementarity will be lost (Friedman 1981: 54-55).

Weber argued that legal authority regimes are legitimized on rational grounds, which in turn, rest upon a congruence between political principles and practices. Friedman explains that the legitimacy of a law is not secured by its formal rationalization (political practice), but first and foremost by its meaning (political principle). Codification and enforcement contribute to the legitimacy of a law, but paramount are the values upon which a principle rests. Values produce a normative yardstick by which to evaluate propositions and other forms of action. Contemporary debates over immigration reform are not "refereed" by a clear list of values, but are deliberated against a hazy backdrop of probationary ethics.

Fluctuations in Nativism: A Weberian Analysis

The specific values (ideas about what is right or wrong) and beliefs (the application of these values to particular situations) applied to immigration reform are difficult to enumerate. As one might suspect, existing immigration and immigrant policies are based on a number of values, but as emphasized earlier, laws incongruent with their intended meanings risk delegitimation if their contents are not brought into line with the values of the political community. The legitimacy of laws and regimes varies with their substantive rationales, but on what value premises are these rationales based? *It is argued that U.S. immigration and immigrant policies secure their legitimacy by placing the sovereignty and interests of the nation-state and its members above the interests of the international community.*

U.S. immigration and immigrant policies represent complex choices made among competing values. The legitimacy of these laws inheres in the principle of national sovereignty—the moral obligation of states to promote and protect the interests of its members (Weiner 1997).[7] Although recognized by national and international laws, this belief is challenged by postnational realities. Some researchers suggest that the reconfiguration of citizenship, emergence of diasporic public spheres, electronic capitalism, and *permanent* framework of refugee bureaucracies and refugee-relief movements—and other transnational processes—call into question notions of national sovereignty and citizenship. These phenomena provoke new definitions of membership and rights which are based on ideas of universal personhood and human rights, rather than national sovereignty (Appadurai 1996; Soysal 1994).

While these realities may signal the emergence of "postnational sovereignties" (Appadurai 1996: 176), these reflections are contemplated in a world comprised of sovereign states, where the concept of national sovereignty is regarded by most citizens as commonsensical (Weiner 1997; Hollinger 1995: 143-46). "While current international law imposes important limitations on the exercise of the sovereign power to control entry, overall there is little disagreement as to the state's authority in this matter" (Sassen 1996:

---

[7] The interests of the nation-state are not objectively settled, but subject to change and power relations (see discussion below).

66). National sovereignty is an organizing principle of immigration and immigrant policies.

The Helsinki Accords and United Nations Universal Declaration of Human Rights affirm the universal right of emigration, "yet all governments and international organizations agree that governments have the right to determine those to admit and to whom citizenship should be granted" (Weiner 1995: 171-75; 1997: 171). The primary objectives of U.S. immigration policies are to facilitate the social and economic betterment of U.S. citizens and legal residents, encourage diversity, promote human rights and control illegal immigration (Fix and Passel 1994: 13). By formulating immigration, refugee and asylum policies, the federal government seeks to strike a balance between, among other things, the principles of national sovereignty and human rights.

However, the scale used to balance international human rights against the right of national sovereignty is decidedly tilted in favor of the latter. Even though the Refugee Act of 1980 sought to align U.S. policies with international practices, the status of refugee nevertheless reflects the decision of a government, not an individual (Portes and Rumbaut 1996: 23). Refugee admissions are not considered moral imperatives, but humanitarian acts in an ungenerous world. The principle of national sovereignty legitimizes the authority of nation-states to promote and protect the rights of natives over and above the interests of aliens.

The national self-interest, however, is rarely unambiguous. Immigration policies symbolize, to various degrees, the tradeoffs made between competing visions of national self-interest (see Chapters 5-7). The people and organizations promoting these visions often contend that the national interest is best served by their national visions, implicitly recognizing that legitimate arguments for reforming immigration are congruent with the principle of national sovereignty (Light 1996; Calhoun 1994). Even open borders positions can be explained in terms of the national interest (e.g., see Isbister 1996: 12). Ideas of national sovereignty and national interest are embodied in national and international laws and, at this point in time, serve as the definitive arbiters of what is, and what is not, legitimate with respect to immigration reform. These laws and declarations will be revised in accordance with new interpretations and emerging realities. Nativism is, and will always be, historically variable so long as the values upon which it rests are probationary, that is, so long as the principle of national sovereignty is reinterpreted in light of transnational processes and regimes.

The National Narrative

The histories of nation-states are presented in narrative form. The events leading to their formation and eventual standing in the world are explained as the fulfillment of a collective project (Appadurai 1996; Anderson 1991; Balibar 1991; Wallerstein 1991). In the United States, immigration constitutes a major theme in the national narrative. From the colonial period to the present, America has imagined itself as a land of immigrants (e.g., Fuchs 1990; Ueda 1981). Immigration reform is frequently understood in relation to this collective representation even though legitimacy ultimately inheres in the principle of national sovereignty. Even though legitimacy does not "reside" in the national narrative, it can be regarded as a social fact having the force of social morality (Appadurai 1996: 5; Durkheim 1982: 52). This point will be illustrated by comparing the national narrative to Robert Merton's analysis of the American creed.

In his classic essay, "Discrimination and the American Creed" (1949), Robert Merton argues there is an American creed which asserts "the indefeasible principle of human right to full equity—the right of equitable access to justice, freedom and opportunity, irrespective of race or religion, or ethnic origin" (1949: 100). Americans are expected to comply with this set of values and principles which are embedded in American culture, and though it is practically immune to direct attack in particular times and places, it can be reinterpreted or evaded by individuals and institutions. The gap between creed and conduct, however, is more than a discrepancy between esteemed principles and inappropriate conduct, but is a relation between three variables: (1) The cultural creed recognized in cultural traditions and lawmaking, (2) The beliefs and attitudes of individuals pertaining to the creed's principles, and (3) The actual behavior of individuals with respect to the creed.

Merton used this formulation to demonstrate that conforming to, and deviating from, the American creed is not a simple function of one's beliefs and attitudes (1949: 102). Adapting his thesis to the idiosyncrasies of nativist discourses *uncovers the social expectations surrounding immigration reform* (intentional actions designed to produce or prevent change in current immigration realities) by analyzing the varying degrees of acceptance accorded to restrictionist and expansionist arguments.

The national narrative is similar to Merton's American creed in matters of immigration reform. The national narrative resembles the creed to the extent that it, too, is a:

> set of values and precepts embedded in American culture, to which Americans are expected to conform. It is a complex of affirmations, rooted in the historical past and ceremonially celebrated in the present, partly enacted in the laws of the land and partly not. Like all creeds, it is a profession of faith, a part of cultural tradition sanctified by the larger traditions of which it is a part. It is...dynamic, subject to change...[and does not] exert the same measure of control over behavior in diverse times and places (Merton 1949: 100-01).

Unlike the creed, however, the national narrative is not a legitimation source, but a myth.[8] It is a story of how immigrants, through self-reliance and an unwavering commitment to republican principles, established a nation where liberty was granted and hard work rewarded.

Like most founding myths, the national narrative chronicles past events and cultivates a national identity congruent with the more laudable aspects of American history (e.g., see Fuchs 1990; Knobel 1996). While some events are ignored, fallacious, or idealized, many of the accounts are accurate and serve to explain, *in part*, why efforts to curb immigration levels or abridge the "rights" of foreign-born residents are described as nativistic. In the United States, immigration almost seems integral to the nation-building process. These initiatives are, at times, at odds with this "nation of immigrants" imagery.

---

[8] A myth is a traditional story of purportedly historical experiences that serves to explain why people see the world from a certain vantage point or act in particular ways. A myth can be an unfounded story, but I am using the word in the sense thought to have been first used in English.

Of course, the national narrative is not intrinsic to any kind of history, but is a matrix of interpretations and inferences derived from the historical record.[9] But whether or not this image is "deserved" or historically "correct" is largely irrelevant from a sociological point of view. As W.I. Thomas explained, if people "define situations as real, they are real in their consequences" (1928: 572). It is not the accuracy of the national narrative, *but the perception of it*, that influences an individual's evaluation of initiatives designed to maintain or change current immigration realities. Restrictionists are keenly aware of this interpretation, often challenging the argument that the United States is, or should be, a nation of immigrants (e.g., see Auster 1997: 42-45; Beck 1994: 113-134).

The implicit assumption of the national narrative is that immigrants augment the economic and political interests of the United States. Religious, cultural and racial interests have also been advanced throughout American history, but these considerations are rarely accorded the same level of legitimacy as that bestowed on economic and political interests.[10] Additionally, the boundaries of the national narrative extend beyond the foreign-born and apply more generally to those perceived as "alien" in some sense. Native-born Americans have been perceived, and treated as, aliens throughout American history.

---

[9] Despite their relatively similar histories of immigration, the United States and France have, for example, come to see, and act upon, their histories in dissimilar ways. Whereas the U.S. is "overtly a country of immigrants, France is only covertly and partially such a country. The French do not regard themselves, in the way that Americans do, as the descendants of immigrants" (Horowitz 1992: 11).

[10] For instance, racial interests were openly discussed in the debate surrounding the 1924 Immigration Act (which established the national origins quota system), but were, by and large, articulated in "scientific" terms (i.e., eugenics) (e.g., see Ludmerer 1972; Morgan 1987), thereby providing a modicum of legitimacy to the proposed reductions. Secondly, the House Committee on Immigration understood the imprudence of justifying their bill on the grounds of Nordic superiority and, as a result, devised a way to discriminate against immigrants from southeastern Europe without appearing overtly racist (e.g., see Higham 1992: 319-320).

The internment of Japanese Americans during the Second World War is a poignant example.

Restrictionists wrestle with the implications of the national narrative in their writings, fully aware that unwanted labels ("nativist," "racist," etc.) are headed their way for suggesting that America's relatively liberal immigration policies be reversed (Brimelow 1996: 9-13; Beck 1992; 1996: 12). Arguments about the "costs" of immigration are generally considered legitimate because the material interests of natives supersede those of aliens. America's "basic openness to outsiders who wish to become members of the national society...presumes that American openness to immigrants serves American material interests" (Bosniak 1996: 289). It is assumed, when considering the implications of the national narrative (i.e., relative openness to immigration) that the material interests of natives supersede those of aliens. To use Blumer's (1958) terminology, it is a proprietary right of natives.

If arguments about nativism are indeed arguments about legitimacy, then what kinds of reasoning and conduct are legitimate? Merton assumes that discrimination is always illegitimate, but in the case of immigration reform, some forms of "discrimination" are legitimate if they "balance" the needs of natives and aliens in favor of the former. For example, few would repudiate the deportation of aliens convicted of terrorism. Unlike the American creed, the principle of national sovereignty does not assert that all humans are entitled to full equity, but presupposes the priority of "natives" over "aliens."

Attitudinal and Behavioral Responses to Legitimate Principles

Political struggles over immigration reform cannot be understood only in terms of legitimacy and a founding myth. The legitimacy of a given social order or practice, and the normative import of the national narrative, are useful for analyzing the content and contentiousness of the discourse, but are less useful for examining the structural basis of nativism and the variety of individual motives and actions predicated on the distinction between natives and aliens. Legitimacy is a core structuring element in numerous social and political hierarchies, but its presence is not indicative of a common will (Albrow 1990: 158-196; Weber 1968: 22-26).

The acceptance and use of an argument does not solely depend upon its perceived legitimacy (e.g., see Blau 1963). Individuals may accept a line of reasoning simply out of self-interest, and thus, only recognize it to the extent that it is in their best interest to do so. Others may comply out of mere habit. Adapting Merton's typology of prejudice and discrimination to the idiosyncrasies of immigration reform underscores this point.

Merton's typology of prejudice and discrimination can be modified to help account for *some* of the discrepancies we find between an individual's beliefs and their actual actions. Even though I have changed Merton's terms, I borrow heavily from his descriptions of the "all weather liberal," "fair-weather liberal," "all-weather illiberal," and "fair-weather illiberal" to construct a typology more suited to the complexities of immigration reform. On the attitudinal dimension, *deny* refers to those beliefs which dispute the principles of national sovereignty and *accept* refers to those beliefs in it. On the behavioral dimension, *expansion* refers to efforts to maintain or increase immigration levels and *restriction* refers to those efforts intended to lower immigration levels.

FIGURE 2
Adaptation of Merton's Typology

	Attitude Dimension: accept (+) and reject (-) principle of national sovereignty	Behavior Dimension: Expansion (+) and restriction (-)
All-weather immigration advocate	–	+
Fair-weather immigration advocate	+	– / +
Timid nativist	–	+
All-weather xenophobe and nativist	–	–

The conduct of *all-weather immigration advocates* seems to coincide with the import of the national narrative, but their underlying rationales can contradict the principle of national sovereignty. As noted earlier, the implicit assumption of the national interest is that immigrants advance U.S. interests, but not at the expense of natives, whose interests supersede those of immigrants. But all-weather immigration advocates do not defer to the interests of natives. Their desire to enlarge the "circle of we" (Hollinger 1995) is not dictated by the "weather," but by a belief that people have the right to emigrate *and immigrate*, or that open borders is in the national interest. This conflicts with the United Nations' *Universal Declaration of Human Rights* and Helsinki Accord, which affirm a universal right of emigration, but not of immigration (Weiner 1996: 171; Lutton and Tanton 1994: 148).

The reasoning of all-weather advocates conflicts with the notion that native interests are paramount in establishing and adjusting immigration policy.

> For anyone who publicly argues that American interests should not be the only relevant interests at stake in formulating national immigration policy—anyone who dares to contend that America's normative obligations extend beyond the national community's formal members and that the interests of immigrants or would-be immigrants should also be taken into account—will not merely be dismissed as a soft-headed utopian but will inevitably be charged with "supporting open borders"—a charge whose pejorative weight begins to rival that of "nativism" itself...Far from being illegitimate, in fact, the assumed priority of citizens over foreigners, of nationals over strangers, lies at the absolute core of contemporary political thought (Bosniak 1997: 290).

Weighing the interests of natives and non-natives in equal measure, or ignoring the interests of natives altogether, conflicts with the "national priority thesis" (Bosniak 1997: 289), but does the charge of "supporting open borders" really rival that of "nativism"?

The insinuation of favoring "open borders," compared to the accusation of "nativism," seems, relatively speaking, inoffensive. Brimelow characterized high immigration advocates in *Alien Nation* as "immigration enthusiasts." But perhaps realizing his characterization did not censure high immigration advocates in the same way that "nativism" admonishes low immigration advocates, he sarcastically suggested that the "moral equivalent" of nativism is "treason," and that it should be used instead (1997). But why the uneven evaluation? All-weather advocates may be accused of promoting "open borders," but their *behavior* seems consistent with the national narrative because the *process* of immigration is thought to be consistent with the national narrative. Because the continuation of immigration is, *in some form*, almost a foregone conclusion, the *behavior* of all-weather advocates appears legitimate. Secondly, open border adherents can express their rationales in terms of the national interest by arguing that immigrants enrich America, materially and culturally.

Fair-weather immigration advocates are willing to widen the "circle of we" (Hollinger 1995), but unlike all-weather immigration advocates, only when the weather permits. For example, if immigrants seriously threaten the employment opportunities of natives, the circumference of "we" stays put. While they may wish things were different, it is the proprietary claims of natives that come first. Requests by American math scientists to curb the immigration of foreign mathematicians for the benefit of native-born mathematicians is an example of fair-weather advocacy (e.g., see Philips 1996).

The majority of expansionists and restrictionists fall into the fair-weather category, but their disparate responses to aliens originate—not in separate rationales—but in different worldviews. As will be illustrated in Chapters 5-7, restrictionists regard the forecasts of expansionists as dangerously optimistic, whereas expansionists view the forecasts of restrictionists as selfishly pessimistic. However, notwithstanding their different decisions, each side generally believes that their recommendations, given their analyses and projections, are the most appropriate.

The explanations of fair-weather immigration advocates are consistent with the national narrative so long as their underlying reasons are considered legitimate—that is, their calls for restriction are grounded in cost arguments and not racial or national identity-based arguments. Because they do not oppose immigration in and of itself, but only in certain circumstances—circumstances viewed as legitimate grounds for restricting immigration—their behavior is not nativistic.

Expansionists may dispute the accuracy of cost arguments but they rarely question their relevance (Bosniak 1997).

The principle of national sovereignty has little bearing on the reasoning of *timid nativists*. They do not accept the implications of the principle, but promote expansion for fear that doing otherwise will entail some kind of cost. Unlike fair-weather immigration advocates who propose reductions when immigration policies are allegedly at odds with the welfare of natives, timid nativists only support the principle of national sovereignty when it is in their best interest to comply. The behavior of timid nativists is, of course, also conditional—they will cease to abide by the principle of national sovereignty when certain sanctions are removed. One can imagine a personnel director who does not believe in the principle of national sovereignty, yet favors expansionist policies—regardless of their impact on natives—because her corporation's competitiveness is thought to hinge on their enactment.

All-weather xenophobes and nativists are the unabashed discriminators, because discrimination does not represent a gap between their rationales and behavior (Merton 1949: 109). *Xenophobes* do not accept the implications of the national narrative, and no matter what the weather, their response to aliens is the same—the "circle of we" is maxed out. The true xenophobe, the one who fears and/or dislikes *all* foreigners, belongs here.

Nativists, on the other hand, may not have an irrational fear of immigrants, but favor restriction for *illegitimate* reasons. Many of Peter Brimelow's (1996) arguments are fair-weather driven, but much of his reasoning is decidedly illegitimate, and therefore, nativistic. According to Brimelow, legal immigration should be drastically reduced, but some immigrants should be let in, so long as they are highly skilled and "assimilable" (e.g., see pp. 257-74).

His concern with assimilation, however, is betrayed by a number of racial arguments and references. For instance, Brimelow asserts that race and ethnicity are "destiny in American politics," refers to the "demographic mutation" America is inflicting upon itself (p. xxi), or even more pointedly: "Just as when you leave Park Avenue and descended into the subway, when you enter the INS waiting rooms you find yourself in an underworld that is not just teeming but is almost entirely colored"(1996: 28). His racial logic was not only criticized by expansionists, but by restrictionists as well. Mark Krikorian, the executive director of the Center for Immigration Studies (a restrictionist organization), sharply criticized Brimelow for equating race and nationality and even questioned the sincerity of his apparent concern for black Americans (1995).

The Social Organization of Nativism

Regarding nativism strictly as an ideological phenomenon overlooks its structural foundation, that is, the social relations and practices influencing the life chances of those categorized as natives and aliens. These processes are subject to redefinition and intervention, but once social relations between natives and aliens are institutionalized, individual volition is circumscribed. Specifically, social relations between natives and aliens are largely organized by, and through, the institutions of citizenship and immigration policy. These national practices, however, are considered legitimate, unlike the institutions thought to perpetuate racial and ethnic stratification. The concepts of identifiability and group position can untie the knot of ideas and practices embodying nativist activities. It is the identification of aliens by natives which makes the entire process possible, but it is the diagnosis of threat, grounded in a sense of group position, which precipitates the process.

Identifiability

Legal boundaries (citizen, immigrant, alien, border, etc.) and social boundaries (race, ethnicity, etc.) reflect relations of culture and power. They are not fixed, primordial distinctions, but culturally constructed boundaries that, despite their changing qualities, "are given meaning and sentiment by those who reside in them" (Basch, Glick Schiller, and Szanton Blanc 1995: 32-33). Conceived as "natural" distinctions, the meanings assigned to these social constructions influence people's attitudes and behaviors and can be reformulated and/or politicized for various purposes, economic or otherwise (Basch et al. 1995: 33). Because meaning does not inhere in the constructions themselves, but is, in part, developed by the people who reside within them, being a "native" begins with the perception that one is a native, not necessarily with one's place of birth or legal status. Although one's birthplace and citizenship influence one's national identity, relative power, and perceptions of others, to think and respond like a "native" is not a simple function of nativity or legal status.

A subpopulation's degree of identifiability is influenced by their phenotypic and cultural distinctiveness (Aguirre and Turner 1995: 31). The religious beliefs and practices of Catholics, political persuasions of "radical" immigrants, and "swarthy" complexions of southern and eastern Europeans were all used, at various times throughout American history, to identify each group as "alien." The selection of these symbols, at the exclusion of others, can in some measure be attributed to the ways in which Americans have "imagined" themselves (Anderson 1991).

Race and gender have figured prominently in U.S. immigration and naturalization laws (cf. Glenn and Parreñas 1996; Pedraza 1991; Ueda 1981) and continue to influence notions of who an American is, or at least should be (e.g., see Brimelow 1996). Because notions of "race" and "Americanness" are intertwined (cf. Almaguer 1994; Frankenberg 1993: 195-202) and our general understanding of what constitutes racism has become less clear since the 1960s (Sánchez 1997), it has become increasingly difficult to distinguish nativism from racism in a time when most immigrants are non-white. Secondly, Hondagneu-Sotelo (1995) argues that many of the proposed restrictions are aimed at women and children (e.g., Proposition 187 and the new welfare laws passed 1996). If nativism is to retain its utility in the social sciences, and avoid the kind of confusion that currently surrounds the concepts of racism and sexism, its meaning needs to be made more clear.

But a group's visibility, in and of itself, is not the cause of nativist activity. Seeing oneself and others as "natives" and others as "aliens" effectively places the groups in relation to each other, providing them with what Blumer (1958) calls a sense of group position. It is this sense of group position, emerging from the definitional process, that is fundamental to understanding the perceptions of natives.

Native as a Sense of Group Position

In his well-known essay, "Race Prejudice as a Sense of Group Position," Blumer theorizes that hostility between dominant and subordinate racial groups is initiated and sustained by a collective process of racial identification where racial groups form images of themselves and others. By characterizing each other, the groups define their positions *vis-à-vis* one another, and in so doing, contribute to what he calls a "sense of group position" (Blumer 1958: 3-4). This sense of group position provides the dominant group with "its framework of perception, its standard of judgment, its patterns of sensitivity, and its emotional proclivities" (1958: 4). It is from this sense of social position where feelings of competition and hostility emerge (Bobo and Hutchings 1996).

The notion as to where a group belongs—socially, economically, and so on—is linked, in part, to a definitional process. Leaders, spokespersons, intellectuals, and interest groups contribute to a group's image of itself and other "subordinate" groups. These individuals and organizations characterize and interpret significant events for their various audiences and constituencies, thereby contributing to the multiple—and often contradictory—perceptions of where one's group should stand in relation to various issues, or even more fundamentally, to other groups. When a dominant group forms a collective image of a subordinate group, they create an "abstract image" of that group. This image fosters the impression that the subordinate group is a "vast entity," and encourages members of the dominant group to eschew their various experiences or interactions with outsiders and rely instead on "their" leaders and spokespersons to interpret events and interactions for them (Blumer 1958: 5-6).

For dominant groups, such as "natives," the sense of group position consists of four perceptions: (1) a feeling of superiority, or ethnocentrism, (2) the perspective that out-group members are fundamentally "alien" or "different," (3) the view that one's group is entitled to privileged (or prior) rights, resources, and statuses—or to use Blumer's phrase, "a feeling of proprietary claim to certain areas of privilege and advantage" (1958: 4), and (4) a fear that out-group members are threatening, or will threaten, "their" rights and resources. Prompted and justified by feelings of superiority and entitlement, the dominant group assumes that certain resources belong solely, or at the very least, primarily, to them. When the dominant group senses a challenge to these exclusive claims, a hostile response is likely (Bobo and Hutchings 1996: 955; Blumer 1958:4; Quillian 1995: 588).

Explaining why certain people in the United States come to define others as "aliens" and develop exclusionary practices to limit their entrance into the nation-state—or participation in certain areas of "native privilege"—can be developed by modifying Blumer's notion that racial prejudice stems from a defense of group position. The importance of his work to nativism lies in its emphasis on group position and the multiple ways this position can be challenged. But how do we account for this sense of group position among natives, and secondly, for the fact that not every native responds to aliens in the same way? With some qualifications, I offer Conner's argument that the proprietary claims of natives are rooted in notions of ownership and entitlement:

> Nativism has appeared at both low and high points in the business cycle, at times of labor shortage and surplus. In some cases, recent large-scale immigration appears to have been a factor giving rise to nativism. But in other cases, a diaspora which had been resident for generations was suddenly targeted as unwanted aliens...The complexity of the pattern therefore frustrates attempts to anticipate outbreaks of nativism. *But this lack of pattern in itself tells us such considerations as the business cycle, the rate of immigration, cultural distance, historic animosities and the like are at most potential/ likely triggers or exacerbators but are not the root force.* Their relationship to nativism may be caustic, but it is not causal. *Explanation ultimately lies in the primal title to a homeland claimed by the indigenous ethno-racial group.* Though it may never be exercised, the power of eviction that is inherent in such a title to the territory may be translated into action at any time. Members of a diaspora can therefore never be at home in a homeland. They are at best sojourners, remaining at the sufferance of the indigenous people (1986: 19-20, italics added).

The basic core of nativism begins to unfold if the word "indigenous" is replaced with "native." Histories of colonialism and migration clearly demonstrate that one need *not* be indigenous to make proprietary claims. Rather, colonizers and immigrants can come to define themselves as "natives," and on that basis, arrogate certain rights unto themselves.[11]

For example, in 1790 the first federal naturalization law stipulated that only a "free white person" was eligible for naturalization. Through a gradual accumulation of judicial decisions, the courts concluded that American Indians were noncitizens because "although they were born in the U.S. territory, their allegiance remained to the tribe." (Ueda 1981: 737). In 1868, *citizenship* was guaranteed to all persons born in the United States, "excluding Indians not taxed," and in 1870, Congress amended the *naturalization* law of 1790 by allowing "aliens of African nativity" and "persons of African descent" to naturalize. Native Americans were not granted U.S. citizenship on the basis of jus soli (where citizenship is acquired by birth in the U.S. or one of its possessions) until 1924 (Ueda 1981: 738-43). The 1882 Chinese Exclusion Act introduced the infamous category "aliens ineligible for citizenship" to prohibit all foreign-born Chinese from naturalizing (Lee 1989: 376; INS Statistical Yearbook 1994). This category was applied to other "Asian" groups as well, and though exceptions were made in the following years, the category was not officially abolished until the enactment of the McCarran-Walter Act in 1952 (Ueda 1981: 746).

While certainly racial, these judicial and executive decisions were attempts to exclude aliens from the institution of citizenship. Racial politics shaped, and continue to shape, the status of white people (Winant 1997). In many ways, whiteness and national identity became synonymous. Racial considerations frequently determine who the "aliens" and "natives" are, but not always. During World War I, German-Americans were seen viewed as aliens—not because of their ethnicity—but because their national organization assumed a pro-Germany posture (Higham 1992). Throughout American history, whites (primarily men in power) have clearly viewed an inclusive

---

[11] This often requires a kind of historical amnesia. "Omission and historical error are central to creating a nation; the advancement of historical knowledge is often a threat to nationhood" (Ernest Renan, 1882, cited in Noiriel 1996: 1).

definition of citizenship as a threat to their material and symbolic interests (e.g., see Almaguer 1994).

A population's status as "natives" entitles them to certain claims, one of which is the "right" to exclude, for various reasons, those they define as "alien." But anyone can have claims. Without the power to enforce them, or more specifically, without the consent or support of the group in power, efforts to exclude or mistreat aliens will be difficult to implement. This definitional process does not, however, in and of itself explain nativist behavior. Natives can feel threatened by those they define as alien and have the power to discriminate against them, and still refrain from nativist behavior. There is a need to understand the conditions under which heightened nativist activity occurs and who promotes it. These issues will be addressed in Chapters 4-7, but for right now it is important to recognize that a sense of group position—native or otherwise—only provides its members with a general orientation, not with a script for behavior and beliefs (Blumer 1958: 5-6). A full understanding of nativism requires that a sense of group position be situated within the contexts of threat, perceived legitimacy and legality.

Defining Nativism

The concept of nativism simultaneously describes and stigmatizes certain beliefs and behaviors. And because these attitudes and actions are *portrayed* as illegitimate, the process and perception of nativism are fundamentally connected. The normative assumptions underpinning the concept, however, should not dissuade researchers from analyzing the phenomenon as a social and legal process. The preceding discussion examined the process and perception of nativism separately for ease of analysis, but the two components can, and will be, combined into one definition.

When a subpopulation is considered alien by those who consider themselves to be natives, and can be *identified* as such, nativism becomes *possible*. This is a necessary, but not sufficient, condition. It is the visibility of difference that allows natives to police systems of domination. Of course, "native" and "alien" are largely matters of perception, but like matters of "race," the categories preferred by the dominant group are usually decisive, regardless of their precision (e.g., see Wright 1994; Omi and Winant 1994: 55). Because they are socially and politically constructed, the images of "aliens" and "natives" will vary. A nativist can be a native-born American, a naturalized citizen, or even a recent immigrant, just as a recently arrived immigrant or third-generation American can appear "alien." The conceptions natives have of themselves and others—products of history and everyday life—contribute to their sense of group position and provide them with frameworks of perception and patterns of sensitivity that are "native" in orientation.

Because nativism is not precipitated by identifiability, a sense of threat (perceived or actual) must also be sensed if discrimination is to occur (Aguirre and Turner 1995: 34; Blumer 1958). Like "race prejudice," the source of nativism "lies in a felt challenge to this sense of group position" (Blumer 1958: 5). Aliens can challenge a group's position by threatening their racial dominance, cultural symbols (e.g., language and customs), encroaching on their privileged resources (e.g., certain jobs and public benefits), and threatening their sense of individual or national security (Blumer 1958; Zimmermann 1995; Aguirre and Turner 1995: 34). In many respects, these threats represent threats to privilege (e.g., racial, economic, and environmental privileges). These are only a few examples of how the behavior or sheer presence of aliens can threaten a populations' sense of group position.

However, as a *system* of exclusion and privilege, nativism requires more than a fear that one's proprietary claims are threatened. Unless a population has the *power* to enforce its claims, nativist attitudes will be present, but not the actual behavior of native-*ism*. Nativism implies the ability to exclude or discriminate against those who, for whatever reason, are deemed to be "non-natives"—aliens, in other words.[12] National citizenship and immigration policy are the primary institutions through which natives enforce their power over aliens. Without the power to define and enforce one's view of who is to be included or excluded from such proprietary entitlements, nativism will not emerge as a form of stratification. Noel (1968) argues that the emergence of ethnic stratification usually requires ethnocentrism, competition, and differential power. Similarly, the process of nativism requires a

---

[12] I am referring to power in the Weberian sense of the word.

definitional process, a perception of threat, and differential power. Without a definitional process, aliens and natives would quickly merge and distinctions would not be structured along native lines. Without a sense of threat there would be little reason to limit immigration or abridge the rights of resident aliens. Without differential power it would be difficult for one group to impose its will upon another (Noel 1968: 163; also see Aguirre and Tuner 1995).

Placing this process within a politically contested context (e.g., to define what is legitimate and what is not), I define nativism as *an illegitimate defense of native proprietary claims over and against the encroachment of aliens*. The terms "native" and "alien" are not immutable categories or natural, but ones of perception and identifiability. Aliens can be an internal and/or external population. Newly arrived immigrants as well as third-generation residents can be perceived as "alien" and "threaten" the proprietary claims of natives.

Attempts to exclude or discriminate against aliens, even if they are "unsuccessful," qualify as "defense." Even if a group has the power to initiate discrimination, resistance to it (from aliens or other natives) can limit its effectiveness. It is the attempt to use power that reveals one's intentions. When aliens encroach upon the proprietary claims of natives, the responses of a native population will vary according to their relative power, the *perceived* legitimacy of the proposed actions, and the overall social and legal contexts.

Because of its implicit evaluation, Bosniak contends that the meaning of nativism "is in important respects indeterminate" (1996: 282-83). The preceding exercise argues that nativism can and should be defined. Nativism is rooted in the notion that a population's status as "natives" entitles them to exclude or restrict "aliens" from certain spheres of importance or privilege. When this idea is put into action it becomes a process, and when the claims being protected are considered illegitimate by the general population, the process is considered nativistic. This will almost always occur within contexts perceived as threatening. The principle of national sovereignty is "well established by treaty law and constitutionally" (Sassen 1996: 65) and in many respects the current arbiter of appropriate and inappropriate conduct with respect to immigration reform. The national narrative describes the congruency between immigration and the national interest and also serves, although with less authority, as a gauge of what is right and wrong with respect to immigration reform. Because the principle of national sovereignty is the standard by which the attitudes and actions of Americans are gauged with respect to migration-related issues, the attendant evaluation is not something to be remedied, but something to be examined sociologically.

The concept of nativism sheds light on the dynamics of immigrant reception and incorporation (Portes and Rumbaut 1996). Its usefulness, however, can be improved. If nativism is to become a sharp analytical tool by which the reactions of "natives" to "aliens" are analyzed, further work—theoretical and empirical—is needed. To this end, the historical review in Chapter 3 illuminates the conditions under which heightened nativist activity typically occurs.

American Nativism in Historical Perspective

Analyzing the constitutive properties of nativism, those elements common to nativistic events, is the central purpose of this chapter. Although these properties are specified in the definition of nativism provided in the previous chapter, this review is designed to illustrate their interrelations. Special attention is given to the conditions under which nativism typically occurs. This research does not systematically analyze every nativist event in U.S. history, but places some of the more infamous incidents into one of three nativist eras. The contextual character of nativism is highlighted in each era, as well as the underlying interests and concerns typically sighted in heightened periods of nativist activity.

A Review of American Nativism

Because nativism is regularly associated with a number of beliefs and behaviors (cf. Bosniak 1997), there is no single study to consult when deciding if a certain event belongs in a survey of American nativism. This situation has been remedied, in some measure, by defining nativism as an illegitimate, native defense of proprietary claims over and against the encroachment of aliens. Applying this definition to the historical record, however, is fairly complex. The propriety claims of the American populace have changed throughout American history, as well as the definitions of "aliens" and legitimacy. Last year's alien can be this year's native, and yesterday's nativism can be today's immigration reform. In short, definitions of aliens and legitimacy change. This quandary is compounded by the fact that secondary materials, which are utilized in this review, are an inseparable blend of documentation and interpretation. These limitations are partly mitigated by relying on multiple sources to examine the same events and attendant conditions.

At the most general level, nativism is impelled by a perception of threat. The following analysis of nativist episodes, from the colonial era to the present, underscores how this perception has intersected with various contexts and ideas throughout American history. The following review does not examine every nativist incident in American history, nor does the inclusion of an event necessarily signify nativism. Some of the more prominent examples of nativism are juxtaposed with a diverse set of sociohistorical settings at the end of this chapter. In many ways, this review demonstrates how some natives have, in the words of Benedict Anderson, "imagined" their national community. Such communities "are to be distinguished, not by their falsity/genuineness, but by the style in which they are imagined" (1991: 6). This "style" is the subject of the following review.

The Ebb and Flow of Religious Nativism: 1600-1859

Anti-Catholicism was the most prevalent form of nativism in the colonial period. Distilled from "No-Popery" laws and a series of real and imagined Catholic conspiracies in seventeenth century England, English settlers tried to limit the immigration and rights of Catholics (Bennett 1995: 17-18; Billington 1963: 1-31; Curran 1975: 12-13). Religious intolerance varied from one colony to the next, but Catholics were routinely barred from entering certain colonies, holding public office, and voting (Fuchs 1990: 7-12; Leonard and Parmet 1971: 11-19; Muller 1993: 18). Even though it is impossible to chronicle and characterize every instance of anti-Catholicism, colonial nativists generally viewed Roman Catholicism as an "authoritarian" religion endangering the political stability of their settlements. To guard against this presumed danger, colonists strove to minimize their numbers and participation in civic affairs.

Catholics were prohibited from naturalizing throughout much of the colonial era, and until 1806, did not assume public office in most states, largely because of objectionable oaths (Leonard and Parmet 1971: 19; Ueda 1981: 735). England's Glorious Revolution of 1689 (where Parliament overthrew the Catholic King, James II) exacerbated anti-Catholic nativism in the colonies, precipitating rumors that Catholics were conspiring with Indians to massacre the Protestants (Bennett 1995: 19; Leonard and Parmet 1971: 12). In 1690, during the French and

Spanish Wars, Catholics were viewed as potential saboteurs, a fifth column.[13] "Every Catholic within the colonies was looked upon as a potential enemy who might let his papal allegiance supersede his loyalty to the crown by co-operating with the armies of French Canada and Spanish Florida against the settlers" (Billington 1963: 9). As a result, Catholics were—in some of the colonies—burdened with additional taxes, forbidden to settle in large groups, and disarmed (Bennett 1995: 20; Billington 1963: 9-16; Curran 1975: 16). Later, in 1755, Britain deported more than six thousand Acadians (French-speaking Catholic peasants from Nova Scotia) to the southern colonies. Their reception was a hostile one, and some even became indentured servants (Jones 1992: 26; Leonard and Parmet 1971: 13).

The conflation of Protestantism and republicanism in the colonial era contributed to conflicts between Protestants and Catholics. Puritans often saw themselves as a "Chosen People" in a "New Israel," where the virtues of liberty and commitment to the public good were republican *and* Protestant, secular and sacred. This perspective tended to cast secular events into sacred, pivotal phases in the "Holy Commonwealth," elevating republican virtues to the level of "sacred," and who better to guard these virtues than Protestants? (Hughey 1992: 538-541). Some Protestants viewed the Catholic church as a menace to their God-given liberty, and Catholics as pawns of the Pope. For a number of Protestants, it was the "secretive" and "conspiratorial" religion of Catholics which precluded their equal participation in the civic culture (Bennett 1995: 18-20; Jones 1992: 127; Leonard and Parmet 1971).

But the dominance of a Protestant-republican ideology cannot account for every nativist episode, even during the colonial era. If it could, nativism would have been an almost permanent, rather than sporadic, feature of colonial America (Hughey 1992: 542). Catholics were not entirely excluded from the civic culture, but tended to endure nativist hostilities during wartime and periods of relatively high immigration. They were not the only ones, however, to encounter opposition.

---

[13] The origin of the fifth column metaphor stems from the "column of supporters which General Mola declared himself to have in Madrid, when he was besieging it in the Spanish Civil War, in addition to the four columns of his army outside the city" (Oxford English Dictionary 1989: 890).

Jews, French Huguenots, Protestant Irish,[14] and Germans also faced native hostility. Like the Catholics, Jews were often barred from voting and holding office (Curran 1975: 13). The Protestant French Huguenots seemed more French than Protestant to the colonists, particularly during the Anglo-French wars in 1689. One of their settlements in Rhode Island was attacked by a mob, some were "compelled" to leave their homes in New York, and others were unjustly imprisoned in Pennsylvania (Curran 1975: 15; Jones 1992: 37).[15] German loyalty was questioned during the French and Indian Wars. Their large numbers and "clannishness" were especially resented in Pennsylvania. Benjamin Franklin worried that they might "Germanize" Pennsylvanians rather than assimilate—a fear clearly shared by the Pennsylvania, Delaware, and New Jersey legislatures (Curran 1975: 16; Leonard and Parmet 1971: 15, 115-116). In his 1751 *Observations Concerning the Increase of Mankind* Franklin asked, "why should the Palatine Boors be suffered to swarm our Settlements, and by herding together establish their Language and Manners to the Exclusion of ours" (cited in Leonard and Parmet 1971: 15). Lastly, the poverty and "large" numbers of the Protestant Irish drew nativist accusations and violence. In Boston, they were blamed for the increase in wheat prices, and in 1734, had their new Presbyterian church in Worcester destroyed (Curran 1975: 15).

Support for the new government replaced religion as the litmus test for loyalty as Catholics joined the revolutionary army and Catholic France became the colony's ally against the British (Bennett 1995: 20-21). Not until the mid-1830s would a strident anti-Catholicism reemerge. In the interim, two short ruptures of nativism occurred in the 1790s—one against foreign ideas, the other against foreigners. In the late 1790s, secret societies of Illuminati (composed mainly of

---

[14] The Protestant Irish are sometimes erroneously referred to as "Scotch Irish." Little "serious scholarship exists about the Protestant Irish...and all statements about their ethnic identity and integration into America need to be viewed somewhat critically" (Diner 1996: 171).

[15] By the eve of the revolution, however, the Huguenot's assimilation was so extensive that they were often indistinguishable from the general colonial population, and in many cases had "Americanized" their surnames, such as Paul Revere, who came from the Huguenot family of Rivoire (Jones 1992: 43).

Freemasons and other anti-Catholics) were accused of trying to abolish the republic's political and religious institutions. Their zeal to bring all people under the rules of reason, and secretive manner, allegedly violated—among other things—property rights, organized religion, and the innocence of women (Hofstadter 1996: 10-14). But by 1799 the thesis of an "Illuminism conspiracy" could not endure public scrutiny and the movement fell into disrepute (Bennett 1995: 23-25). The second rupture, the passage of the Alien and Sedition Acts in 1798, was primarily directed against the foreign-born and was propelled in part by the Federalist's resentment and distrust of the many foreigners who sided with the Jeffersonians (Bennett 1995: 22; Leonard and Parmet 1971: 22-23; Muller 1993: 21). The first *federal* immigrant (naturalization) and immigration policies were established in the 1790s (INS 1994).

Between 1815 and 1860 the rapid transformations surging through the young republic had Americans asking questions and restrictionists giving answers. Over five million immigrants arrived between 1820 and 1860, dwarfing the estimated 250,000 who arrived between 1776 and 1820 (INS Yearbook 1991: 13, 47). Many of the newcomers were Catholic—between 1841 and 1850 their numbers swelled from 663,000 to 1,606,000 (Leonard and Parmet 1971: 34). "Dramatic changes in population, territory, transportation, industry, and urban growth transformed the United States from a small, primarily agricultural and rural nation of about 10,000,000 in 1820 into an industrial-urban giant of 31,000,000 in 1860" (Leonard and Parmet 1971: 34). While these changes would set the stage for nativists in the early- to mid-1800s, the threat of secession and public's impatience with established political parties proved to be even more decisive (Holt 1973).

The destruction of churches and convents, Catholic scare literature, and violent clashes between Protestants and Catholics were standard fare in the 1830s. In New York, St. Mary's was set afire in 1831—the first in a series of church burnings and desecrations that would continue up until the Civil War (Leonard and Parmet 1971: 57). The 1834 burning of the Ursuline Convent School in Charlestown, Massachusetts on August 10 was perhaps the most notorious example of Protestant violence. Drawing from Samuel F.B. Morse's books warning of an international Catholic conspiracy, the Reverend Beecher delivered three anti-Catholic speeches in Boston during the day and incited forty to fifty Bostonians to cross the river and torch the school (Bennett 1995: 40-41; Leonard and Parmet 1971: 57). Other anti-Catholic publications followed, often excusing these acts of violence and encouraging new ones. *The Awful Disclosures of Maria Monk* (1836) falsely alleged that priests were raping young women and killing their offspring after baptizing them. The book sold 300,000 copies by the Civil War, and until surpassed by *Uncle Tom's Cabin*, was the best-selling book in American history (Bennett 1995: 42-43; Leonard and Parmet 1971: 58).

A controversy over the funding of New York parochial schools took place between 1840 and 1842. Comparable debates later emerged in Philadelphia and Cincinnati, contributing to the formation of local restrictionist organizations and sparking riots in Brooklyn and Philadelphia (Leonard and Parmet 1971: 66-84). Restrictionist organizations, particularly the American Republican party, tasted political success in mayoral and congressional races in New York, Pennsylvania, and Massachusetts in 1844 (Bennett 1995: 53-59). But such victories were short-lived. Support for restrictionist activities faded as riots between native-born Americans and Irish erupted in Philadelphia and Brooklyn. Respectable middle class Protestants were apparently displeased with the violence and a number of other Americans began, in 1846, to focus on the Mexican War.[16] The movement itself was also to blame, however, as political amateurs and opportunists lacked the organizational skills needed to sustain the campaign (Leonard and Parmet 1971: 79-80). While the militia was able to curb the riots in Brooklyn, approximately a hundred people were wounded and thirty were killed in Philadelphia (Bennett 1995: 56-58; Leonard and Parmet 1971: 74-79; Purcell and Poole 1941: 29-30).

The restrictionist movement regained momentum by the early 1850s. The looming sectional crisis and general public's dissatisfaction with the Whigs and Democrats provided them with the opportunity to actualize their agendas (Bennett 1995: 106-134; Holt 1973). Historians have tended to place context (e.g., sectional discord, high immigration)

---

[16] Throughout the war "there never materialized a national Protestant sentiment directed at transforming the struggle into a Protestant jihad south of the border...[although] most southern Protestants, particularly the Methodists and Baptists, were vigorous in their support of the war" (Hinckley 1962: 121-122).

at the center of their reconstructed, "causal" analyses of nativist activity in the 1850s. While recognizing that context is critical to understanding the variety and intensity of nativism at a given locale and time, overemphasizing its importance can obscure the different motivations people bring to a nativist organization or event. Holt raises a related point in his research on the origins of "Know Nothingism," observing that the public's displeasure with the government and political parties are endemic in American history, and that there are hazards in using such constant phenomena to interpret discrete events (1973: 312-313). As much as these conditions contributed to the appeal of nativism, other factors must also be considered, such as the nativist organizations themselves.

The nativist societies born in the 1840s, such as the Order of United Americans (OUA) and Order of United American Mechanics (OUAM), carried the nativist "seed" into the fifties, facilitating the development of what later became known as the Know Nothing movement (Bennett 1995: 106). In 1850, the Order of the Star Spangled Banner was founded in New York, and their ranks quickly swelled, often with OUA members. Instructed to say they "know nothing" when outsiders asked about their society, Horace Greeley of the New York Tribune contemptuously labeled them as such in 1853 (Bennett 1995: 110-112). At one time, the Know Nothings had over 1.25 million members and ten thousand councils (McCauley 1990: 87). Most effective as a local movement, their council system doubled as a political system for the American Party (the official name of the Know Nothings) to elect seven governors, eight U.S. senators, and 104 U.S. Representatives by 1856 (Fuchs 1990: 41; Leonard and Parmet 1971: 99). So effective and popular was the American Party in 1855 that the *New York Herald* unhappily predicted a presidential victory in 1856. But the very issue which helped unite the American Party in the early 1850s—slavery—proved too divisive just a few years later (Bennett 1995: 116, 123-25; Anbinder 1992: 162-219).

Unable to ignore the slavery crisis in their own national meetings between 1854 and 1856, and accentuated by regional differences in group membership and objectives, consensus in the American Party began to wane. In the West, antislavery forces in some states brought immigrants into the restrictionist fold, while other state parties excluded them (Bennett 1995: 136; Leonard and Parmet 1971: 95; Pitt

1961). Convinced that immigrants opposed slavery and favored free soil, the South tended to be more anti-immigrant than anti-Catholic. Immigrants supposedly "disrupted" their southern culture by violating race relations etiquette and gaining entrance into city politics (Bennett 1995: 141-142; Miller 1985: 46-51). West of Buffalo, the Know Nothing party frequently focused on foreign Germans instead of the Irish because they apparently resented their economic achievements. In Texas, Germans and Catholic Mexicans were targeted, but in New Orleans, Catholics belonged to the American Party (Bennett 1995: 135, 144, 147). While the Know Nothings generally disliked Catholics and immigrants, the regional differences underscore the multiple interests of restrictionists. Some exploited the nativist theme for its political and economic dividends, others merged it with dissimilar agendas, and still others entered as American patriots.

In 1856, the party's candidate for President, Millard Fillmore, came in a distant third, bringing the party's activities to a close in most states. Except in a few border states, the Know Nothings were little more than a shell by 1860. It would take a Civil War, one fought by Catholics and immigrants alike, to expunge the anti-immigrant and anti-Catholic sentiment of the sixties (Bennett 1995: 154-155; Miller 1985: 52). But the transformative power of war could only last so long—new contexts and ideas would once again bring nativists to their feet.

"Racial" and "Radical" Nativism: 1860-1929

The Civil War may have brought organized nativism to a transitory halt, but it was the expanding economy and frontier that allowed immigrants to retain their wartime laurels for the next two decades (Higham 1992: 13-14). Suspicions of disloyalty did however emerge during the war. General Grant expelled Jews from his military jurisdiction in 1862, but revoked the order three weeks later at Lincoln's request. In 1863, an effort to revive the Know Nothing movement failed in New York as discontents from the Irish working class participated in the four-day "draft riots" which were "widely interpreted as a disloyal Irish conspiracy inspired by Confederate agents" (1992: 13). During the 1860s and 1870s, European immigrants seemed to be a national blessing, but on the West Coast, the Chinese were attacked by mobs and saddled with discriminatory laws (cf. Almaguer 1994; Higham 1992; Hing 1996; Lane 1987).

The Chinese, and later Japanese, encountered "racial nativism" much earlier than did immigrants from southern and eastern Europe. Many of the actions directed toward them bore the imprint of a racial and nativist logic generally not seen when examining the receptions encountered by European immigrants during the same time period (cf. Blauner 1972; Barrera 1979: 34-57; Almaguer 1994). Not until the eugenics movement of the early 1900s were southern and eastern European immigrants exposed to a pervasive racial logic. This is perhaps why Higham concluded that no "variety of anti-European sentiment has ever approached the violent extremes to which anti-Chinese agitation went in the 1870's and 1880's" (1992: 25).

Anti-Catholicism and anti-radical sentiment briefly flared in the 1870s, although both lacked "nativistic significance." In 1875, Republicans in Ohio and New Jersey successfully exploited the anti-Catholic theme for election purposes, but instead of blaming immigrants, nativists directed their gaze toward the Catholic clergy. Among the rioting immigrants in the railroad strikes of 1877 nativists saw the specter of communism at work, but little was done to address this fear (Higham 1992: 30-31). Nativist agitation also cropped up in the urban areas of the Northeast and older Midwest in the 1880s (Higham 1992: 63-64), but in 1882 the Chinese Exclusion Act suspended almost all Chinese immigration and also barred foreign-born Chinese from naturalizing, thereby creating the infamous category "aliens ineligible for citizenship" (Lee 1989: 376; INS Statistical Yearbook 1991). Anti-Chinese sentiment on the West Coast had been building at least since the mid-1800s, thanks in part to the efforts of California's white working class (Almaguer 1994: 178-180). The Chinese Exclusion Act was not repealed until 1943, when the U.S. and China were allies during the Second World War (Ueda 1981).

In May 1886, "the Haymarket Affair was to go down as the most important single incident in late nineteenth century nativism" (Higham 1992: 54). In the midst of a national strike for an eight-hour day, a meeting was called by Chicago anarchists in the Haymarket Square. A bomb exploded as the police closed in on the peaceful group. "Instantly, a torrent of nationalist hysteria coursed through the cities of the Northeast and Midwest" (1992: 54). Even though the police were unable to determine the bomber's identity, six immigrants and one native-born American were sentenced to death. The aftershock of the Haymarket Affair revived some of the old fraternal organizations of the 1840s and 1850s, especially the Junior Order United American Mechanics, whose membership list quadrupled in just four years. The fraternal orders were anti-radical first, and anti-Catholic second, but local anti-Catholic societies sprang up in the eighties to carry on the crusade. In 1887, the American Protective Association (APA) was established in Iowa, and by 1890 "its local councils were flourishing in communities from Detroit to Omaha" (1992: 63). But nativism never garnered a national following as it had in the 1850s. It seemingly lacked the kind of nationalist formula that equated specific immigrant groups with subversive activity or inherently "un-American" ideas (1992: 54-64).

Following the economic downturns of the mid-1870s and mid-1880s, the depression in the 1890s contributed to a resurgence of nativist activities (Bennett 1995: 165; Higham 1992: 69, 94). European aliens found themselves ineligible for certain jobs and Catholics increasingly became the targets of the American Protective Association. The APA, over a half-million strong in 1894, was particularly active in the Midwest. They accused Catholics of intentionally disrupting the economy for the purpose of facilitating a Roman takeover, boycotted their businesses, and were involved in two Protestant-Catholic riots. They helped re-elect William McKinley as governor of Ohio and aided sympathizers in their bids for Congress (Bennett 1995: 171-178; Higham 1992: 80-87). But by the latter part of 1894, internal dissension racked the organization, and the religious fervor of the organization carried less weight with a changing middle-class. "In an increasingly secular culture, enthusiastic religion was passing out of middle-class life, and without it the belief that popery lay behind the major national perils was hard to sustain" (Higham 1992: 86). To frame this observation in the terminology of C. Wright Mills (1940), the APA's religious vocabularies of motive were "on the wane" and no longer served as an "an unquestioned answer to questions concerning social and lingual conduct" (pp. 907, 910). Their actions had changed little, but their justifications were apparently beginning to lose their appeal among the middle class.

Anti-radical nativism also surfaced in the nineties, but in a much more violent show of force. In 1897, deputies opened fire on a group of unarmed Hungarian and Polish strikers in Pennsylvania, injuring forty immigrants and killing twenty-one. In 1891, eleven Italians were lynched in New Orleans (Bennett 1995: 169; Higham 1992: 88-90). However, an improving economy and the swift defeat of Spain in the 1898 Spanish-American War seemed to dam the current of restriction for a short while, but another crisis would shortly reappear.

The twentieth century began on the restrictionist foot with the Immigration Acts of 1903 and 1907. In response to the assassination of President McKinley in 1901 by Leo Czolgosz, a native-born anarchist of obvious foreign extraction, Congress pushed for the exclusion and deportation of alien anarchists. This objective was incorporated into the more general 1903 bill, which expanded the criteria for excluding and deporting aliens, and for the first time since the Aliens Act of 1798, penalized immigrants for their political beliefs. The Immigration Act of 1907 doubled the head tax from two to four dollars and authorized the President to deny admission to immigrants that he deemed detrimental to U.S. labor conditions. This provision was primarily aimed at Japanese laborers (Higham 1992: 111-130; INS 1994: A.1-4 - A.1-5) and was followed by the Gentlemen's Agreement of 1907-08, which sharply curtailed Japanese immigration (cf. Hing 1993: 54).

Not until the second decade of the twentieth century were specific European groups systematically filtered through a racial lens. The American Breeders' Association incorporated eugenics into its field in 1907, and in 1910, Sir Francis Galton launched the eugenics movement in England. He and a host of others were committed to race improvement through selective breeding. The National Committee for Mental Hygiene, a group of psychiatrists fearful that "mental defectives" would pollute future generations, added a provision to the immigration bill of 1914 excluding people of "constitutional psychopathic inferiority" (Higham: 1992: 151-152). But it was not until Madison Grant published his *Passing of the Great Race* in 1916 that eugenicists and other race thinkers received what later was to become an indispensable tool in reducing legal immigration—a racial typology (Higham 1992: 152-157). Grant warned that the extinction of the Nordic race was inevitable unless the hordes of Alpines, Mediterraneans, and Jewish hybrids were turned back. Even though

Grant's book was relatively insignificant when it debuted in 1916, "its appearance before America's entry into the First World War indicates that the old Anglo-Saxon tradition had finally emerged in at least one mind as a systematic, comprehensive world view" (Higham 1992: 157, 201).

This world view was put on hold by America's entrance into the First World War. Although the circulation of *The Menace*, an anti-Catholic weekly, rose to over 1.5 million by April, 1915, it lost a million subscriber's in little over a year as the war with Germany diverted the public's attention to another "fifth column"—German-Americans (Higham 1992: 200-214). The German-American Alliance's bold support for Germany, the virtually unanimous pro-Germany stance of the German-American press, and a few blundered attempts at sabotage by a group of Germans, was intolerable to a country drunk on "100 per cent Americanism" (Conzen 1981: 422; Harrington 1981: 685; Higham 1992: 204-207). Federal agents used the 1798 Alien Enemies Act to arrest 6,300 Germans ("enemy aliens"), of whom 2,300 were interned. Congress also enacted the 1917 Espionage Act and 1918 Sedition Act to prosecute U.S. citizens of German origin who "criticized the war effort or obstructed the draft" (Ellis and Panayi 1994: 242). During the war, German-Americans not only "swatted" the hyphen, but also Americanized German names—for example, Schmidt became Smith, East Germantown, Indiana was renamed Pershing, and sauerkraut became "liberty cabbage" (Ellis and Panayi 1994: 245). Nonetheless, these last minute demonstrations of loyalty did little to pacify official or public sentiment. Volunteer "spy-hunting" organizations, such as the American Protective League, continued to harass German Americans, and by early 1915, fifteen states passed laws requiring that English be the language of instruction in all public and private schools (Higham 1992: 211; Harrington 1981: 685; Kamphoefner 1996: 157; Ross 1994).

After the war, Attorney General Palmer preserved America's fear of foreign subversives by creating the General Intelligence Division in 1919 to weed out "radicals." In a series of "Palmer raids" conducted between 1919 and 1920, agents from the Department of Justice stormed Russian worker meeting places in twelve cities. Thousands were arrested and hundreds of aliens were deported to Russia. Some were even forced to leave their families behind (Higham 1992: 229-231;

Bennett 1995: 190-195). A false prediction of terrorism by Palmer in 1920, however, brought the Red Scare to an abrupt end (Bennett 1995: 195-196). This debacle marks a transition in nativist apprehension, where a fear of foreign radicals was increasingly overshadowed by a general uneasiness with "inferior races."

Between 1920 and 1927 Henry Ford's *Dearborn Independent* deplored the control allegedly exerted by "International Jews" and, at one point, reached a circulation of 700,000. Two new editions of Grant's *The Passing of the Great Race* also appeared in the early twenties (Bennett 1995: 205-210; Higham 1992: 272-284). The Ku Klux Klan stepped up its restrictionist and racist initiatives in the early twenties and acquired somewhere between two and three million recruits by 1924 (Bennett 1995: 223; Higham 1992: 297). Although white supremacy played an influential role in the twenties, their ideas converged on populations that seemed especially "foreign." Catholics, Jews, and foreigners were the Klan's main targets (Higham 1992: 290-291). Eastern European Jews faced discrimination in housing, employment, and college admissions in the twenties (Gold and Phillips 1995: 184-185). Eugenicists were also hard at work, conducting experiments in the laboratory and lobbying for less immigration in the nation's capitol.

The Immigration Act of 1924, which did not assume its full form until 1929, barred "aliens ineligible for citizenship" and instituted a "national origins quota system." Primarily designed to limit immigration from southeastern Europe, the system used 1890, then 1920, as the base year for determining annual quotas for eligible nationalities (INS 1996; Higham 1992: 300-330; Simon 1993: 67). The House Committee on Immigration intended to discriminate against immigrants from southeastern Europe but realized they could not openly defend the bill on grounds of Nordic superiority nor shift to an older census base without revealing their bias for immigrants from northwestern Europe. Using 1920 as the quota base instead of 1890 proved to be equally restrictive without appearing overtly racist (Higham 1992: 319-24).

The racial tone characterizing previous immigration dates, starting as early as 1918, is unmistakable: "Out of the rising vigor of the racial tradition in the early twenties came one plea after another for an immigration law designed specifically to keep the old stock from being 'hopelessly bogged down in the mire of mongrelization'" (Higham 1992: 313). President Coolidge captured the sentiment well when he signed the National Origins Act of 1924 by declaring that "America must be kept American" (cited in Gould 1981: 232). Such opinions were widely held and discussed in the early 1920s, and contrary to being the ravings of a few xenophobes and racists, were considered intellectually sound.

The research and lobbying efforts of eugenicists helped to secure the passage of the Immigration Act of 1924. During World War I, 1.75 million army recruits were given mental age tests by Harvard Professor Robert M. Yerkes. Although his research design was conceptually unsound and methodologically flawed (see Gould 1981: 199-222), Yerkes and his assistant, E.G. Boring, had little problem accounting for the low mental age of Nordics—the intelligent native stock was being swamped by the "dregs of southern and eastern Europe" (Gould 1981: 196). This conclusion was followed by an even more "scientific" finding—European immigrants could be ranked by their country of origin. "The darker peoples of southern Europe and the Slavs of eastern Europe are less intelligent than the fair peoples of western and northern Europe" (1981: 197). These results were later transformed into a social prescription by C.C. Brigham's *A Study of American Intelligence* (1923). Relying on Grant's typology of three races, Brigham concluded that the only way to arrest the deterioration of "American intelligence" (i.e., Nordic intelligence) was to regulate reproduction and restrict immigration (1981: 227-230). Brigham's political advice and "hard" army data were used to help justify the national origins system. Recognizing that he had measured one's fluency in English and culture, and not intelligence, Brigham recanted in 1930. But it was too late. Numerous Jewish refugees, anticipating the holocaust, could not emigrate (1981: 232-233).

Wartime Nativism and Emerging Concerns: 1930-1998

"The darker, often understated, sides of the immigrants' woes of the 1930s involved those who elected to stay and were forced out and those who sought to enter and were kept out" (Barkan 1996: 44). The deportation or repatriation of 500,000 to 600,000 persons of Mexican ancestry in the decennial wake of the Great Depression symbolizes those who desired to stay but were forced out (Barkan 1996: 47; Samora 1971: 41). It is estimated that by the end of the decade more than half of those who returned to Mexico were American citizens and that a third of the Los Angeles Mexican community emigrated to Mexico (Barkan 1996: 47; Sánchez 1993: 210).

Those who tried to enter, but were kept out—primarily Jewish refugees—encountered a President and State Department hesitant to admit them as refugees or expand the immigration quotas. However, these two offices are not solely to blame. Public opinion polls between 1938 and 1941 reveal a pervasive anti-Semitism that clearly influenced Roosevelt's position (Barkan 1996: 50-53; Bennett 1995: 265; Simon and Alexander 1993: 31; Simon 1993: 68). Anti-Semitism was steered through the air waves by Father Coughlin, a Detroit-area Roman Catholic priest. While his Christian Front against Communism focused on "the problem of the American Jews," Coughlin reprinted the speeches of Nazi propaganda minister Joseph Goebbels in his widely-read newspaper, *Social Justice* and personally praised the "social justice" meted out by the Third Reich. With an estimated 30 million listeners by the mid-thirties—not to mention a wide readership—Coughlin amassed the largest radio audience in the world. But his support for Germany against the "British-Jewish-Roosevelt conspiracy," and the banning of *Social Justice* from the mails—for violating the Espionage Act—contributed to his downfall (Bennett 1995: 253-266).

Fearful of a fifth column, Congress established a set of internal and external barriers when war erupted in Europe. "Admissions from Nazi-occupied countries were reduced by 75 percent" and Congress enacted the Alien Registration Act in 1940, requiring all resident aliens fourteen and older to be fingerprinted and register annually (Barkan 1996: 58-59; Daniels 1993: 24). On 8 December 1941, the day the U.S. declared war against Japan, President Roosevelt directed the FBI and other related agencies to arrest all Italian and German aliens they regarded as a threat to national security (Fox 1988: 410; 1990: 52). By 4 February 1942 the FBI had arrested 261 Italians and 1,361 Germans, and by 5 October 1943, 5,300 Japanese, 3, 503 Italians and 5, 977 Germans had been taken into custody. Of those arrested, none were convicted of sabotage, although 228 Italians were interned for various lengths of time (Fox 1990: 151-163; Nelli 1981: 558).

On 19 February 1942, President Roosevelt signed Executive Order 9066, authorizing the army, under the Secretary of War's direction, to "prescribe military spaces" and exclude "any or all persons" as military necessity required (Executive Order 9066, cited in Myer 1971: 307). While the words "Japanese" and "Japanese American" are never mentioned in the order, they alone were interned en masse (Daniels 1972: 70-71). By 7 August 1942, nearly all of the West Coast Japanese (112,704 in all, nearly two-thirds of whom were American citizens) were either in War Relocation camps or in Wartime Civil Control Administration (WCCA) Assembly centers (Daniels 1972: 104). The camps were scattered throughout the U.S. interior and reached as far as Jerome, Arkansas (Daniels 1993: 56). Life in the camps was not unduly harsh, and with the exception of barbed wire and armed sentries, bore little resemblance to the concentration camps in Germany (Daniels 1972: 105). However, they dwelled in barracks, ate in mess-halls, used communal toilets and showers, dressed in identical clothing, and endured days marked with monotony, tension, and violence (Kitano 1981: 567-568). By 1943, the WRA began to release "evacuees" who satisfied certain requirements, and by January 1945, most Japanese were allowed to leave the camps (Polenberg 1980: 67-70).

The fate of German and Italian aliens came frightfully close to that of the Japanese, but in the end took on a much smaller course. From January to May 1942, various officials at the local, regional, and federal level requested that "all 'enemy' aliens and their families be interned for the duration of the war" (Fox 1988: 407-408; 1990: 41). The failure to realize this objective can be attributed to, among other things, bureaucratic infighting between the War and Justice Departments, racism, the logistics of relocating and/or interning possibly millions of Germans and Italians, and the recognition that such an action would inevitably interrupt the war effort (Fox 1988: 435-438; 1990: 183-187). All three groups were ordered to evacuate certain military areas in March 1942 (approximately 2,500 to 3,000 Italians were required to leave Monterey Bay alone), but in April, while the Japanese were being transported to concentration camps, German and Italian aliens endured "silly indignities," such as a 9 p.m. to 6 a.m. curfew, travel restrictions, and the confiscation of their cameras, radios, and firearms. The restrictions lasted approximately nine months and affected most of the German and Italian aliens on the West Coast (Fox 1990: 59-88).

Mexican Americans in Los Angeles were also portrayed as a fifth-column, albeit for a shorter period of time. Between 1942 and 1943, descriptions of "Mexican juvenile delinquency either replaced or were printed alongside stories of supposed disloyalty among interned Japanese Americans. Chicano youth were increasingly depicted as the 'enemy within'" (Sánchez 1993: 267). Such press accounts continued to inflame public opinion, and in June 1943, Anglo servicemen and Mexican American youth clashed for ten days in the "Zoot Suit Riots." Tearing off the youths' oversized suits and assaulting them, Anglo servicemen were joined by civilians in their provocations and confrontations with the "zoot suiters" (Sánchez 1993: 267; Barkan 1996: 70).

Primarily because of the Cold War, a fear of foreign radicals did not subside with the war's end. Passage of the McCarran Internal Security Act in 1950 made membership "in any subversive organization...grounds for exclusion, deportation, denial of citizenship, and even the loss of citizenship" (Barkan 1996: 76). The McCarran-Walter Immigration and Nationality Act of 1952 brought this policy and the preceding myriad of immigration and naturalization laws under one legislative roof. Although the act preserved the basic national origins formula and fortified the federal government's deportation powers, it removed race as a barrier to naturalization, thereby eliminating the infamous category "aliens ineligible for citizenship" (INS 1994: A.1-12; Barkan 1996: 77; Ueda 1981: 746). However, the act continued to emphasize what wartime actions had already made clear—that the rights of naturalized citizens were not quite equal to those of native-born citizens. Membership in a supposedly subversive group was grounds for denaturalization, as well as deportation and exclusion (Barkan 1996: 104).

Another initiative connected to the wartime effort was "Operation Wetback." At the request of U.S. employers, the "bracero program" began when the U.S. and Mexico "signed an international agreement to allow Mexican contract laborers (braceros) to work in agriculture, railroad construction, and maintenance" (Romo 1996: 92). Although the agreement was extended several times until its cessation in 1964 (Romo 1996: 92), an increasing number of border apprehensions in the early fifties prompted Eisenhower to appoint a new INS Commissioner to curb illegal border crossers. In 1954, the INS launched "Operation Wetback" and "apprehended more than one million undocumented Mexican persons and nearly one-quarter million more the following fiscal year" (Barkan 1996: 84).[17]

Although not fully implemented until 1968, the national origins system was finally abolished with the non-controversial passage of the 1965 Immigration and Nationality Act Amendments, thereby removing the ban on Asian entry. However, a ceiling on Western Hemisphere immigration impeded the legal migration of Latin American immigrants for the very first time (Daniels 1991: 338; Massey 1995: 637-638; INS 1994: A.1-14).

Nevertheless, between the end of World War II and the early 1980s, immigration received (relatively speaking) scant attention from the public and policymakers (see Table 1). America apparently had more pressing matters to deal with—the "blight of affluence," poverty, juvenile delinquency, communism, and civil rights (cf. Ehrenreich 1990; Fuchs 1990). However, by the mid to late seventies, another wave of "neorestrictionist" sentiment emerged (Daniels 1991: 388; Espenshade and Hempstead 1996: 538-539). Beginning in April 1980, and ending the following fall, 125,000 Cubans arrived in the United States. Precipitated by a three-way dispute between the U.S., Cuba, and Peru—and Castro's declaration that people could leave as long as they went directly to the U.S.—thousands of Cuban exiles violated U.S. law by chartering boats in Miami and traveling ninety miles to Cuba's Mariel Harbor to pick up "relatives, friends, and anyone else there was room for" (Daniels 1991: 347; Pedraza 1996: 269). According to the INS, about nineteen percent of the Mariel refugees admitted to having been jailed in Cuba, although it "considered only 7 percent to be serious criminals—less than 2 percent of all the Marielitos" (Pedraza 1996: 271). The press, however, accentuated the criminal element in their portrayals of the Marielitos (Pedraza 1996: 269-271), and even afforded Al Pacino the opportunity to complement his performance in *The Godfather* by assuming the role of another gangster in *Scar Face*.

---

[17] Apprehension statistics are based on events, not individuals. A person apprehended three times during a fiscal year "will appear three times in the apprehension statistics" (INS 1996: 159).

In 1983 Senator Hayakawa and John Tanton, a Michigan ophthalmologist, founded U.S. English for the purpose of establishing English as the nation's official language. Although an "anti-bilingual ordinance" had already been approved in Dade County, Florida in 1980, and other official language laws had been passed in several states before 1980, the organized and well-financed U.S. English immeasurably contributed to what became known as the "English Only" movement (cf. Draper and Jiménez 1990/1992; Crawford 1992). Between 1981 and 1990, ten Southern and Midwestern states established English as their official language, and by 1990, seventeen states "had adapted laws or constitutional amendments designating English as their official language" (Crawford 1992: 16; Tatalovich 1993).

The objectives of U.S. English and other related groups were questioned by expansionists because of their association with restrictionist, and allegedly racist, organizations. During Tanton's tenure as chairman of FAIR, the Federation received approximately half a million dollars from The Pioneer Fund, an organization which funds eugenics and race-IQ research. U.S. English may have also received funding from The Pioneer Fund, but this allegation remains at the level of speculation (Stefancic 1997; Torres 1993: 255-58; Crawford 1992: 160). Tanton denied any knowledge of their eugenics agenda, but a 1986 memorandum to participants of an upcoming WITAN meeting (a forum where prominent restrictionists met to discuss matters of culture, language, immigration, and population) confirmed, for expansionists, suspicions of racism.

The "thought-provoking" memo became public in 1988 when the *Arizona Republic* published portions of it shortly before Arizona voters approved the "Official English" initiative. Tanton wrote: "Will the present majority peaceably hand over its political power to a group [Hispanics] that is simply more fertile?...Perhaps this is the first instance in which those with their pants up are going to get caught by those with their pants down!..." (cited in Crawford 1992: 151). Tanton explained that the memo was written for "a group of people who were already initiated into immigration, population, and language issues," but nonetheless decided to resign from U.S. English before the excerpts were published "in hopes that the crest of the controversy would pass by election day" (FAIR *Tenth Anniversary Oral History Project*, Tanton: 76).

Numerous authors have portrayed the agendas of U.S. English and other "English Only" organizations as surrogates for racism and/or immigration restriction because of their connection to non-linguistic organizations (e.g., see Torres 1993), but others have found it difficult to infer motives because of the organizations' members and their explanations:

> Sponsors of Official English initiatives became a moving target for anyone seeking to pin them down about their goals. One day they appeared as jackbooted language police, the next as high-minded seekers of ethnic harmony...Some prominent advocates of Official English have foreign accents and liberal politics; surprisingly few have Anglo-Saxon surnames...Some of these assimilated first- and second-generation Americans are among the most militant exponents of English Only. Which makes it problematic to pin charges of nativism, ethnocentrism, or racism on those who hold such views (Crawford 1992: 18-19, 24-25).

Investigating motives requires researchers to look beyond individuals and contexts if they are to leave analytical room for the diversity of motives and vocabularies found within each restrictionist organization and/or event.

Just as the Mariel incident exhibited a sizable gap between immigration policy and the reality of migration (Daniels 1991: 347), so too did the events following the passage of the 1986 Immigration Reform Control Act (IRCA). Although IRCA was restrictionist in intent, the status of nearly 3 million formerly undocumented immigrants was legalized and "did not stop the flow of unauthorized migrants, despite a big drop immediately after 1986" (Rumbaut 1996: 27-28; Hondagneu-Sotelo 1994: xiv). During this time, restrictionist sentiment "represented less a response to undocumented migration per se than to undocumented immigrant settlement...Claims...of the 'Mexicanization,' or *reconquista* (reconquest) sometimes animated this discourse" (Hondagneu-Sotelo 1994: xv). Accusations that settled immigrants were "unassimilable," stealing jobs from U.S. citizens, and weakening the economy through their use of social services, helped to lock in the legislation (Hondagneu-Sotelo 1994: xv).

In early 1991, a number of events in the Midwest resembled those taken by the public and U.S. government during the First and Second World Wars. Arab Americans were the target of numerous hate crimes during the Persian Gulf War, including physical assaults, two bombings of an Arab American owned grocery store in Cincinnati, and a bomb threat to a Detroit area high school where students of Arab descent constituted almost half of the student body (Edmonds 1991b: 3A). In addition to these reactions, FBI agents questioned hundreds of Arab Americans in the Detroit area and throughout the country about their political views and knowledge of potential terrorists (Cook 1991: 12A; Edmonds 1991a: 8A).

On 8 November 1994, voters in California passed Proposition 187 by a 59% to 41% margin, an initiative designed to exclude all "illegal aliens" from tax supported benefits, such as public education and welfare. "According to exit polls, 64 percent of whites, 57 percent of Asian Americans, 56% of African Americans, and 31 percent of Latinos voted in favor of Proposition 187" (Martin 1995: 255-59). Although some sections of the proposition were immediately challenged, a dozen other states were not dissuaded from considering similar measures (Martin 1995; Espenshade and Hempstead 1996: 536). The "Save Our State" (SOS) initiative developed in a context of rapidly increasing non-white immigration to the state and a prolonged recession, although Hondagneu-Sotelo reasons that the provisions were largely directed at women and children because "they are central to making settlement happen" (1995: 170).

The publication of Peter Brimelow's *Alien Nation* (1995) helped disseminate the symbolism of Proposition 187. Recommended for serious consideration by some reviewers, the book secured multiple headlines and television appearances for Brimelow. One of Brimelow's suggestions—that U.S.-born children of unauthorized residents be denied automatic citizenship (1995: 265)—was even adopted by the 1996 Republican platform. Although it had been introduced to Congress prior to the Republican convention (e.g., see Delgado 1997), the guidance was apparently too controversial for presidential politics, as the recommendation was later repudiated by Bob Dole, the Republican candidate for President.[18]

Controversy did not end with the proposal, however, as Congress remade immigration law in 1996. It enacted anti-terrorism and welfare reform legislation in April and August, respectively. The bills included provisions concerned specifically with non-citizens, but in September, Congress enacted the broad-gauged Illegal Immigration Reform and Immigrant Responsibility Act (IIRAIRA). The bill, in large measure, dealt with illegal immigration, but also addressed—among other issues—asylum adjudication, crime, and judicial review. Many of the provisions were considered fair, although some portions of the bill were viewed as unduly harsh, especially those pertaining to asylum claims (Legomsky 1997). Lastly, in 1998, California voters overwhelmingly approved Proposition 227 (60.9% in favor of the ballot measure). The initiative requires that "all students in public schools be taught primarily English unless their parents requested otherwise."[19]

Group Position and the Context of Nativism

The definition of nativism developed in chapter two is largely guided by the perspective and approach of symbolic interactionism. On the surface, this does not seem to be the case—nativism is an illegitimate defense of native proprietary claims over and against the encroachment of aliens." Below the surface of this terminology, however, lies various assumptions, arguments, and observations concerning the thoughts and feelings of natives. In the final analysis, nativist behavior pivots on *their* definition and evaluation of the situation, not on the researcher's judgment of the matter. If natives *perceive* the conduct or presence of aliens as a threat to their proprietary claims and seek to defend these claims, then nativism has occurred if these claims are generally *perceived* as illegitimate by the native populace. As emphasized earlier, definitions of aliens and legitimacy are variable.

---

[18] Sample, Herbert A. Dole: Allow citizenship for illegal immigrants' kids. [Online] Available http://sacbee.com/news/election/daily/daily082496.html, August 24, 1996.

[19] Streisand, Betsy. Is it hasta la vista for bilingual ed? [Online] Available http:www.usnews.com/usnews/ news/enghigh.htm, November 18, 1997.

But the question still remains: Under what conditions does heightened nativist activity occur? Natives may feel threatened by those they define as "alien" and have the power to enforce their claims, but the appearance of nativism is not guaranteed by the presence of such contingencies. There is a need to contextualize these processes. Nativism scholars frequently attribute the occurrence of nativism to increases in immigration and worsening economic conditions (e.g., Bennett 1995; Calavita 1996; Muller 1997; Perea 1997), but can one ever really know the "cause" or "causes" of nativism? Probably not, but one can recognize the conditions that give rise to its occurrence.

Table 1 correlates some of the cultural, demographic, economic, and social conditions typically associated with nativist behavior. These include the relative size and composition of immigration waves, size of the foreign-born population, business cycles, and domestic and international conflicts. These are not the only factors associated with nativism, but are some of the more regularly imposed terms. Pertinent data before 1830 are unavailable, and therefore preclude a comparison of prior historic events.

Table 1 Timeline of American Nativism

1821-1840: Anti-Masonic Movement (late 1820s though mid-1830s); St. Mary's burned in 1831 and Ursuline Convent in 1834; "Nunnery literature" published and numerous riots and confrontations between Catholic immigrants and Protestant natives (1831-1840)

Census Year (Decade)	1830 (1821-30)	1840 (1831-40)	1850 (1841-1850)	1860 (1851-60)
US Population[a]	12,866,020	17,069,453	23,191,876	31,443,321
% Foreign-born of Total US Pop.[b]	*[c]	*	*	*
Legal Immigrant Arrivals[d]	143,439	599,125	1,713,251	2,598,214
Annual Rate of Legal Immigration per 1000 US Population[e]	1.2	3.9	8.0	9.7
Region of Last Residence (% of total)[f] N/W Europe and Canada (NWEC)[g] S/E/C Europe (SECE)[h] Latin America (LA)[i] Asia (AS)[j] Africa (AF)[k]	NWEC: 68.3% SECE: 2.2% LA: 6.5% AS: _[l] AF: –	NWEC: 84% SECE: 1.0% LA: 3.3% AS: – AF: –	NWEC: 95.4% SECE: .3% LA: 1.2% AS: – AF: –	NWEC: 95.9% SECE: .8% LA: 0.6% AS: 1.6% AF: –
Largest Countries of Last Residence (1, 2, 3)	Ireland, U.K, Mexico	Ireland, Germany, U.K	Ireland, Germany, U.K	Germany, Ireland, U.K.
Business Cycles	⊠°	⊠	⊠	1854↓57↑ 58↓60↑
Domestic/International Conflicts	Texas War of Independence (1835-36)		Mexican-American War (1846-48)	

1841-1860: 1844 Philadelphia and New York riots; 1850 Order of the Star Spangled Banner formed (later referred to as "Know Nothings" and the American Party); 1855 American Party divides over slavery issue but secures victories in state elections

Table 1 Timeline of American Nativism (cont'd)	1861-1880: 1862 Expulsion of Jews from Union army; 1863 Draft riots in NYC; Anti-Catholicism flares up in Northeast and Midwest; Anti-Chinese agitation in the West			
Census Year (Decade)	1870 (1861-70)	1880 (1871-80)	1890 (1881-90)	1900 (1891-00)
US Population[a]	39,818,449	50,155,783	62,947,714	75,994,575
% Foreign-born of Total US Pop.[b]	14.0	13.3	14.7	13.6
Legal Immigrant Arrivals[d]	2,314,824	2,812,191	5,246,613	3,687,564
Annual Rate of Legal Immigration per 1000 US Population[e]	6.3	6.3	9.3	5.3
Region of Last Residence (% of total)[f] N/W Europe and Canada (NWEC)[g] S/E/C Europe (SECE)[h] Latin America (LA)[i] Asia (AS)[j] Africa (AF)[k]	NWEC: 94.4% SECE: 1.5% LA: 0.5% AS: 2.8% AF: –	NWEC: 87.3% SECE: 7.1% LA: 0.7% AS: 4.4% AF: –	NWEC: 79.5% SECE: 18.2% LA: 0.6% AS: 1.3% AF: –	NWEC: 44.7% SECE: 51.8% LA: 1.0% AS: 2.0% AF: –
Largest Countries of Last Residence (1, 2, 3)	Germany, U.K., Ireland	Germany, U.K., Ireland	Germany, U.K., Ireland	Italy, Aust.-Hun., Soviet Union
Business Cycles	1861↓ 65↑ 67↓ 69↑ 70↓	1873↑ 79↓	1882↑ 85↓ 87↑ 88↓ 90↑	1891↓ 93↑ 94↓ 95↑ 97↑ 99↑ 1900↓
Domestic/International Conflicts	American Civil War (1861-65)		Spanish-American War (1898)	

1881-1900: 1882 Chinese Exclusion Act; 1886 Haymarket Affair; 1887 American Protective Association (APA) founded; 1893 APA contributes to McKinley re-election as Ohio governor and sends sympathizers to Congress; 1894 APA involved in two Catholic-Protestant riots

Table 1 Timeline of American Nativism (cont'd)

	1910 (1901-10)	1920 (1911-20)	1930 (1921-30)	1940 (1931-40)
1901-1920: 1905 Asiatic Exclusion League formed; 1907-08 Gentleman's Agreement; 1910 Sir Francis Galton launches eugenics movement; 1916 Grant's *Passing of the Great Race* published; 6,200 German aliens arrested and 2,300 interned by military (1917-1918)				
Census Year (Decade)	1910 (1901-10)	1920 (1911-20)	1930 (1921-30)	1940 (1931-40)
US Population[a]	91,972,266	105,710,620	122,775,046	131,669,275
% Foreign-born of Total US Pop.[b]	14.7	13.2	11.6	8.8
Legal Immigrant Arrivals[d]	8,795,386	5,735,811	4,107,209	528,431
Annual Rate of Legal Immigration per 1000 US Population[e]	10.4	5.7	3.5	0.4
Region of Last Residence (% of total)[f] N/W Europe and Canada (NWEC)[g] S/E/C Europe (SECE)[h] Latin America (LA)[i] Asia (AS)[j] Africa (AF)[k]	NWEC: 23.8% SECE: 69.9% LA: 2.1% AS: 3.7% AF: 0.1%	NWEC: 30.3% SECE: 58.0% LA: 7.0% AS: 4.3% AF: 0.1%	NWEC: 53.8% SECE: 28.7% LA: 14.4% AS: 2.7% AF: 0.2%	NWEC: 58.0% SECE: 28.3% LA: 9.7% AS: 3.1% AF: 0.3%
Largest Countries of Last Residence (1, 2, 3)	Aust.-Hun., Italy, Soviet Union	Italy, Soviet Union, Aust.-Hun.	Canada, Mexico, Ireland	Germany, Canada, Italy
Business Cycles	1902↓ 04↑ 07↑ 08↓ 10↑	1912↓ 13↑ 14↓ 18↑ 19↓ 20↑	1921↓ 23↑ 24↓ 26↑ 27↓ 29↑	1933↓ 37↑ 38↓
Domestic/International Conflicts	World War I (1914-1918)[q]; Mexican-American Border War (1916); World War II (1939-45)[r]			
1921-1940: 1920-1927 Henry Ford's *Dearborn Independent*/peak circulation: 700,000; 1924 Number of KKK recruits increases to 2-3 million; 500,000-600,000 persons of Mexican ancestry (including American citizens) deported in wake of Great Depression; Father Coughlin's Christian Front Against Communism (late 1930s)				

Table 1 Timeline of American Nativism (cont'd)

	1941-1950: 112,000 West Coast Japanese (two-thirds of whom were American citizens) interned. Some German and Italian aliens are interned and/or excluded from certain localities, although many faced restrictions, such as registrations and curfews; 1943 "Zoot suit" riots			
Census Year (Decade)	1950 (1941-50)	1960 (1951-60)	1970 (1961-70)	1980 (1971-80)
US Population[a]	151,325,798	179,323,175	203,302,031	226,542,199
% Foreign-born of Total US Pop.[b]	6.9	5.4	4.8	6.2
Legal Immigrant Arrivals[d]	1,035,039	2,515,479	3,321,677	4,493,314
Annual Rate of Legal Immigration per 1000 US Population[e]	0.7	1.5	1.7	2.1
Region of Last Residence (% of total)[f] N/W Europe and Canada (NWEC)[g] S/E/C Europe (SECE)[h] Latin America (LA)[i] Asia (AS)[j] Africa (AF)[k]	NWEC: 63.8% SECE: 12.8% LA: 14.9% AS: 3.6% AF: 0.7%	NWEC: 51.8% SECE: 16.0% LA: 22.2% AS: 6.1% AF: 0.6%	NWEC: 30.0% SECE: 16.3% LA: 38.6% AS: 12.9% AF: 0.9%	NWEC: 10.2% SECE: 11.4% LA: 40.3% AS: 35.3% AF: 1.8%
Largest Countries of Last Residence (1, 2, 3)	Germany, Canada, U.K.	Germany, Canada, Mexico	Mexico, Canada, Italy	Mexico, Philippines, Korea
Business Cycles	1945↑ 45↓ 48↑ 49↓	1953↑ 54↓ 57↑ 58↓ 60↑	1961↓ 69↑ 70↓	1973↑ 75↓ 80↓ 80↑
Domestic/International Conflicts	WW II (1939-45); Cuban Missile Crisis (1962); Vietnam Conflict[u] (1964-73)			
1951-1980: 1954 INS conducts "Operation Wetback"; 1980 Marielitos reception				

Table 1 Timeline of American Nativism (cont'd)	1981-1990: 1982 Murder of Vincent Chin; 1988 U.S. English scandal; 1989 Murder of Jim Loo and killing of five Southeast Asian children	
	1990 (1981-90)[s]	**2000** (1991-98)[t]
Census Year (Decade)		
US Population[a]	248,718,301	
% Foreign-born of Total US Pop.[b]	7.9	
Legal Immigrant Arrivals[d]	7,338,062	
Annual Rate of Legal Immigration per 1000 US Population[e]	3.1	
Region of Last Residence (% of total)[f] N/W Europe and Canada (NWEC)[g] S/E/C Europe (SECE)[h] Latin America (LA)[i] Asia (AS)[j] Africa (AF)[k]	NWEC: 7.2% SECE: 5.3% LA: 47.1% AS: 37.3% AF: 3.1%	NWEC: SECE: LA: AS: AF:
Largest Countries of Last Residence (1, 2, 3)	Mexico, Other Asian, Philippines	
Business Cycles	1981↑ 82↓ 90↑	
Domestic/International Conflicts	Persian Gulf War (1991)	

1991-2000: 1991 Hate crimes against Arab Americans during Persian Gulf War; 1994 Passage of Proposition 187, the Save Our State initiative; 1995 Brimelow's *Alien Nation* published; 1998 Passage of Proposition 227 in California, the Bilingual Education initiative

Notes and Sources

a Alaska and Hawaii are not included until the 1960 census. For a general analysis of census enumerations, and their limitations, see *Historical Statistics of the United States: Colonial Times to 1970, Part I* (pp. 1-7) and U.S. Bureau of the Census, *Statistical Abstracts of the United States* (116th ed.), 1996, Tables 1-2.

b See Series C 228-295 in *Historical Statistics of the United States: Colonial Times to 1970, Part I* for 1870-1890 and Rumbaut (1994) for 1900-1990.

c Data not available.

d Note: from 1820-67, figures represent alien passengers arrived at seaports; from 1868-92 and 1895-97, immigrant aliens arrived; from 1892-94 and 1898-1994, immigrant aliens admitted for permanent residence. From 1892-1903, aliens entering by cabin class were not counted as immigrants. Land arrivals were not completely enumerated until 1908. Fiscal year 1843 covers 9 months ending September 1843; fiscal years 1832 and 1850 cover 15 months ending December 31 of the respective years; and fiscal year 1868 covers 6 months ending 30 June 1868.

e Annual rate per 1,000 U.S. population. Rate computed by dividing sum of annual immigration totals by sum of annual U.S. population totals for same number of years. Rates for 1901-1994 located in *Statistical Abstracts*, Table 5. Rates for 1830-1900 ascertained by dividing annual immigration totals (*1994 Statistical Yearbook*, Table 1) by annual population estimates (*Historical Statistics*, Series A 6-8) (same formula).

f Data for years prior to 1906 relate to country of birth whence alien came; data from 1906-79 and 1984-94 are for country of last permanent residence; and data for 1980-83 refer to country of birth. Because of changes in boundaries, changes in lists of countries, and lack of data for specified countries for various periods, data for certain countries, especially for the total period 1820-1994, are not comparable throughout. Data for specified countries are included with countries to which they belonged prior to World War I.

g N/W (Northern and Western) Europe and Canada includes: Belgium, Denmark, France, Germany, Ireland, Netherlands, Norway-Sweden, Switzerland, United Kingdom, Canada and Newfoundland. Percentages for 1821-1890 calculated from Table 2, *1994 Statistical Yearbook*. Percentages for 1891-1990 calculated by Rumbaut (1994). The same designations were used for both sets of percentages. Note: (1) Prior to 1926, data for Northern Ireland included in Ireland; (2) Data for Norway and Sweden not reported separately until 1871; (3) Since 1925, data for United Kingdom refer to England, Scotland, Wales, and Northern Ireland; (4) Prior to 1920, Canada and Newfoundland recorded as British North America. From 1820-98, figures include all British North America possessions; (5) Land arrivals for Canada and Newfoundland not completely enumerated until 1908; (6) From 1899-1919, data for Poland included in Austria-Hungary, *Germany*, and the Soviet Union; (4) From 1938-1945, data for Austria included in *Germany*.

h S/E/C (Southern, Eastern, and Central) Europe includes: Austria-Hungary, Czechoslovakia, Greece, Italy, Poland, Portugal, Romania, Soviet Union, Spain, and Yugoslavia. Percentages for 1821-1890 calculated from Table 2, *1994 Statistical Yearbook*. Percentages for 1891-1990 calculated by Rumbaut (1994). The same designations were used for both sets of percentages. Note: (1) Data for Austria and Hungary not reported until 1861; (2) Data for Austria and Hungary not reported separately for all years during the following periods: 1861-1870 and 1891-1910; (3) From 1899-1919, data for Poland included in *Austria-Hungary*, Germany, and the *Soviet Union*; (4) From 1938-1945, data for Austria included in Germany; (5) Designation of Austria-Hungary utilized for all years; (6) No data available for Czechoslovakia until 1920; (7) No data available for Romania until 1880; (8) In 1920, a separate enumeration was made for the Kingdom of Serbs, Croats, and Slovenes. Since 1922, the Serb, Croat, and Slovene Kingdom recorded as Yugoslavia.

i Latin America (LA) includes: Mexico, Caribbean, Central America, and South America. Percentages from Pedraza (1996). Note: (1) Land arrivals for Mexico not completely enumerated until 1908; (2) No data available for Mexico from 1886-1894; (3) Until 1925, data for Cuba reported by region, rather than separately; (4) Until 1932, data for Argentina, Colombia, Dominican Republic, Ecuador, El Salvador, and Haiti reported by region, rather than separately; (5) Data for Jamaica not collected until 1953. In prior years, consolidated under British West Indies, which is included in "Other Caribbean."

j Asia (AS) includes: China, Hong Kong, India, Iran, Israel, Japan, Korea, Philippines, Turkey, Vietnam, and Other Asia. Percentages from Pedraza (1996). Note: (1) Beginning in 1957, China includes Taiwan; (2) Until 1952, data for China and Vietnam reported by region, rather than separately; (3) Until 1925, data for Iran reported by region, rather than separately; (4) Until 1949, data for Israel reported by region, rather than separately; (5) No data available for Japan until 1861; (6) Until 1948, data for Korea reported by region, rather than separately; (7) Prior to 1934, Philippines recorded as insular travel.

k The INS does not identify individual countries within Africa (or Oceania) in Table 2, but does specify them in other, more recent tables. This is of little consequence, however, since the total number of immigrants from each *region* is always smaller than the total number of immigrants arriving from the third largest *country* of origin (1830-1905), last permanent residence (1906-1979, 1984-1994), or country of birth (1980-1983).

[l] Indicates less than 0.05%

[m] Qualifications described in footnotes "g" through "k" also apply to this category.

[n] Business cycle data drawn from Peterson and Estenson (1992: 587-93). A business cycle is defined as a "wavelike movement in the general level of economic activity that takes place over time" (p. 588). A simplified version of a business cycle pattern resembles a bell curve by depicting Gross National Product output in constant dollars (p. 591). For example, the business cycle containing the Great Depression, which began November 1927 and ended March 1993, contained—like other business cycles—an initial trough (November 1927), a peak (August 1929) and a second trough (March 1933). The Great Depression occurred during the long downswing from August 1929 to March 1933. Hence, the time between an up arrow (↑) and a down arrow (↓) is a downswing in the economy and called a recession or depression, and the time between a down arrow (↓) and an up arrow (↑) is an upswing in the economy and called a recovery or boom. Hence, recessions/depressions occur between up and down arrows (e.g., ↑ recession ↓). Special thanks to Dr. Warren Samuels for directing me to this resource.

[o] Satisfactory data are lacking before 1854 (Peterson and Estenson 1992).

[p] Record of domestic and international conflicts recorded in *Timelines of War* (Brownstone 1994). Only the most relevant and significant events are included here.

[q] The U.S. did not officially enter World War I until 1917.

[r] The U.S. did not officially enter World War II until 1941.

[s] "Data include 1,359,186 formerly undocumented immigrants who had resided in the United States since 1982 and whose status was legalized in fiscal years 1989 and 1990 under the provisions of the IRCA of 1986. An additional 1.7 million eligible legalization applicants, already qualified under IRCA, had not yet adjusted their status to permanent residence as of 1990 and are thus not included...they are reflected in INS statistics for fiscal 1991 and subsequent years...in 1991 a record total of 1,827,167 immigrants were legally admitted into the United States; of these 1,123,162 were IRCA legalizees. In 1992 and 1993 respectively, admissions totaled 973,977 and 904,292, of which IRCA legalizations numbered 163,342 and 24,278" (Rumbaut 1996: 25). Also note: these figures reflect immigration levels, not net immigration levels (immigration minus emigration). For example, it is estimated that between 1981-1990, there were approximately 1.8 million emigrants (Passel and Edmonston 1994: 34-35).

[t] Current data (through 1998) unavailable.

[u] In 1964, the Tonkin Gulf Resolution authorized the President Johnson to take the U.S. "into the undeclared Vietnam War, which he immediately did" (Brownstone 1994: 479). The last American forces left in 1973.

Sources: U.S. Bureau of the Census, *Statistical Abstracts of the United States 1996* (116th ed.); *Historical Statistics of the United States: Colonial Times to 1970, Part I*; U.S. Immigration and Naturalization Service, *1994 Statistical Yearbook*, Tables 1-2; Passel and Edmonston (1994); Rumbaut (1994; 1996); Pedraza (1996); Browstone (1994); Peterson and Estenson (1992); [web address/site of INS and Census]. Some footnotes are direct quotations of original source (e.g., footnotes "d" and "f").

Discussion

The history and points of comparison have been necessarily selective because analyzing the unique circumstances surrounding each and every occurrence of American nativism is beyond the scope of this brief survey. Perceptions of aliens, entitlement, and threat were said to undergird nativist activities in Chapter 2, but it was necessary to historicize these processes in order to discern the conditions that help convert these ideas into systems of action. The contextual qualities of nativism are better understood by examining some of these conditions and situating perceptions of threat within these contexts.

Two final notes—the variables specified in Table 1 are only juxtaposed with some of the more notorious examples of American nativism. These correlations do not imply causality, but are designed to show associative relationships. Secondly, the units of analysis are different. For example, the 1994 "Save Our State" initiative took place in California, but the data refer to national contexts. In other words, what is occurring at the regional or local level may have very little to do with events at the national level (and vice-versa). On a related matter, it must be remembered that the definition of nativism proposed in the second chapter primarily theorizes about the perceptions of individuals. While these views are connected to collective processes, it does not attempt to explain the motives of regional and/or national aggregates. It is possible, nevertheless, to note a few general observations about the contexts commonly associated with nativism.

The most egregious examples of nativism occurred during or around wartime. The emergence and success of the Know Nothings took place on the eve of the Civil War and the unnecessary internments occurred during the First and Second World Wars. Such actions are not unique to the United States. During World War II, 2,600 Japanese were "relocated" in British Columbia, Germans were interned in Canada and Australia—and in Britain—Germans, Italians, and Austrians were briefly interned by the Churchill administration (Foster and Seitz 1991; Lafitte 1988: 70-160; Palmer 1982: 2). The kind of nativism which can erupt during wartime belongs to an enduring tradition of intolerance where national and ethnic populations come to be seen as potential subversives because their former homeland is at war with their "new home." In the course of conflict, some are branded as "fifth columnists," internal saboteurs who aid their former homeland through acts of sabotage. Actions unthinkable in times of peace, such as internment, are not uncommon, but instead are standard protocol (e.g., see Daniels 1993; Edmonds 1991a; 1991b; Fox 1988; 1990; Harrington 1981; Higham 1992; Palmer 1982; Panayi 1990).

This is not to say, however, that a fear of disloyalty is the only concern of nativists during wartime or that other factors are not involved. Numerous business associations and labor unions seemingly tried to capitalize on the wartime hysteria during World War II by urging their national representatives to "ship" the Japanese "back to Japan," or at the very least, place them in concentration camps (Grodzins 1949: 19-61; Okamura 1982). In addition to the alleged material interests, the Japanese internment seems to have also been spurred by racism and their small, concentrated numbers (Sowell 1994: 154-55; Daniels 1993; Fox 1990). However, from what I can discern, a genuine concern about the disloyalty of German Americans seems to have been the primary motivation for interning 6,300 of them during World War I (e.g., see Ellis and Panayi 1994; Luebke 1974; Child 1939; Wittke 1936).

Unlike wartime nativism, the correlation between economic downturns and nativist activities is far less clear. Nativist incidents occurred during downswings in the economy (e.g., 1857-1858, 1882-1885, 1893-1894, 1929-1933, etc.) and upswings in the economy (e.g., 1861-1865, 1904-1907, 1914-1918, 1982-1990). Interestingly, many of the nativistic events which occurred during upswings in the economy coincided with domestic and international conflicts. However, it should be remembered that some of these happenings were confined to specific locales and that the national context may have had little bearing on these events. Nevertheless, it is instructive to note that some of the most tranquil time periods in American nativism are marked by strong economies and relatively low immigration (e.g., 1897-1899, 1951-1980), which raises one final observation.

Although the relationship between the annual rate of legal immigration and nativism is difficult to discern (mainly because of the disparate wartime and economic contexts), the number of nativist activities appears to dwindle during prolonged periods of low immigration (e.g., examine 1821-30 and 1940-1990). This is especially the case if the Second World War is temporarily extracted from the picture. Of course, the annual rate is not only relative in a proportional sense, but also relative in a sequential sense. The annual rate of legal immigration for 1990 (3.1) is almost double that of the 1970 annual rate (1.7), even though the annual rate for each decade is decidedly less than the average annual rate for the years 1821-1990 (4.7).

With the exception of the relationship between economic downturns and nativism, few of these observations are surprising. Nativism is frequently attributed to increases in immigration, wartime contexts, and economic downturns (e.g., see Calavita 1996, Ellis and Panayi 1994; Muller 1997). Even a cursory glance at the above juxtapositions demonstrates that the relationships between such conditions and nativist activities is far from straightforward.

While these factors may *precipitate* nativism, they do not *cause* it. A precipitating factor often gives generalized beliefs immediate substance, but in and of itself, is not the cause of anything. "It must occur in the context of...other determinants" (Smelser 1965: 17). For example, the internment of Japanese Americans during World War II was precipitated by Japan's victories in the Pacific, particularly at Pearl Harbor (Daniels 1993: 27). However, racism, historic discrimination, and their small, concentrated numbers on the West Coast made their internment all the more probable (Daniels 1993; Fox 1990).

Scholars use terms like "economic nativism" and "racial nativism" to highlight the contextual character of nativism, but at times, this terminology also implies cause and effect, and tacitly imputes motives to "nativists" (e.g., see Fredrickson and Knobel 1981: 842; Hing 1993: 31). The ironic consequence is that 'nativistic" contexts are often better understood than the very people who construct meaning and act within them. Chapters 5-7 tackle this deficiency by examining the worldviews of those who actively shape such contexts through their work and volunteered time. Before digging into these different visions, however, it is necessary to examine the methodological approach and perspective of this investigation.

CHAPTER 4

Methodology

The research methods required for a given study are suggested by the properties of the problem being examined (Mills 1959: 128). This investigation seeks to answer three central, interrelated questions: What is American nativism? Under what conditions does heightened nativist activity occur? and What does immigration mean to those involved in immigration reform? The definition of nativism provided in Chapter two offers an answer to the first question. The methods used to arrive at this interpretation were intentionally omitted because their validation requires a comprehension of the overall research design, which is described below.

Research Design

The research methods described below are appropriate for collecting the kinds of data needed for discerning *how* and *why* certain groups in the United States come to define others as "aliens" and develop exclusionary practices to limit their entrance into the nation-state or participation in certain areas of "native privilege" (see Chapter 2 for details). Multiple research methods were used to examine the conditions under which heightened nativist activity occurs and understand why certain individuals become collectively involved in organized efforts to reform current immigration policy. Qualitative methods are critical for probing the complex mixture of motives and interests behind such actions, and the contexts in which they are embedded. Rather than being the *means* of research, the categories developed by quantitative researchers, and the conditions stressed by historians and nativism scholars, were the *object* (along with those themes that emerged in the course of field work) of this research project (cf. McCracken 1988).

By synthesizing historical accounts of immigrant reception, I identify the constitutive elements of nativist episodes in Chapter 3 and develop criteria for measuring and comparing the multifarious reactions confronted by immigrants and their progeny. These findings were incorporated into the definition of nativism introduced in the second chapter. This historical-comparative research responds to the second question by examining the conditions typically associated with nativist activities. Understanding the renewed interest in reducing immigration levels and abridging the "rights" of immigrants already living in the United States, however, requires data on the people and organizations promoting and opposing such changes. Interviews with expansionists and restrictionists, along with a content analysis of immigration reform agency documents and archives, furthers our understanding of what immigration means to immigration activists and the roles they play in shaping public policy and opinion. In so doing, an answer to the third and final research question is advanced. The collected data are analyzed in order to develop a conceptual scheme for examining the different discourses, beliefs, and behaviors of immigration activists, and will be compared to dominant perspectives on nativism and intergroup hostility in the final chapter. Many of these observations influenced the arguments set forth in Chapter 2, but a more comprehensive synthesis is presented in Chapter 7.

Historical-Comparative Research and Analysis

A selective history of American nativism is subdivided into three nativist eras. Special attention is given to the plethora of interests and ideologies seemingly present during each time period. This research does not systematically analyze every nativist event in U.S. history, but identifies the constitutive properties of nativism. It unveils the patterns and attendant conditions of nativism. Additionally, this research was used to develop a versatile framework of concepts suited to the complexities and essence of American nativism, as outlined in Chapter 2. This analysis was informed by—above all else—a meticulous dissection of secondary sources (e.g., Almaguer 1994; Bennett 1995; Fuchs 1990; Gould 1981; Higham 1992; Leonard and Parmet 1971; Pedraza and Rumbaut 1996).

One could argue that a tautology has been constructed by providing a definition of nativism at the outset. Identifying the constitutive properties of nativist events, those elements common to most nativist events, is one of the main objectives of Chapter four. One might contend that specifying these components beforehand is the equivalent of a tautological warm up. Any phenomenon matching my pre-established criteria would be, by definition, nativistic. The definition proposed in chapter two, however, is based on historical-comparative research and interviews. My synthesis of historical accounts, and interviews with expansionists and restrictionists, allowed me to propose a working definition of nativism which can be assessed throughout the entire dissertation.

In-depth Interviews

Forty-six semi-structured *interviews* were conducted with immigration "activists" and "allies." *Activists* were defined as those individuals who regularly devoted, at one time or another, thirty[20] or more hours a week to immigration *reform* (i.e., intentional actions designed to produce, or prevent, change in current immigration and immigrant realities) by participating in organizations aspiring to mold such conditions. *Allies* primarily contribute to immigration reform, not by participating in such organizations, but by virtue of their professions. The job requirements of policy makers, immigration officials, congressional staff, and researchers involve them in the maintenance and transformation of immigration policy. Similar to the dilemmas faced by professionals in bilingual education (Crawford 1992: 227), the adversarial climate surrounding immigration can pressure researchers and other professionals to operate like politicians and carefully consider the

---

[20] The idea to define activists as a function of time committed to immigration reform was gleaned from Kristin Luker's study of pro-life and pro-choice activists. Her minimum time requirements for defining pro-life and pro-choice activists were 10 and 5 hours of "activity" per week, respectively (1985: 250). The decision to increase the number of hours was made on the assumption that people devoting a minimum of thirty hours a week to immigration reform were more likely to have seriously thought about immigration reform, thereby exposing me to respondents for whom the issue is especially salient.

political implications of their work. Although these categories are not mutually exclusive, interviewing activists and allies (i.e., those most heavily involved in immigration reform) introduces us to the meanings and interests they attach to immigration and consequently, to some of the more influential beliefs and values shaping the debate. This approach approximates the methodology of Kristin Luker (1985), whose interviews with pro-life and pro-choice activists helped her to relate their conflicting moral positions to divergent worldviews and experiences.

The 46 interviews were completed between March 1997 and June 1998. Of those forty-six, three were conducted with individuals previously interviewed, as the expertise of these respondents proved indispensable for piecing together the politics of immigration reform. The conglomerate of immigration/immigrant-related agencies in the United States is very large, but the actual number of *activists* is quite small compared to the number of *allies* (see definitions above). The decision to conduct forty-six interviews with activists and allies was based on logistical considerations. There are approximately twenty-five national activist organizations currently involved in immigration reform (see Figure 3) and some of these agencies only consist of three or four "employees." This limited the potential pool of eligible activists, particularly the number of activists. Of the forty-three interviewees, twenty-four immigration *activists* and eighteen immigration *allies* were interviewed.

Research Sample Characteristics

As indicated earlier, meaning-related inquires guided decisions of sample and site selection. Because immigration worldviews and the policy-making process were identified as having the maximum potential to provide relevant and rich data on the topics of nativism and immigration reform, respondents were selected on the basis of their association and familiarity with these matters. Some interviewees were initially selected by me, although most respondents were incorporated into the study through a snowball sampling procedure.

Demographic data on the activists and allies are arranged in Table 2. The presentation of individual-level data could jeopardize the guarantee of confidentiality and are therefore not displayed.

Table 2 Research Sample Attributes

	Activists	Allies	Expansionists	Restrictionists
Age range[a]	20-30: 5 31-40: 7 41-50: 9 51-60: 1 61-80: 2 Total: 24	20-30: 0 31-40: 8 41-50: 4 51-60: 7 61-80: 0 Total: 19	20-30: 3 31-40: 11 41-50: 7 51-60: 8 61-80: 0 Total: 29	20-30: 2 31-40: 4 41-50: 6 51-60: 0 61-80: 2 Total: 14
Gender	Female: 5 Male: 19	Female: 7 Male: 12	Female: 11 Male: 18	Female: 1 Male: 13
Native- or Foreign-born[b]	Native: 20 Foreign: 3	Native: 17 Foreign: 3	Native: 25 Foreign: 4	Native: 12 Foreign: 2
Race / Ethnicity[c]	Asian: 1 Hispanic: 1 White: 22	Asian: 1 Hispanic: 3 White: 15	Asian: 2 Hispanic: 3 White: 24	Asian: 0 Hispanic: 1 White: 13
Educational Level[d]	BA: 8 MA: 7 Ph.D.: 8	BA: 4 MA: 9 Ph.D.: 6	BA: 7 MA: 11 Ph.D.: 10	BA: 5 MA: 5 Ph.D.: 4
Political Persuasion[e]	C/R: 4 L/D: 3 Lib: 4 Other: 12	C/R: 0 L/D: 10 Lib: 0 Other: 10	C/R: 1 L/D: 11 Lib: 4 Other: 13	C/R: 3 L/D: 2 Lib: 0 Other: 9

a. Approximate age at time of interview.

b. Of the foreign-born, two were born as American citizens, both of whom were restrictionists.

c. Members of other racial/ethnic groups were not interviewed (see next two paragraphs and Chapter 7).

d. Educational level represents only highest degree completed. "Ph.D." includes law and medical degrees.

e. Political persuasion gauged by respondent's self-description. Symbols: C/R (Conservative and/or Republican), L/D (Liberal and/or Democrat), Lib (Libertarian). "Libertarian" was sometimes used in conjunction with other descriptors, such as "conservative" or "Democrat." These individuals were categorized as libertarian. "Other" represents various labels, such as "moderate," "independent," "centrist," "progressive," and "supporter of human rights." It also represents those who declined to answer and those who were not asked.

The interview sample primarily consists of highly educated white men. Two-thirds of the respondents took an expansionist position on immigration, although some (particularly allies) were more interested in maintaining current policies, rather than expanding upon them. Of the 43 interviewees, 14 had earned doctoral-level degrees (J.D., M.D., Ph.D., etc.), 16 secured masters-level degrees (Masters of Social Work), 12 received bachelors degrees, and only one person had yet to receive a bachelor's degree, although he had completed some college coursework. Only 12 of the interviewees were women, and of those 12, only 5 were activists. The sample was overwhelmingly native-born, and of the 6 foreign-born individuals, 2 were born as American citizens, both of whom were restrictionists.

As stated earlier, the sample was not randomly generated, but formed through calculated choices and respondent referrals. Some interviewees were selected because of their relative prominence or extensive knowledge, but most were drawn in via a snowball sample. Given the exploratory nature of the research, the focus on immigration reform, and absence of an advocate sampling frame, a purposive sample was required. Because the respondents were not randomly selected, generalizations in Chapters 5-7 refer only to those people interviewed for the study. Questions of representation are difficult, if not impossible, to answer. However, akin to Kristin Luker's study of abortion activists in California (1985: 254), it seems that the above sample is fairly representative of national activists, given the immense overlap in themes and referrals. This tentative conclusion does not apply to national representatives or allies. I suspect that had more interviews been conducted at the local level, more women and African Americans would have been interviewed. In addition to structured racial and gender relations, Sylvia Walby (1996) suggests that women's political activities are usually "less nationalist" and more local than those of men.

Interview Settings and Recruitment Procedures

Efforts at immigration reform are largely organized by a complex of active lobbies in the nation's capital. Because immigration is principally a federal responsibility, many of these organizations are concentrated in Washington D.C. for the express purpose of shaping the national debate on immigration and influencing immigration policy. Hence, the Washington D.C. area provided an excellent setting for examining some of the key organizations promoting or opposing changes in current immigration and immigrant policies and programs. In order to comprehend the multiple ideas and discourses adopted by these groups, I began to develop an inventory of organizations active in immigration reform by consulting immigration specialists and asking some of the directors of these designated associations to identify people and organizations they viewed as "key players" in the politics of immigration reform. A listing of these groups, and their general positions on immigration reform, are depicted in Figure 3.

**Figure 3 Field of Primary Organizations Shaping National
Immigration Reform Efforts**

Restrictionist	Nonpartisan/Bipartisan	Expansionist
Environmental-Population Lobby/Awareness -Carrying Capacity Network -Negative Population Growth -Population-Environment Balance -Zero Population Growth **Environmental-Cultural Lobby/Awareness** -American Immigration Control Foundation -Federation for American Immigration Reform -U.S. Border Control -U.S. English **Research/Publications** -Center for Immigration Studies -The Social Contract Press (Umbrella Organization: U.S. Inc.)	**Federal Government and Govt.-related** -U.S. Commission on Immigration Reform -Senate Immigration Subcommittee -House Immigration Subcommittee -Immigration and Naturalization Service -Department of Labor -Congressional Research Service **Education/Research** -Carnegie Endowment for International Peace, International Migration Program -Lewis Center for Regional Policy Studies (UCLA) -New School for Social Research / Urban Institute -The Center for Migration Studies -Social Science Research Council -The Tomás Rivera Polciy Institute -Population Reference Bureau	**General Immigration Advocacy** -National Immigration Forum -Frank Swartz and Associates **Libertarian Orgzs.** -Cato Institute -Center for Equal Opportunity **Business Lobbyists** -American Business for Legal Immigration -American Council on International Personnel -National Association of Manufacturers -National Federation of Businesses **Ethnic Lobbies** -National Council of La Raza -MALDEF Organization of Chinese Americans Council of Jewish Federations **Religious Lobbies** -US Catholic Conference -American Jewish Committee **Legal Lobbies** -American Immigration Lawyers Association

Many of the respondents were also asked, near the end of the interview, if they would recommend someone who might consider talking to me about some of the very same issues we had just discussed. Many of them suggested two or three individuals, and one interviewee even arranged an informal dinner to introduce me to other activists. A few of the respondents, however, first called potential candidates to see if they were willing to talk with me and later provided me with their names and phone numbers. By the thirty-fifth interview, the interviewees usually recommended two or three people I had already spoken with, and in some cases, their suggestions read like a completed checklist. While I did not exhaust the entire population of immigration advocates and allies, I did interview, gauging by the interviewee's referrals, some of the most prominent and influential *activists*. In all, 61% of the interviewees currently work, or worked for, the organizations listed in Figure 3. All of the respondents were selected through this snowball sample procedure on the basis of their relation to the problem areas being investigated.

This procedure contains one exception, however. The majority of "activist" interviews were conducted in the Washington D.C. area, but because interviews were also conducted with "allies" (those people who contribute to immigration reform by virtue of their occupations), some interviews were conducted outside of this locale. Thirteen interviews were conducted in the Midwest, primarily at regional conferences and local offices. Comparing the interviews of those who deliberately chose to devote thirty or more hours a week to immigration reform with those whose professions involved them by necessity (regardless of their own beliefs about the issue) not only diversified the sample, but also allowed me to examine how ideas and vocabularies of motive (Mills 1940) are influenced by one's setting and participation (i.e., from occupational duties to outright activism) in immigration reform.

Interview Format

Eight of the interviews were conducted over the phone because of distance and scheduling changes. To my surprise, some of the most transparent and informative interviews were achieved over the phone. Incidentally, the most candid discussion with respect to race and culture took place during my first phone interview. The other thirty-eight interviews were conducted in-person, and usually in the interviewees' offices, but on a few occasions, at a conference or restaurant. The interviews—both face-to-face and on the phone—lasted anywhere between thirty minutes and three hours, but the average interview lasted approximately sixty to ninety minutes.

At the beginning of every interview I informed the respondents that their responses would be kept confidential and I would do everything I could to guarantee their confidentiality.[21] I also asked for their permission to record the interview. To ensure that the respondents felt no obligation or coercion to comply with any of my requests, I emphasized that their participation was completely voluntary and that they could end the interview at any time. All of this was spelled out on the consent form, which was signed before the interview began (see Appendix 1).

By the second interview, the interview schedule (see Appendix 2) was quickly pared down to a short battery of demographic queries and series of questions concerning their respective professions, political persuasions, views on U.S. immigration and immigrant policy, values, nativism, motives and interests. Some of the interviewees, however, were hesitant to share their opinions without first knowing mine. I initially tried to sidestep such questions by indicating my interest in their perspectives, but more often than not, this proved insufficient, and I briefly shared some of my thoughts on immigration. I usually indicated, in one minute or less, that refugee policy was especially important to me and that numerical limits on legal and illegal immigration were necessary, but difficult to establish in one's mind. This proved satisfactory, as perhaps my own ambivalence on—and openness to—these issues encouraged the respondents to freely express their opinions. This, along with promise of confidentiality, encouraged forthright discussions.

---

[21] The respondent's statements and attributes are disguised as much as possible, but because I am interested in public actions and because a number of these individuals are undertaking activities to influence public policy and opinion, I was very careful to avoid quotes and references (in chapters 5-7) which might jeopardize the subjects' confidentiality.

Comparing the interviews of immigration activists and allies illuminates key differences dividing opponents and proponents of immigration restriction. Analyzing the meanings they associate with immigration contributes to our understanding of how group boundaries (native, alien, etc.) are drawn and redrawn, and highlight the multiple discourses used by coalitions to protect or promote the interests they have in maintaining or challenging the status-quo. Salient themes in the debate, however, were also identified by analyzing the public and private documents provided by the organizations and interviewees.

Collection and Analysis of Written and Visual Records

The interview data were supplemented with an analysis of public relations materials provided by the interviewees and/or their respective organizations. Informational videos, pamphlets, books, articles, research findings, press releases, editorials, and published interviews were examined for the arguments and imagery contained therein. In all, over one hundred and fifty public relations "texts" were examined. Field notes were also taken at three immigration-related conferences, which provided spontaneous and equally rich "texts" for data analysis.

Emerging themes were recorded and developed into a preliminary list of questions regarding: the history of the expansionist and restrictionist organizations, their role in immigration reform, and their financial and intellectual support. Special attention was paid to the natural and social scientists used by the activists in their debates and respective literatures. My first glimpse into their worldviews came, in fact, from their quotes and public relations materials.

Archived documents of the Federation for American Immigration Reform (FAIR), arguably the preeminent restrictionist organization in the U.S., were also reviewed and analyzed.[22] This data contains written

---

[22] These documents are on deposit at George Washington University's Gelman library. This collection is referenced only by a preliminary finding aid and has not undergone formal archival processing. Because there are sixty-three boxes of documents and videos, it is impossible to conduct a quick, systematic search for specific materials, but of the boxes I inspected, I found numbers 1, 10, 26, and 27 to be the most informative and organized. I would like to thank Cheryl Chouiniere, the manuscripts librarian at the Gelman library, for her assistance.

accounts of the associations' official views and documents many of their activities, beginning in the early 1980s. Over two hundred press releases issued between 1987 and 1996 were examined. The press releases consisted primarily of legislative updates, formal positions on pending and passed legislation, summaries of "Borderline" (a television program hosted by the current Executive Director of FAIR, Dan Stein), fact sheets, research reports and commentary, and rebuttals to allegations advanced by expansionist agencies. One set of documents studied, but apparently not included in the collection, is FAIR's "Tenth Anniversary Oral History Project." This project contains interviews with five of FAIR's original board members and executives and supplied information not contained elsewhere.[23]

Lastly, selected back issues of the *Social Contract*, "the restrictionist movement's house magazine" as Peter Brimelow calls it (1996: 298), were also examined. The articles and book advertisements in the magazine deepened my understanding of the positions taken by restrictionists and expansionists and illuminated blank spaces in my own thinking. Most of these "texts"—public relations materials, FAIR documents, and *Social Contract* issues—were gathered prior to the fifteenth interview and were later used to construct additional interview questions, and hone those already developed.

Data Analysis

The preceding discussion alluded to a general research philosophy and methodology, but did not specify my initial expectations or explain my position on interviewing people associated with immigration reform. These particulars undoubtedly influenced the structure and direction of my analysis and require some elaboration.

Initial expectations

A distaste for intolerance and untested assumptions, and appetite for understanding and balance, necessitated interviews with immigration activists. First, little is known about the individuals who influence

---

[23] The 456 page single-spaced transcriptions are only available, to the best of my knowledge, at FAIR's headquarters in Washington D.C.

public policy and American attitudes toward immigration and immigrants. Although researchers have used interviews to examine a wide range of immigration-related phenomena, such as ethnic identity, language politics, and relations between the native- and foreign-born (e.g., see Waters 1990; Crawford 1992; Portes and Stepick 1993), they have not systematically examined the worldviews of immigration activists, although LeMay (1994) interviewed "allies" (my term) for their expertise on the legislative process.

Secondly, some recent analyses have been decidedly ignorant and partial. For example, there is the widely held, but untested assumption in the nativism literature that proponents of restricting immigration disguise their "real" motives (e.g., racism) with other, more acceptable arguments (e.g., immigration depresses the wages of the working poor). Scholars often characterize these arguments as "covers" or "surrogates" for other motives (e.g., see Crawford 1992). Johnson's (1997) analysis typifies this practice:

> ...modern restrictionists regularly deny that race is the reason for their dismay with immigration. *They instead employ other non-race-based arguments*—that too many people are immigrating to the United States, that immigrants (particularly "illegal aliens") take jobs from U.S. citizens, especially the poor and minorities, that "they" overconsume public benefits and adversely affect already-strapped state and local government budgets, that "they" contribute to the crime problem, and that "they" cause interethnic conflict and refuse to assimilate. Some restrictionist arguments approach the boundaries of racism, such as claims that today's immigrants speak languages other than English, which is "un-American," and that the new immigrants come from different, "un-American" cultures (Johnson 1997: 174, italics added).

Because organizations cannot use race-based arguments if they hope to secure legislative and public support, Johnson's skepticism is understandable. But such assumptions are unwarranted. Johnson (1997) has no way of knowing what "motivates" restrictionists without first developing a study to research their rationales.

Restrictionists also impute motives. Lutton and Tanton contend that immigration lawyers and government bureaucrats welcome the influx of immigrants because they have an economic stake in maintaining a steady stream of new arrivals (1994: 139-146). These allegations also make sense—most people are concerned about their jobs—but again, such analyses are heavy on insinuation and light on data.

I examined the interviews of immigration advocates in terms of their "vocabularies of motive" (Mills 1940), but was much more cautious in my analysis. Mills (1940) would likely argue that we can *never* know what really motivated an individual to do something at a given point in time. We cannot peep behind explanations and opinions (verbalized motives) and look for the supposedly "real attitude or motive" at work inside of an individual. "When we ask for the 'real motive' rather than the 'rationalization,' all we can be meaningfully asking for is the controlling speech form which was incipiently or overtly present in the performed act or series of acts" (Mills 1940: 910).

This distinction between interest as an *impetus* and interest as a *vocabulary* is necessary if we are to keep the *influence* of ideas and *usage* of ideas analytically separate. In so doing, we avoid the assumption that people's explanations for their behaviors are the causes of it. Clearly, the forces "behind" an action and the ensuing explanations that are used to justify it are not always the same. Motives frequently arise, not from within individuals, "but from the situation in which individuals find themselves..." (1940: 906).

This is not to say I approached the study of nativism and immigration reform with a blank slate. I had observed a variety of phenomena and held a number of assumptions. It appeared that the vocabularies of motives typically used by expansionists and restrictionists could be captured by one of four rationales. Expansionists seemed to defend their position (or privileges) by referring to (1) free market principles, (2) economic and diversity "needs," (3) human rights, and (4) specific ethnic groups. Restrictionists seemed to defend their position (or privileges) by referring to (1) economic "needs," (2) American culture, (3) native-born racial-ethnic groups, and (4) personal and national security.

With reference to the immigration advocates themselves, I suspected that their views were largely shaped by ethnicity, experiences with immigration and immigrants (or lack thereof), feelings about (and perceptions of) the United States as a nation and its role in the world, economic interests (from personal to national), and various ideological and religious perspectives. These assumptions allowed me to organize my analysis from the very start, but—in hindsight—were incomplete and somewhat misplaced. The interviews examined in Chapters 5-7 will aptly demonstrate this observation.

A Perspective on Interviewing Immigration Advocates and Allies

The works of Mills (1940) and Goffman (1959) are particularly sensitive to some of the dilemmas faced by social researchers. Trying to understand social phenomena by relying on a respondent's *words* and *appearances* can be a risky business, but we are left with few options since this is all we really have. The purpose of this research is, in part, to come to terms with these limitations and to suggest a perspective and method that makes the best of this quandary.

Mills (1940) argued that "vocabularies of motive" accompany certain behaviors and that individuals use them to legitimate their conduct. Motives are not the cause of behavior, but the explanation of it. "Rather than fixed elements 'in' an individual, motives are the terms with which interpretation of conduct *by social actors* proceeds" (1940: 904, italics in original). Motives are not explanations for behavior, but are themselves in need of explanation since they are usually verbalized only when certain forms of behavior are questioned. Individuals use learned vocabularies of motive to comprehend situations and anticipate the questioning of their conduct (1940: 905-06). "There is no need to invoke 'psychological' terms like 'desire' or 'wish' as explanatory, since they themselves must be explained socially...Institutionally different situations have different *vocabularies of motive* appropriate to their respective behaviors" (1940: 906, italics in original). The objective here is to consider the implications of using this perspective for analytic purposes and for organizing interviews with participants in immigration reform.

Nativism and Vocabularies of Motive

In *The Age of Migration*, Castles and Miller (1993) lamented the disunion of research on *immigration* and *ethnic diversity*. To develop linkages they urged that the migratory process be analyzed in its totality. Although this has been accomplished by some scholars (cf. Portes and Rumbaut 1996; Pedraza and Rumbaut 1995; Massey 1993, 1995), *motives* continue to be an understudied topic in both sets of literature (Gold 1997). Gold's recent examination of Israeli motives for emigrating to the United States begins to address this omission.

Gold observes that many of the categories and concepts used to understand immigration, such as "refugee" and "economic immigrants," are generally interpreted in light of migrant's motives. Instead of scrutinizing these motives, they are often assumed by researchers and attributed to migrants. In some cases there is sufficient reason to assume a population's motives for migrating (as in the case of Cambodian refugees), but more caution is warranted when considering other groups, such as Jewish Israelis. Their "comments [on their presence in the U.S.] bear little correspondence with the economic and political motives referred to in most literature on international migration" (1997: 411). Analyzing Israelis' comments from the perspective of transnationalism allowed Gold to link their explanations to the multiple contexts and networks bearing on their various decisions and explanations.

Gold examines the vocabularies of motives used by immigrants to explain their decisions to migrate, but what about the vocabularies of "natives" who explain their decisions to, in the terminology of Woldemikael (1987), *accommodate* newcomers or *assert* their dominance? Although adapting to a new environment is a social process requiring *both* the native- and foreign-born to decide how much they are willing to change (Woldemikael 1987), it is the judgments of immigration advocates that concern us here. What matters is motives. "When immigration policies are reviewed, the final judgment depends upon what *motivates* voters and policy makers, who often hold different conceptions of national self-interest" (Light 1996: 62, italics added). Investigating these motives requires that one look beyond individuals and their respective contexts to see how linguistic behavior fulfills "ascertainable functions in delimited societal situations" (Mills 1940: 904).

Nativism scholars have struggled with the question of motives. The motives of racists and nativists are frequently assumed (e.g., see Wellman 1994; Crawford 1992). Terms like "economic nativism" and "racial nativism" are often used by scholars to highlight the contextual character of nativism, but sometimes implicitly double as sociological analysis. While these concepts underscore the significance of context and the tendency of nativism to intersect with other processes (such as racism), they tell us little about the worldviews of "nativists," or more generally, of immigration advocates. Interviews with expansionists and restrictionists were needed in order to understand their different perceptions and justifications. When researchers rely on context to explain the motives of nativists, they often see causation in a correlation and leave little room for the diversity of *interests* and *vocabularies* within each restrictionist phase.

The passing of California's Proposition 187 aptly demonstrates this. The drive to exclude "illegal aliens" from tax supported benefits developed within the context of a prolonged recession. Some reporters and researchers assumed that the economic slump supplied nativists with the necessary motives (cf. Johnson 1995). But not all proponents of the initiative were solely concerned about the fiscal impacts of immigration. Some of the S.O.S. supporters referred to the hygiene of immigrants and alluded to an "alien" conspiracy (Kadetsky 1994: 418-420). While the recession may have contributed to their positions, the above comments illustrate how California's sagging economy was not their only concern. (See Chapter 2 for details.)

Clearly, the motives of nativists will vary from one context to the next and also *within* each context. Determining when nativism is the primary organizing principle in ethnic conflict is necessary for developing a program that can minimize its occurrence. An overreliance on context to explain the motives of nativists misdirects such efforts by assuming that nativists are nativistic for the same reason. Nativistic contexts are better understood than the nativists who construct meaning and act within them. Rather than treating them separately, our aim should be to delimit the contexts under which motives are declared and attributed.

The Interview

Goffman's (1959) dramaturgical perspective is especially relevant when examining vocabularies of motives. Like Mills (1940), Goffman stressed that people are concerned with the *appearance* and *acceptance* of their behavior. Individuals who cooperate to project a definition of a situation are called "teams," and manage their impressions so that they will be accepted, or more precisely, so that their "performances" will be.[24] Goffman likens social encounters to a series of performances where teams attempt to foster a certain image through the art of impression management. These performances are susceptible to a variety of disruptions which have the potential to discredit a team's performance. Performances are usually designed to "express the characteristics of the task that is performed and not the characteristics of the performer" (p. 77). Instead of trying to reach certain ends by acceptable means, performers can manage the impression that they are realizing their objectives by acceptable means (p. 251).

Teams manage their impressions for the benefit of audiences. Their concern with the presented expressions is tied to their concern with the audience's opinion of them. To paraphrase William James, for every group about whose opinion we care, we have a different self (Goffman 1959: 48-49). This creates a multitude of standards by which a team and their actions can be judged.

> In their capacity as performers, individuals will be concerned with maintaining the impression that they are living up to the many standards by which they and their products are judged. Because these standards are so numerous and so pervasive, the individuals who are performers dwell more than we might think in a moral world. But, *qua* performers, individuals are not concerned with the moral issue of realizing these standards, but with the amoral issue of engineering a

---

[24] A performer and an audience constitutes a team, but an individual can also be a team. Individuals can be an audience to their own performance or can think about absent audiences, such as reference groups. Like teams of two or more, they also try to have their performances accepted, albeit by a non-present audience (1959: 79-82, 104).

convincing impression that these standards are being realized. Our activity, then, is largely concerned with moral matters, but as performers we do not have a moral concern with them. As performers we are merchants of morality...To use a different imagery, the very obligation and profitability of appearing always in a steady moral light, of being a socialized character, forces one to be the sort of person who is practiced in the ways of the stage (1959: 251).

Goffman essentially argues that people hide or underplay those actions and motives which violate an audience's moral standards (pp. 48-49). These arguments are highly compatible with the basic thrust of Mills' (1940) position.

Because vocabularies of motive arise in certain contexts for the purpose of making one's actions appear acceptable, we can see these vocabularies as one aspect of impression management. Goffman argues that the self is not the cause of a scene that comes off, but the product of it (p. 253). "In analyzing the self then we are drawn from its possessor, from the person who will profit or lose most by it, for he and his body merely provide the peg on which something of a collaborative manufacture will be hung for a time" (p. 253). Similarly, Mills argues that vocabularies of motive are not the cause of behavior, but the legitimation of it. "As a word, *a motive tends to be one which is to the actor and the other members of a situation an unquestioned answer to questions concerning social and lingual conduct*" (1940: 907, italics in original). Given this perspective, how then should interviews with immigration advocates proceed and *what can we know*?

It is important to remember that performances are designed, to varying degrees, to achieve a "veneer of consensus" where *both* the team and audience conceal their own wants "behind statements which assert values to which everyone present feels obliged to give lip service" (Goffman 1959: 10). The audience often helps performers to save their own routine by employing a number of protective practices, such as by readily accepting an excuse for a performance-threatening exhibition (pp. 229-31). These observations are familiar to social scientists who often reflect on their roles in the research process, particularly in interviews and participant observation. An interview designed to obtain a respondent's vocabularies of motives in various situations is asking for his or her view of the world in a context fraught with dramaturgical dangers. Instead of being a liability, this situation is desirable (one could even say a requirement) because this is where vocabularies of motives are typically utilized.

Another issue concerning the researcher is the analysis of the interview. Sociologists are accustomed to framing vocabularies of motives with sociological concepts and theories, but these can, at times, impede our understanding of certain circumstances. "The languages of situations as given must be considered a valuable portion of the data to be interpreted and related to their conditions. To simplify these vocabularies of motive into socially abstracted terminology is to destroy the legitimate use of motive in the explanation of social actions" (Mills 1940: 913). This is particularly easy to do when analyzing the interviews of people with whom we disagree.

In *Portraits of White Racism*, David Wellman argues that racist beliefs surface, not so much in the form of outright prejudice, but in beliefs that are "culturally sanctioned, rational responses to struggles over scarce resources; that they are sentiments which, *regardless of intentions*, defend the advantages that whites gain from the presence of blacks in America" (1994: 29, italics added). He goes on to demonstrate that whites defend their racial privileges and explain their opposition to institutional change in ways *"that do not explicitly contradict egalitarian ideals"* (p. 53, italics in original). In order to justify their privileged position, all white Americans have learned to do this (pp. 60-61). Although Wellman did not begin with the notion that whites developed strategies for maintaining privilege (p. 76), his analysis is largely one of a vocabulary of motives used by whites to defend the racial status quo in the context of interviews.

Focusing on the consequences (and not the intentions) of whites allowed Wellman to demonstrate the social nature of motives. But one has to wonder—would his analysis have emerged if it were not for the dominant vocabulary of motives used by sociologists? Could it be that the attribution of "negative" motives to people with whom we disagree is more a product of not what is said, but *who* it is said by? "Sometimes when we ask whether a fostered impression is true or false we really mean to ask whether or not the performer is authorized to give the performance in question, and are not primarily concerned with the actual performance itself" (Goffman 1959: 59). Is Wellman's analysis derived more from his assessment of whites' performances than it is from the actual interviews?

Wellman observes that each respondent's position was "formulated in very acceptable, almost liberal, American terms," but that all of their solutions required little or no social change (1994: 208-209). Obviously, it would be a great mistake to only focus on what is said and ignore who said it. It is the job of the sociologist to connect a person's perceptions with their position in social space (Bourdieu and Wacquant 1992: 11). This challenge, however, becomes increasingly difficult when sociologists fail to consider why some vocabularies of motives are more acceptable than others. This oversight becomes especially problematic when they are attentive to the vocabularies used by their respondents but not themselves.

> Individualistic, sexual, hedonistic, and pecuniary vocabularies of motives are apparently now dominant in many sectors of twentieth-century America. Under such an ethos, verbalization of alternative conduct in these terms is least likely to be challenged among dominant groups...A medieval monk writes that he gave food to a poor but pretty woman because it was "for the glory of God and the eternal salvation of his soul." Why do we tend to question him and impute sexual motives? Because sex is an influential and widespread motive in our society and time. Religious vocabularies of explanation are now on the wane. In a society in which religious motives have been debunked on rather wide scale, certain thinkers are skeptical of those who ubiquitously proclaim them (Mills 1940: 910).

The use of certain vocabularies makes it very easy for researchers to impute motives to their respondents, especially those that are dominant, those which are "the least likely to be challenged." But Mills (1940) is not only talking about the vocabularies of respondents. He is also referring to the vocabularies used by those who analyze the statements and actions of others, as indicated by his question, "Why do *we* tend to question him and impute sexual motives?"

I would argue that the motives of white restrictionists are more suspect than not when issues of race and immigration are being considered. I only suggest that this is the case right now and not that these suspicions are unwarranted. Perhaps this point can be illustrated by the example of the late Barbara Jordan, former chairperson of the U.S. Commission on Immigration Reform. A former congresswoman from Texas, Jordan made her position quite clear on illegal immigrants: "Illegal aliens don't have the right to be here...They broke the law to get here. They never intended to become a part of our social community and they are not entitled to benefit" (Rosenthal 1994). Had this statement been made by a white person, he or she could potentially be accused of not only being nativistic, but racist as well since illegal immigrants and Mexican nationals are synonymous in the minds of many Americans. For many Americans, I would venture to say that Jordan would not be suspected of couching her racist sentiments in the motives of legality by virtue of her status as an African American. But even if she were to be branded "nativist," her position would still be defensible because she is speaking, symbolically at least, on behalf of an oppressed group. Whether or not Jordan's explanation "truly" matches her reasoning at the time she first concluded that "immigrants don't have the right to be here" is difficult to assess without having interviewed her.

The theories and concepts we encounter as sociologists help us to frame people's vocabularies of motive in terms that may say more about the theories we use than about the people we are interested in understanding. Mills observation about practitioners of psychoanalysis is applicable to most of our theories. "To converted individuals who have become accustomed to the psychoanalytic terminology of motives, all others seem self-deceptive" (1940: 912). Sometimes "economic immigrants" and "racial nativism" are the appropriate concepts to use, but sometimes they are not, *and we can only determine when this is the case by observing how people explain their behavior in response to the questioning of their conduct.*

It has become increasingly difficult to distinguish between racism and nativism. Both terms are used interchangeably to described restrictionist efforts or are combined into the term "racial nativism." But why is this? Part of the reason, of course, is that today's immigrants are predominantly non-white. It was much easier to distinguish between racism and nativism at the turn of the century when the majority of incoming immigrants were phenotypically white.[25] People "opposed" to immigration or immigrants were simply nativists, but now that today's immigrants are mostly non-white, it is becoming harder to determine which process/attitude is primary. This brings us to the important question of "what can we know?" and the challenge of seeking that information.

Situated Actions and Vocabularies of Motive as an Approach

Goffman (1959) emphasized that the information we need in order to comprehend situations is generally unattainable.

> When one individual enters the presence of others, he will want to discover the facts of the situation...To uncover fully the factual nature of the situation, it would be necessary for the individual to know all the relevant social data about the others...Full information of this order is rarely available; in its absence, the individual tends to employ substitutes—cues, tests, hints, expressive gestures, status symbols, etc.—as predictive devices. In short, since the reality that the individual is concerned with is unperceivable at the moment, appearances must be relied upon in its stead. And, paradoxically, the more the individual is concerned with the reality that is not available to perception, the more must he concentrate his attention on appearances (Goffman 1959: 249).

If we must rely on appearances for much of our information about situations and the people involved in them, what can we do? Mills (1940) argues that we cannot peep behind explanations and opinions (verbalized motives) and look for the supposedly "real attitude or motive" operating inside of an individual. "When we ask for the...'real motive' rather than the 'rationalization,' all we can be meaningfully

---

[25] The Irish and Italians were not initially thought of as being "white" by some native-born Americans (cf. Ignatiev 1995; Alba 1996). This is something that needs to be considered when comparing the intersection of racism and nativism at the turn of the century with today's nativist movements.

asking for is the controlling speech form which was incipiently or overtly present in the performed act or series of acts" (pp. 909-10). However, Mills contends that there is an empirical way to "guide and limit, in given historical situations, investigations of motives. That is by the construction of typal vocabularies of motives that are extant in types of situations and actions" (p. 910). But where does this leave us and what can we do as researchers with these forms of speech?

Mills emphasizes that motives are not necessarily the source of behavior, but are social phenomena that need to be explained because they are attributed and/or declared in situations where one's behavior is, or can be, questioned (1940: 904-5). He argues that we need to examine the functions of motives in certain situations and not simply ask someone what "motivated" them and then place their answer at the beginning of a causal chain. Rather, motives are data that can be examined within an analytic framework where their functions in legitimating past and present actions, and guiding future ones, can be studied. By asking respondents about their work and asking them to reflect on the issues surrounding immigration reform, the interview schedule (see Appendix 2) was designed to draw out the kinds of data needed for examining verbalized motives.

The method described above is only a preliminary attempt to understand, not locate, motives. This is an uncomfortable position to be in—morally and intellectually. Mills' suggestions take us to the very edge of relativism where we try to come to grips with the limitations of social science by developing a method that fights them at the stage of inquiry. His perspective and method allows the researcher to avoid choosing between accepting a respondent's words as true and reading between the lines as Wellman (1994) tends to do. But from a practical standpoint, does it matter if we can never know what "really motivates" a person's behavior? Mills argues that our objective is to develop an analysis of "the integrating, controlling, and specifying function a certain type of speech fulfills in socially situated actions" (1940: 905). If we succeed in this endeavor, and if Mills' argument that vocabularies of motive affect *present* and *future* behavior, the perspective and related methods used in this study are ideally suited for connecting the views of immigration advocates to the contexts in which their perspectives are refined and actions initiated.

Immigration and the Politics of Reform: An Analytical Preview

At this point, expansionist and restrictionist depictions of the immigration debate are briefly introduced. Their worldviews are thoroughly examined in Chapters 5 and 6, but the broad political and ethical contexts framing the debate are primarily considered in this chapter. The immigration debate, taken as a whole, rotates on different perceptions of national needs and wants: How, and on what basis, should the national interest be defined?

Ivan Light argues that the national interest is typically ambiguous and settled by complex tradeoffs. When countries formulate immigration and immigrant policies, they prioritize their cultural, demographic, economic, environmental, political, and racial interests. Presidents Taft and Wilson, for example, both vetoed what was to become the Immigration Act of 1917 (which created an Asian "barred zone") because they "did not think California's racial purity was compensation enough for antagonizing the Japanese..." (1996: 60). To this day, restrictionists and expansionists are still arranging the national interest in dissimilar ways and competing for political leverage and public support.

One expansionist explains that their objectives originate in competing visions: "The 1990s are all about competing visions...Here [in Washington, DC] you really have visions in conflict." The metaphor of competing visions is apt for two reasons. First, it is a sociological truism that our worldviews, our visions, exert a tremendous influence on our perceptions, attitudes, and behaviors. Second, Thomas Sowell uses the same metaphor to classify different "visions of how the world works" (1987: 13). In *A Conflict of Visions* he examines the theoretical underpinnings of political struggles by contrasting what he calls "constrained" and "unconstrained" visions. Different visions of human nature, human potential, and social causation provoke different perceptions and consequently, different policy proposals. Sowell admits to having dichotomized a continuum, but suggests that "constrained" and "unconstrained" be qualified with the words "more" or "less" (e.g., *more* constrained, *less* constrained).

In like manner, "expansionist" and "restrictionist" do not represent all-or-nothing postures, but signify tendencies. Expansionists, for example, favor the maintenance or expansion of current immigration quotas, but many of them believe that restricting illegal immigration and reducing the number of fraudulent refugee and asylee claims is imperative. Restrictionists, on the other hand, would like to see the numbers reduced, but some oppose recent attempts to restrict immigrant access to American social services.

In short, restrictionists are more or less restrictionist and expansionists are more or less expansionist. If given the option, expansionists would probably call themselves "pro-immigrant," and restrictionists would likely pick "immigration reform" to describe their efforts. However, these terms are more political than descriptive. Some expansionists view welfare as a "disservice to immigrants" and believe immigrants should be thoroughly "Americanized." Are these positions unequivocally pro-immigrant? And for most "reformers," "reform" means "restriction." One expansionist put it this way: "The other side always calls themselves "reformers"...you don't get that word "reform." What you mean by reform is less immigration...What makes that a reform?...I think that's deform." While "expansionist" and "restrictionist" are not perfect, they are empirically and metaphorically more accurate than the above terms.

Questions of admittance and membership have, historically, attracted vocal interests. Like two side-by-side trains traveling in opposite directions, projections and arguments fly past each other. Spectators see the cars pass, hear the rumble, and feel the vibration, but in the end have a difficult time—with all of the noise and commotion—deciding which train is headed in the right direction. Like matters of admittance and membership, legitimate national interests are debated within a decidedly political, and complex, context.

Restrictionists and expansionists acknowledge the importance of passing an amorphous, but certain, legitimacy test. One expansionist explains: "Washington confuses...kinetic energy for progress...Here, you have to keep some legitimacy...If they [organizations] pass the plausibility test, then you're in business." Some expansionists claim restrictionist objectives are normatively out of bounds by referring to them as "racist" and "un-American." Some restrictionists do the very same thing by asserting that expansionists advocate "open borders" (read "un-American"). Both sides insist their proposed norms are in line with society's expectations or "right" in some sense. The binding character of norms are used to register social disapproval, secure public acceptance, and improve political standing (Bosniak 1997: 284; Habermas 1975: 97-110).

Legitimacy

Restrictionists use analogies to illuminate the congruence between their policy recommendations and the opinions of ordinary Americans. Their ideas, they suggest, are already endorsed by the American public, although in different areas of life. Here are two examples:

> I think it's perfectly legitimate for me when I write my will to include my children in my will, but not all the other children in the world. Is that nativism? Is that preferring my own? Yeah, well it's true I do prefer to take care of my own and beyond that I have other closer associations—I take care of my own community. I left some money in my will for my local community foundation. I do believe that there are hundreds of other community foundations around—this is the one I know, I prefer it. It's not that I say the others are "bad" or "mean spirited" or beneath me or something...so...do I prefer the things that are closest to me and most important to me? Of course I do, and so does everybody else in the world. Is that nativism? If that's nativism, then everybody I know is a nativist.

> The one [accusation] you hear most often [from expansionists] is racism..."Because you want to block immigration you must therefore not like people that are different than you. Therefore, you're a racist."...If I had to judge on the actual racists, between all the people that are countering and saying they're not...my take would probably be 10% probably are racists, maybe more, but it's such a slippery term, anyway. Are you a racist just because you like your family better than someone else's family...?

Restrictionists emphasize the resemblance between what people are already doing and their suggestions for reform. There's nothing intrinsically wrong with preferences, they maintain, because they're a part of life. In fact, they arise naturally: "The other side tries to give you the idea that if you have these natural preferences, that you're a Nazi or a Fascist or whatever words they throw at you..." It is an understatement to say that restrictionists are familiar with the charges of racism and "anti-immigrant."

One prominent restrictionist explains that he is not "anti-immigration" simply because he would like less of it:

> ...I think that it's legitimate to have restrictions on the operations of an automobile. I think it's okay to have to be sixteen before you get a license and to have speed limits and to say that you can't...drive drunk and that you need to be able to read the chart down at the drivers license bureau. So, does that make me anti-automobile? So, I'm not anti immigration. I'm interested in one set of regulations...somebody else is interested in a different set. So, that doesn't make either one of us "anti" or "pro"—it's a question again—what are the rules going to be? Let's get beyond this accusing each other and rhetoric...

Another influential restrictionist concurs. Wanting fewer immigrants is not inherently "anti-immigrant" or "un-American," but simply a different objective:

> I consider ourselves to be a pro-immigrant organization. We just want fewer of them in the future...The other side tries to come up with "nativist," "xenophobic," you know, "anti-immigrant"...for them, that's just sort of an empirical description...And to be perfectly honest, there's too many people on our side who "anti-immigrant" accurately describes...And immigration really is part of our national heritage, but there's no reason that immigration of 300,000 a year is somehow not part of our national character...What it really boils down to is there's nothing intrinsically un-American about cutting immigration to 300,000 a year, say. The other side has very successfully made the argument that immigration restriction is un-American. And because the low immigration side has been so heavily represented, for so long,

by people who really don't think of themselves in any fundamental, emotional sense, as patriotic Americans, the other side has...sort of wrapped themselves in the flag in a sense, because people on the low immigration side don't want to salute the flag...That is really what it boils down to and we've gotten clobbered because of that...

Even though restrictionists and expansionists argue there is "nothing magical" about the number of annual admissions, they nevertheless align their proposals with America's immigrant tradition. Restrictionists argue that lower levels largely square with American history (particularly before 1965) and expansionists contend that current numbers are not, relative to the U.S. population, historically high (e.g., see Beck 1994: 113; Brimelow 1996: 38; *Cato Handbook for Congress* 1997: 315).

Like restrictionists, expansionists are quick to point out what is legitimate and what is not. But rather than lobby for a new arrangement or perspective, they usually bring up specific policies or the immigration system. By and large, they give restrictionists the benefit of the doubt, but draw the line at race. Peter Brimelow (author of *Alien Nation*) and the Federation for American Immigration Reform (FAIR) are popular targets:

And I think many of them [restrictionists] are operating on good motives too...You...have a sort of cultural, conservative argument which can, I think, be a very disciplined kind of argument...versus one that's very undisciplined, like Peter Brimelow's...I think Peter Brimelow doesn't like people who aren't white...There's sort of a fear of foreign subversion [in Brimelow's book], particularly a fear of American becoming a majority minority country. And again, I don't think these fears are completely irrational or stupid or necessarily racist in and of themselves so long as we think them through because I think there are good responses to each of these kinds of worries. It's when they're taken to rather bizarre degrees that you begin to see some of the ugliness...

I feel it's legitimate to have a debate in this country about how many immigrants and who they ought to be and based on what relations...I think that's legitimate. I think it's legitimate to take a view we're bringing in too many people. I don't think it's legitimate to use the immigration issue to create and stir up racial and ethnic conflict, which is what their [FAIR] game is.

I very much understand where they [FAIR] are coming from—much more the Center for Immigration Studies than FAIR. Interestingly enough, even with individuals with the FAIR organization—particularly earlier people—I can understand, you know, what it is that they think that they would accomplish. That's where we part company...They worry about things—some of which are legitimate and some of which [are] not...The element of FAIR that has to do with race, that has to do with supremacy, that has to do with all of this, you know—what fully represents the uglier parts of everyone's soul—you know, what is there to understand? That should be condemned openly...but you know, that part that comes from, in a sense, a misguided sort of bleeding heart liberalism, you know, for the downtrodden, for the minorities, etcetera, etcetera—I understand that...So, is there part of the FAIR message that I think is legitimate? Yes. Do I think they have a right to do what they are doing. Absolutely yes...I find some of the people at the Center for Immigration Studies, you know, much more easier to take than the people at FAIR...The head of the Center for Immigration Studies has his heart in the right place in many, many of the things that he's concerned about.

Instead of proposing significant changes in immigration policy, expansionists typically focus on the subtleties of the debate and immigration system. Generally content with the current arrangement (see Chapter 6), they rarely suggest fundamental changes or emphasize the legitimacy of their efforts, but instead develop political strategies or recommend ways to improve, or "tweak," the system. As one expansionist put it: "I'd probably leave our general immigration numbers alone and maybe tweak the system in a few areas."

The very idea of "tweaking" the immigration system is typical of expansionists and exemplifies their *general* satisfaction with present policies. Although restrictionists prescribe various changes, their suggestions usually belong to more encompassing and sweeping sets of reforms (e.g., a moratorium on immigration, replacement-level migration, etc.). Expansionists rarely propose sweeping changes. The current system works pretty well: "...I do feel we have sort of inadvertently, in this country, stumbled upon a pretty good immigration policy. It's not perfect...You know, I'd tweak it here or there, I'd increase the numbers, but you know it seems to work pretty well." If immigration policy were a home stereo requiring adjustment, expansionists would likely fine-tune the receiver and calibrate the speakers. Restrictionists, however, would probably replace the receiver and speakers with more modest, rebuilt components.

Not surprisingly, notions about "reasonable" or "proper" policies are closely tied to values and the evaluations they engender. Because restrictionists are predominantly concerned with overpopulation and environmental degradation, the current flow of immigration is, in their estimation, at crisis levels (see Chapter 5). They typically use words like "flood" and "invasion" to describe the situation. One expansionist explains that restrictionists value the environment more than economic growth:

> I think in some ways they're [expansionists and restrictionists] talking past each other because you're talking about people who really want vigorous economic growth, perhaps at the expense of other things versus people who may be willing to do without vigorous economic growth in order to preserve something...I think what you've got are people who have different assumptions, different values...and so they talk past each other... [Restrictionists] value having a national environment they see disappearing and that they understand is disappearing because of population growth.

Determinations of legitimacy are rooted in the value systems which give rise to them, and as discussed in Chapter 2, in their formal codification. The standards implied by beliefs and legal codes are, however, negotiated and set within a decidedly political context. This setting can also influence the progression and regression of an issue along the "legitimacy continuum."

Working the Context

The struggle to recognize, define, and legitimate social problems is political. And ongoing. Expansionists and restrictionists look to empirical, moral, ethical, and historical justifications to secure public consideration, to have their perspectives become the public's perceptions. But in Darwinian-like fashion, some arguments are ignored, others avoided, and some are "rushed along to legitimacy by a strong and influential backing" while others claw their way to respectability (Blumer1971: 303).

The very first sentence of Chapter 1, in fact, considers the subject of immigration reform problematic: "Does international migration undermine the well-being and progress of host countries, as some people argue, or is the problem the reactions of those who express such views?" Simply because a set of social conditions is perceived as perilous by a certain segment of society does not mean it will enter the public arena, let alone be taken seriously. A problem must gain recognition and legitimacy before it can even enter the public ring as a serious contender for debate and discussion (Blumer 1971).

While public recognition and respectability are needed to mobilize the public, they exact a price. Immigration researchers, in particular, recognize the costs. They see accurate information in the corner, taking a beating. Researchers from a nonpartisan organization explain:

> The big battle here...is that people...demand oversimplification. We refuse to give them black and white. The real knowledge, the real understanding of immigration, comes from toiling in the gray areas...Everything is in the context. The entire explanation is in the context...There are different ways of looking at all of this, but of course, nobody wants a complicated picture...Washington is concerned with...instant experts who know nothing about the issue, but [who] have access to some of the major...news magazines, who ultimately become immigration experts. I am shocked, okay, I'm shocked by all of these instant immigration

experts—all of these elite opinion shapers...Well, you can get expertise, you know, for a couple thousand dollars and an investment of about 30 days in research...And yet these are the people, and these are the outlets, that make the most difference in the debate...Over here, you know, you have Brimelow become an expert on U.S. immigration. And, you know...you realize that he doesn't know a damn thing, but that's not the issue...Now, there are lessons there. One of those lessons is we haven't done a good enough job, in terms of playing the public game, of which they are so good...

The problem with experts like us is that...there's all kinds of credentialed people out there with opinions. So you can find whatever opinions you're shopping for and find someone who's got a credential that enables you to call that person an expert. It doesn't matter whether they've...made their calculations on the back of a napkin at lunch....The Social Science Research Council had a big report that came out and...because the discussion about immigration in the country is framed as a debate...this was not seen as...a definitive statement about immigration but was instead immediately transformed. It's conclusions were immediately transformed into one side of an ongoing policy debate. So...the opening leads of the stories I saw in the newspapers and in CNN and so on was inevitably "the Social Science Research Council," you know, "which is comprised of 25 very distinguished economists and social scientists and demographers and sociologists...have come out with this...However, Jack Spratt at FAIR, or whoever it is, has got really...meaningful credentials"...The...sort of equal weighting of a intellectual featherweight and...this incredibly thorough, massive, tome really did a tremendous disservice...Work that aims for impartiality and objectivity immediately just becomes grist for the political...all research is seen as advocacy research or is portrayed as advocacy research, unintentionally perhaps by the media, and that's how it enters the debate, so I think that...in today's climate, the sort of quiet, rational voice tends to get left behind...Clearly people on both

the open borders side of the fence and the *Alien Nation* side of
the fence are going to view us as belonging to the wrong side.

The conversion of impartial reports into advocacy broadcasts may
muddy the issue and annoy researchers, but activists say the debate is
not won with facts and figures, but with emotions. The debate is
driven—not by research and rationality—but by gut-level reactions and
values.

When presenting (not refuting) an issue, some expansionists and
restrictionists try to steer clear of research reports. Published studies
reassure fellow believers, but neglect the people who are "up for
grabs." After two years of traveling the country, a prominent
expansionist explains why he "got away from a recitation" of facts and
figures: "The only people interested were people who already
agreed...This is an emotional, value-laden debate and when we started
to engage it on those terms...we started to diffuse and neutralize the
advantage of the restrictionists." A restrictionist concurs: "We need to
address [people] on an emotional [basis]... Frankly, I think that...we're
too intellectual, we're too rational...We spend...time on that level
when there isn't any debating to be done on that level..."

The emotions of restrictionists and expansionists are, however,
quickly stirred by racial matters and questions of organizational
funding. Both issues are intimately connected in the minds of both
parities. Some expansionists believe the restrictionist movement is
backed, in part, by eugenicists and racists: "My take on [FAIR] is that
they are eugenicists... Look at the people from the environmental-
population control movement that control FAIR and U.S. English." In
his mind, they "think there are too many people in the world, there's
too many people in the United States, and they're the wrong kind of
people and that white folks are being taken over." For expansionists,
suspicions like these were confirmed in the late 1980s when John
Tanton's WITAN memo was leaked to the press (see Chapter 2) and
FAIR acknowledged the acceptance of money from the Pioneer Fund.
In the past, the Pioneer Fund has funded race-IQ and eugenics research
(Stefancic 1997).

One restrictionist contends that Cordelia Scaife May, the largest
contributor to the restrictionist movement, is well-intentioned, but
believes FAIR diminished its efforts and polluted the restrictionist

skyline by accepting money from donors like the Pioneer Fund. Actions like these make them "morally ambiguous":

> The principle funder for the immigration reform movement in America, for every single organization in the immigration reform movement in America, is a woman by the name of Cordelia Scaife May...Cordelia...is a very nice woman. I like her personally...She's worth 700 million, or 800 or 900 million dollars...She is an environmentalist who is tired of the simpering, pandering, bullshit of the environmental movement...But none of these organizations, the environmental organizations, talk about the underlying disease. You see, if you were coughing up blood and I...gave you cough syrup, you'd think I was a shitty doctor wouldn't you? You'd say what's the underlying problem? Underlying problem in the environmental debate is population...And Mrs. Mae is correct that that's the name of the tune. She's also correct that immigration is a huge driver in all of this...They've [FAIR] made a pack with the Devil. They've made a pack to take money from racist foundations. They made a pack to keep people on the board who, in my opinion, have nativist tendencies. Don't misunderstand me, I'm not a guy who throws his words around that easily...If she [Cordelia Scaife May] wants the debate to go to the show, it [FAIR] has to say "fuck you" to the nativists, it has to stick to some core arguments and a principled position...It has to say "no" to donors like the Pioneer Fund, and if it doesn't, it sets itself up. *It compromises everything... It also makes you morally ambiguous...Will you sleep with me for $5, will you sleep with me for $50,000—now we're just arguing over the price.* FAIR's argument with the Pioneer Fund was that it only represents 2% of its budget—bullshit. Okay, we won't even go into that stuff...If it's such a small percentage of the money, then drop the rock...[italics added]

The idea of moral ambiguity highlights the link between authority and legitimacy. The legitimacy of an argument depends, in part, on the person delivering it. If a spokesperson is perceived as an appropriate representative of a given position, his or her authority and intentions are given only a cursory glance. In other words, he or she has the moral or legal authority to raise the issue. Identity politics are often an offshoot of this link.

Unlike the above observation, restrictionists usually reprimand expansionist organizations for their ties to the Ford Foundation. Ethnic lobbies like the Mexican American Legal Defense Fund (MALDEF) and National Council of La Raza are roundly criticized for their foundation origins and support: "These are not just a bunch of ragtag people without resources. They get millions of dollars from the Ford Foundation. Ford is apparently taken over by this left-wing clique...They created MALDEF—that's a Ford Foundation creation there." Even some expansionists disapprove of La Raza and MALDEF: "...to this day, they're not membership organizations...they don't have members, they don't have dues...La Raza claims to represent all Hispanics, yet has no members and relies almost entirely on foundation grants and federal grants for its funding."

One restrictionist believes that some ethnic lobbies are used by foundations and business groups to advance their financial interests:

> As a Mexican American, I wasn't searching for political correctness, I was searching for truth...What you have...in my opinion, is an immigration policy that...tends to benefit certain liberal interests, including ethnic interests...ethnic politicians, ethnic professionals... When all is said and done...the points of view of a limited Hispanic leadership is used by the business community and by libertarians ideologues to promote an expansive immigration policy...That is essentially what I have come to believe about what's driving immigration today...If you sit back and consider the millions of dollars that flow from Northeastern, liberal foundations, and business groups, into putatively civil rights-oriented ethnic organizations (that reflexively lobby intensely against any kind of immigration reform in the country) and who make their reputations on trying to persuade liberal Americans that any kind of immigration reform is a throwback to the kind of persecution that African Americans suffered in the days of Jim Crow—then you can see that the organizations that

want...immigration [are] somehow benefiting. It really doesn't make sense because the beneficiaries in this debate...from decade to decade...are deriving [an] enormous amount of financial support from foundations...whose orientations [are] not so much liberal, in the traditional sense, but rather libertarian, in [their] business objectives. And to be specific—objectives that are grounded in expanding the size of the labor supply in order to depress wages and working conditions...

In the late 1960s, MALDEF and La Raza were basically produced within the walls of the Ford Foundation. Restrictionists regularly sharpen this detail into a point: they (unlike expansionists) represent the majority of Americans. "Right now," Peter Brimelow asserts, immigration policy is "unusually *undemocratic*, in the sense that Americans have told pollsters long and loudly that they don't want any more immigration; but the politicians ignore them" (1996: xviii, italics in original).

The same cannot be said of immigration researchers. Many of them study the public's attitudes toward immigrants and the policies affecting them (e.g., see Espenshade and Hempstead 1996; Huber 1997; Johnson, Farrell, Guinn 1997). This research design, however, examines the worldviews of immigration activists. Before examining this data in the next two chapters, a brief description of their organization and contents is in order.

Expansionist and Restrictionist Worldviews

The photographs of restrictionists (Chapter 5) and expansionists (Chapter 6) are duskier, but also clearer than conventional images. Because the photographs were developed with an eye toward the most evident features, idiosyncrasies sometimes blur into the background. Exceptions, nuance, and details appear, but they always make room for the more prominent themes that emerged during data collection and analysis. The content and contours of these representations are particularly distinct because the interpretive systems of expansionists and restrictionists were used to filter their own portraits. In some respects, the snapshots are more precise than if I had simply pointed my camera and clicked.

Of course, the pictures I have taken are second-order interpretations of first-order interpretations. That is, they are reconstructions of people's ideas and meanings (Neuman 1994: 324). The worldviews captured by my lenses are intended to reflect, as much as possible, the perceptual and interpretive systems of immigration activists. I will not be correcting what I consider to be misrepresentations of immigration policies and research, inaccurate facts, or errors in logic. They're all in there and I leave them alone. Kristin Luker, in the preface to her research on abortion activists writes:

> If I have done my job well, both sides will soon conclude that I have been unduly generous with the opposition and unfairly critical of themselves. They will become annoyed and perhaps outraged as they read things they know to be simply and completely wrong (1984: xiii).

I hope to receive the same kind of backhanded complement. Using the activists' ideas, interpretations, and logic to symbolize their own worldviews was the objective. These representations are not representative of all restrictionists and expansionists, but only refer to the people interviewed for this investigation. If the representations seem too generous or critical (depending on the reader's vantage point), then perhaps, I have also done my job well. The arguments of expansionists and restrictionists are presented from their vantage points, and I often write as if I agree with their assessments. I am a restrictionist in Chapter 5, an expansionist in Chapter 6, and a sociologist throughout.

Expansionists and restrictionists are compared along three dimensions: entry points, human nature/human nurture, and nationalism/globalism. Adherents on both sides of the debate enter through different doors, or entry points. A prominent restrictionist explains:

> When [I sit down with fellow activists] I say...something like, "Well, you know there's about eight major ways people get

involved with this issue...What was your entry point?" And I'll always tell them...mine was environment and population...because...in a lot of ways the entry point is the one...position you won't budge from...

In general, restrictionists are unwilling to "budge" from two overriding concerns: (1) overpopulation and its contribution to environmental degradation and (2) demographic changes curbing the political power and cultural influence of European Americans. Unlike restrictionists, who view immigration in terms of depletion, expansionists see immigration in terms of completion, or more specifically, augmentation. Expansionists argue that (1) the American experiment with immigration has been "a godsend" and that (2) immigrants contribute to the economy and culture of the United States.

Both sides also espouse different conceptions of humans and nature. For some restrictionists, the relationship between humans and nature is one of limits. Humans are not exempt from physical laws or their own nature. Prudent immigration and foreign aid policies will, in their estimation, yield to *natural* laws: "...you can't have growth in anything on a finite, closed, materially-limited world forever." Expansionists, on the other hand, contend that the relationship between humans and nature is one of potential. Americans can exceed natural "limits" by *nurturing* human ingenuity and can nurture generosity and tolerance "by extending ourselves out and by...engaging and struggling."

Lastly, restrictionists are more national, and expansionists more global, in their outlooks. Restrictionists assert that the U.S. cannot admit all of the world's dispossessed (either through foreign aid or immigration) and needs to place national rights in front of human rights. Lines have to be drawn in a world of limits. Expansionists, however, see immigration as an inevitable outcome of globalization. In their minds, immigration can be managed by developing flexible and humane policies. In this global "race" for human and investment capital, the United States should import both as quickly as possible.

In comparing the worldviews of natural scientists and "literary intellectuals," C.P. Snow concluded in his now classic *Two Cultures* that words "are always simpler than the brute reality from which they make patterns: if they weren't, discussion and collective action would both be impossible" (1964: 66). Similarly, the themes noted above admittedly make patterns of a very complex and rich reality. But the perceptions and suggestions of restrictionists and expansionists do fall into general patterns. These themes are the subject of the next two chapters.

Summary of Research Methods

Comparing immigration reform efforts—intentional actions designed to produce or prevent change in current immigration realities—and the worldviews which fundamentally incite and interpret these maneuvers—to a contextualized review of immigrant reception, elucidates the *essence* of American nativism.   This research reconceptualizes the concept of nativism for the purpose of explaining how and why nativism occurs in the United States and deepens our understanding of the people and organizations who currently contribute, directly and indirectly, to American immigration and immigrant policies. The relationship between context and meaning is studied in the next three chapters by examining the worldviews of expansionists and restrictionists and situating these perceptions within a variety of social contexts.

CHAPTER 5

Restrictionist Worldviews

Restrictionists propose a reduction in U.S. immigration levels. Annual admissions are, in their estimation, a threat to the American environment and the people it sustains. Some restrictionists stress the dangers of overpopulation and environmental degradation, while others contend that the demographic and cultural trends fueled by immigration are disrupting the country's ethnic balance, values, and polity. Some emphasize both hazards. In general, cultural decline and overpopulation require significant reductions in U.S. immigration levels. The United States needs to square its immigration policies with natural laws and human nature if it's going to ensure the well-being of its citizens. A country cannot sustain a population larger than the one offered by its habitat and should not compromise the integrity of its lifeboat in order to ease the overcrowding of other countries. Like any other nation-state, the United States has the right to align numerical quotas and admittance criteria with its own needs and preferences. Even in this age of globalism, national rights supercede human rights. The time has come, restrictionists argue, for the United States to recognize the environmental and social costs of immigration and reduce it accordingly—before today's damages become tomorrow's hardships.

Entry Points

The impact of immigration on the size and growth rate of the United States absorbs the attention of many restrictionists. Pulled in by concerns of overpopulation and environmental degradation, they consider current immigration levels a threat to humans and the environment. Widened by a collision between ecological objectives and immigration levels, this opening has become a main entryway in the last thirty years. Other restrictionists are taken in by demographic projections. Apprehensive about political and cultural trends, they believe incoming immigrants exacerbate interethnic relations and diminish the political power of native-born whites. While other misgivings certainly exist, restrictionists generally enter the debate through one, or both, of these doors.

Population and Environment

According to Feagin (1997), nativists (his term) have been trying to restrict, exclude, or attack immigrants for the last two hundred years because of their presumed racial inferiority, improbable assimilation, and exacerbation of economic and social problems. The title of his review suggests that contemporary nativism is merely "old poison in new bottles." However, Feagin overlooks a primary concern among today's restrictionists—U.S. population growth. Many restrictionists attribute environmental degradation and a shrinking resource base to a growing U.S. population. Reducing immigration levels is necessary, they insist, because immigration and immigrant fertility accelerate the U.S. growth rate. Historically speaking, this contention is relatively new. One expansionist explains: "You know, we're talking about the debate being the same eighty or ninety years ago. The economics were there, the culture was there—the environment and population control stuff is the only new twist..."

This "new twist" is not insignificant. The entry points through which restrictionists enter the debate are many, but restrictionists active at the national level largely enter through an entrance marked "population growth." An overriding concern with population control, not immigration per se, brings them to the issue. Asked to explain their interest in reducing immigration levels, restrictionists repeatedly refer to the consequences of population growth:

> Over the next fifty-five years, we're looking at having 400 million Americans. Right now, we're about 267 [million]. So that's a 130 more million Americans we're going to have to educate, feed, house, employ...It's gonna really be a huge drain on our environment. Right now, with 267 million Americans, 40% of our lakes and streams aren't even swimmable. What's gonna happen when we add another 50% to our population?

That's the main reason we're looking at the issue. You'll have folks come out and say, "Well, no, you're anti-Mexican or anti-European or anti-South American." No, we don't really care where people come from. We just want to see the numbers reduced. The whole reason I got into this issue is I just think that population is the key issue, and if we can do something about it now, we're gonna be much better off in the future...A lot of people see the environment as one issue, population as another issue, and immigration as another issue—no one really understands that linkage.

It struck me [at a conference in 1989] that [population]...is really the underlying problem...The concern about not only rapid population abroad, but of course at home we have...environmental problems that...are really the symptoms of population pressure on everything—on land and water resources and air and atmosphere and habitat...Everything that we do to protect and preserve the environment—any victories that we have—will be swept away by continuing growth...

Any problem that you point out that America has today, or most anywhere else in the world, at root cause there's some population issue...I see everything important, or most things important, as relating somehow to some kind of population issues.

More and more, I realized that most of the issues I was covering in Congress, where Congress was trying to make something better for people—child poverty, dropout rates, education problems, clean air, clean water, biodiversity, urban sprawl, traffic problems, infrastructure...I began to see that every one of those issues was being affected by immigration policy, and that Congress was undercutting...all of its efforts... I personally don't want to live in the United States with double the population. You see, that's the bottom line with me...I do not believe it's possible to retain the American style of life...and to protect the environment like we want to, with double the population...Basically, we're on target to double the 1970 population by 2050...I'm talking about doubling it from 1970, Earth Day. Of course, it's not going to stop even if we double...It just keeps growing...All those other things [e.g., cultural and economic concerns] can be solved, but until you can prove to me that...we can meet all of our standards right now with the current population, then I'm opposed to any governmental policy that forces population growth.

Restrictionist estimates of natural resources, overpopulation, and quality of life are usually based, either implicitly or explicitly, on the concept of "carrying capacity." Carrying capacity is "the number of individuals who can be supported without degrading the natural, cultural and social environment, i.e., without reducing the ability of the environment to sustain the desired quality of life over the long term" (Durham 1997).

If the carrying capacity of a given area is 1,000 then approximately 1,000 people can enjoy a specified quality of life within that zone without reducing the environment's ability to sustain that level of living over the long term. Restrictionists admit the concept is variable and somewhat vague, but argue that "current levels of per capita environmental impact" are already exceeding the environmental carrying capacity of the United States. A noted restrictionist, Roy Beck, contends that "if sustainable living can be defined as enjoying the fruit without harming the tree that produces it, then there is ample evidence that 260 million Americans are already hacking vigorously at the trunk" (1994: 14-20).

The concept, however, has its detractors. The Cato Institute, an expansionist organization, contends that every person in the world could live in Texas and occupy 1,400 square feet. Restrictionists argue this exercise is misleading: estimates of overpopulation are not based on land area but on carrying capacity. Overpopulation is more than a space problem—Texas could not sustain the world's population without depleting the resources beyond their capacity to replenish. People would begin dying. Another variation of this reasoning is expressed in the "empty lands" argument: "What if the U.S. population were dispersed to relatively unpopulated areas? Whenever I fly over the United States I see a lot of open space" (Beck 1994).

One expansionist, for example, relies on the logic of open space to explain his dismissal of restrictionist warnings: "...you know, when I fly across this country from Washington to California, what impresses me is the vast emptiness of the place, so I'm not particularly worried [about population growth in the United States]..." Most expansionists, however, rarely discuss population growth or environmental degradation. They know restrictionists worry about these things, but see little or no reason why they should. Most regard their conclusions as nonsense, but others are "agnostic" in that they don't know what to think: "...the...concern about the environment and population, I'm agnostic about. Fundamentally, I think they're silly concerns, okay? But, you know, since I don't study these things...I'm essentially, fundamentally, agnostic." Not convinced, but not indifferent, expansionists devote little attention to restrictionist warnings. They prefer the persuasion of their cultural and economic arguments over restrictionist scenarios of environmental degradation and overpopulation.

Because not all experts are convinced that the United States has exceeded its carrying capacity, restrictionists then ask, why take the risk? The prudent approach is to "stop short of full carrying capacity" (Beck 1994: 29). The argument of worthwhile risk, emerges time and time again among population restrictionists. The logic of Pascal's Wager is applied to population options:

> If the nation wants more people later on and discovers it can handle more without harming the environment or diminishing the quality of life, it always can increase the population then. There will be no shortage of people wanting to come. But decreasing population after discovering its long-term carrying capacity has been exceeded is a much tougher and slower task, and that may not be possible at all (Beck 1994: 29).

Population restrictionists generally believe lowering immigration levels will not sufficiently curb population growth without the complements of abortion and family planning. During a dinner meeting with three population restrictionists, the first topic of conversation was not immigration, but abortion. The two topics are inextricably connected for many restrictionists. Many are active in organizations like Planned Parenthood, although some participate in family planning initiatives via the intermediacy of environmental associations. This issue is discussed later under the heading of "public image," as some cultural restrictionists believe population restrictionists diminish their reputation and hobble their political efforts.

Demographic Forecasts

Familiar with the charge of racism, many restrictionists acknowledge the presence of racists on their side of the debate, but argue that racists are the exception and not the rule. Some are very straightforward about the matter and even discuss cultural and racial issues without prompting. The topics usually emerge in discussions over motives and potential demographic projections. A smaller number of restrictionists also address group relations and political power in terms of race and culture. Demographic changes propelled by immigration, they submit, can diminish the culture and political influence of European Americans.

Restrictionists understand that voicing these concerns can be viewed as out of bounds. Pulling out a map of California and table of demographic projections, a prominent restrictionist explains:

> Here's the demographic situation in California. In 1970—population of California by ethnicity—is seventy-seven percent Anglo, fifty years later—twenty [percent]. So is that a legitimate concern?

> Brian: What do you think?

> Well, see, some people would say "Well, if you're concerned about that sort of thing it's racist." But most people are concerned about political punch and power and being in the demographic majority. It's common all around the world so why would somebody decide that they want to become subject to some other people?

After stressing the connection between political power and majority status, he emphasizes that the absence of an ethnic majority is politically ineffective:

> I'm not really...interested in giving up control over my political future by becoming a minority group that's relegated to no political importance—in a country that I think probably won't work. One of the questions that's raised in all this is Bill Clinton's vision, as he put it in the paper the other day, the future of the United States no longer having a majority population—it's all just gonna be a bunch of little groups contending with each other. Is that really a workable situation?...How well does it work in Switzerland? Switzerland's only got five or six million people, and it doesn't even work there very well. Four language groups don't get along. How well does it wok in the Baltics? Not very good. How well does it work in the Middle East? Not very good. How well does it work Sri Lanka? How does it work in India? Doesn't work anywhere. And yet we've had the blessings of having a majority population that was generous enough—maybe not fast enough or maybe not big enough—but to try to grant minority rights and bring a whole lot of people along. So is this the future that works? I don't think it is...If...to be concerned about this is racism, then what are we to say about Israel?...Jews in Israel, justifiably in my view, are not interested in being a minority group in their country. The Jews make up two thirds of Israel and have one third of the babies. The Arabs make up one third of Israel and have two thirds of the babies—now where does that take you after a couple of generations, you see? It takes you into political illegitimacy because one of the most powerful ideas in the world today is majority rule. So if you lose your majority, you lose your political legitimacy. Is that a good thing?

Some restrictionists see political struggles as a byproduct of human nature, a consequence of living in a world that is inherently competitive. This understanding of human nature is not only applied to politics, but to expansionists as well.

One restrictionist explains that some expansionist organizations enter the debate for purposes of family reunification, but contends that a number of them—particularly the ethnic lobbies—enter the ring in hopes of expanding their political power. The natural desire to enlarge one's power base is a legitimate objective, but should not be sought at the expense of the country and other co-ethnics:

At two levels, people do have relatives. They want to get in here—you can't begrudge them that, but on the other hand, the country has the right to decide who and how many people to let in and we just can't let everyone in who would potentially like to come here. But there's also at a more basic, fundamental, political level, a struggle of a group to get more power. And you get more power by getting more numbers first and foremost...So when you get these different groups talking among themselves...they're quite up-front, or unabashed about what their aim is—to get more people like themselves here who will get more political power for that group, and I wouldn't say that is racist, or that there's anything unseemly or unnatural about that. Every group attempts to do that. We'd like to be bigger and more powerful by getting like-minded people to join this organization. And the reality of ethnic and racial politics in this country anymore is that if you have a large group of people who identify with you ethnically or racially, it's a point in your favor as a politician. That's why you find Hispanic politicians being elected from Hispanic areas, whites from white areas, blacks in black areas, etc. So the politicians know this. So I don't begrudge a group wanting to enlarge its own power base. What bothers me is that they're doing it at the expense of not only the country as a whole, but even members within the community. Because by bringing too many people over, by enlarging the population of the country and flooding labor markets, they're damaging Hispanic or Asian people—a lot of whom as recent immigrants are working in low-skilled professions—damaging their ability to ever get ahead in this country.

Expansionists often respond to projections like these with a great deal of skepticism. One expansionist, in fact, characterizes restrictionists as "pessimists" and expansionists as "optimists." Expansionists look to the country's immigration history and are optimistic about the future. They are willing to take "a little bit of a risk," he explains, because "that's what America is built on...it'll work out somehow—it always has."

But restrictionists see a history unlikely to repeat itself. The American experiment worked, in large part, because the last great wave of immigration was followed by a forty year breather and because assimilation, not multiculturalism, was the modus operandi. Comparisons of the past and present are misleading because the current stream of immigration continues unchecked:

> ...it's alleged that "Look, look at this last great wave [in the late 1800s and early 1900s]—the wonderful things that it did for America."...One thing that's always ignored by the people who make that claim is that the last great wave was brought to an end. Arguably, the reason we can afford to wax nostalgic now, and talk about what a wonderful thing immigration is for the country, is because, yes, there were the twenty or thirty million people who were brought in, but after twenty or thirty years of it, that wave was brought to an end. It gave that mass of people and their descendants here a chance to get ahead in the country.

With no end in sight, meaningful comparisons between the past and present are few and far between. Unlike the last great wave, today's flow is entering a country brimming with people. To use the metaphor of one restrictionist, Americans are no longer advancing on the frontier, "but the frontier is now advancing on us." Apple to apple comparisons are hard to come by and the country is full of people—what is there to be optimistic about?

Restrictionists also question the content and value of diversity. A speech made by President Clinton at a NAACP meeting, stressing the benefits of a multicultural society and [multiethnic nation], drew heavy fire:

"Diversity being our greatest strength," the Bill Clinton cliché, is silliness, it's folly. Diversity is something that you tolerate. Diversity is something you try to make work for you, and you try to make a strength, but your unity is your strength. Diversity is only helpful insofar as it helps make a stronger union, but if you can't bring the parts together, all you got is diversity and balkanization.

There's also the dissatisfaction brought on by bilingualism, I think...The language question, I think, is a big one...When I was living in Honduras as a Peace Corps volunteer, I saw it as a sacred trust, a sacred mission to learn Spanish, so I could deal with people on their own terms in their own country. I would not have imposed my English on them—to me it would have been an affront, an example of an ugly American...But then coming back to this country, I began to get the impression that a lot of social and cultural liberals here were saying that, "Well, no, immigrants no longer have to adapt to American norms, customs, language, etc. We have to have adopt to theirs." And to me that was just the opposite of the message I had gotten as a Peace Corps volunteer from our staff going to Honduras...And so I think that feeling I felt in these instances is probably shared by a lot of other Americans too...There's a lot of subcultures in this country—this is part of the diversity that President Clinton will speak about—it is part of our heritage, and it makes this country what it is, and it is something to be proud of, but what I worry about is that...if you're trying to hold a nation together, have national unity and social cohesion, but if you promote diversity that's one thing, but if you go out of your way to promote it too much...it can produce divisiveness, separatism, balkanization...which ultimately is really dangerous for a country.

These changes are especially serious because the United States, in addition to its rapidly growing population, is having a difficult time managing the diversity and cultural changes that are already taking place.

Incoming immigrants exacerbate problems that are already out of control. In general, they make matters worse:

...we have the highest levels of legal immigration that we've ever had—just bringing all kinds of problems that we don't need. In America, I don't think we've solved the racial problems between black people and white people. On top of this problem, we're now dumping even more potential racial problems and this, to me, is just crazy...Well, we haven't solved those problems, yet we're bringing in more problems to deal with and the numbers that we're bringing in will certainly make these problems worse...So here we are bringing in unskilled people who are lowering the living standards of our own people ([and] many of them are minorities)...And again, you bring in all these people from Third World cultures, you're going to displace the values of this country. Assimilation worked in the past to some extent because it was understood that the immigrants would conform to Anglo-Saxon values. I'm not saying Anglo-Saxon values are superior, but I'm just saying, historically, that was the standard of assimilation and everyone understood this and the American people insisted that immigrants assimilate to that standard...[With multiculturalism] there's ceasing to be a standard of assimilation at all...I think immigrants assimilate to certain aspects of American culture. I mean, there are two dominant cultures in America now, as I see it. There's the traditional culture of, for lack of a better term, Anglo-Saxon values, self-control, self-restraint, self-discipline—this kind of thing. And then you have the Madonna culture...the culture of TV, movies...self-gratification, sexuality, violence, sports mania, this kind of stuff. I think a lot of immigrants are assimilating to that. They're learning English and at the same time, they're learning these values that are not the values that made America great. Now, they're assimilating again, but is this the kind of assimilation that's beneficial? I think it's horrible that native-American born children are assimilating to that culture rather than traditional culture. If we're not even assimilating our own young people how are we going to

assimilate immigrants?...There's a recent study by a
sociologist named Alejandro Portes...He made the point that,
from one of his recent studies, that children of immigrants are
learning English fairly well—they're assimilating in that
sense. But on the other hand, more and more of them are
adopting the idea that they're hyphenated Americans...that
they really aren't identifying completely with the country.

Of course, not all restrictionists are not concerned about cultural
differences or assimilation. Restrictionists focusing on population
growth and environmental degradation sometimes have little or nothing
to say about diversity or integration. They refer to population pressure
and carrying capacity, but stop there. Everything else is of secondary
importance: "If truly there are vast horizons and there's no end to the
resource base, then I guess we really are down to talking about things
like language and how people get along..." The substance of this
inclination is observable in the convictions of many restrictionists. The
first order of business, for many of them, is population growth. Human
relationships are relevant, but the relationship between humans and
nature is much more important.

Human Nature

Natural scientists generally see more "nature," and social scientists
more "nurture," in human behavior. While not all restrictionists and
expansionists were asked about their areas of study, most restrictionists
received formal training in philosophy or one of the natural sciences.
Expansionists, on the other hand, tended to congregate in the
humanities and social sciences. Although one's worldview is not
entirely shaped by one's college curriculum, both sides clearly embrace
different conceptions of humans and nature.

From the restrictionist point of view, the relationship between
humans and nature is one-sided. Human potential is checked by natural
laws. Humans are not exempt from the laws of nature, but subject to
their boundaries. Like other animals, human behavior is circumscribed
by physical laws and human nature—no amount of browbeating,
nurturing, or socialization can trump the limits and dispositions of
nature. This set of beliefs, however, does have its detractors. Some

restrictionists, especially cultural restrictionists, consider these ideas, and the people that push them, a political handicap.

American Exceptionalism

Restrictionists are critical of "American exceptionalism" or what Garrett Hardin (1995) describes as the "hypothesis of human exemptionism"—the notion that natural laws have little or no bearing on America, or on human beings in general. Expansionists think they are "exempt from the basic laws that govern the behavior of other animals" (1995: 79). Restrictionists frequently comment on this notion of "exemptionism" by emphasizing that human ingenuity, while impressive, cannot overcome natural laws.

The following comment on human exemptionism refers to Julian Simon, the now deceased economist from the University of Maryland, College Park. To many restrictionists, Simon's work typifies the expansionist mindset:

> ...You've probably heard of Julian Simon in the immigration debate. He also been involved in the environmental limits to growth debate...He believes that, as he puts it, the human mind, the brain, is the ultimate resource—that there really are no limits to copper or to oil. Even if those resources ultimately—if not run out, but at least get prohibitively expensive to use...then we'll simply, automatically, come up with replacements. This is the genius of the human mind at work...What we would say is that these people operate on a faith that this process can occur forever...These people enjoy a lot of favor because, I think, they give a very comforting, business-as-usual sort of message. We can go on without any basic changes in lifestyle...It really does come down to a matter of a faith that people can continually pull rabbits out of the hat like magicians...And I don't think nature or reality works that way...They have made some really good points. One is that human beings are flexible, one is that it is possible to substitute or replace resources that are growing scarce. In fact, environmentalists hope for this themselves. We are also...prone to, I think, [the] sort of techno fix mindset. In the

case of environmentalists, it tends to be with renewable technologies like solar energy or recycling...They [environmentalists] don't want to face that either...that we have to deal with the second law of thermodynamics, that you can't have growth in anything on a finite, closed, materially-limited world, forever...And yet somehow we [humans] think that human beings...will face no limits to growth, like everything else in nature has to. It's almost a form of American exceptionalism...it's almost sort of a Homo sapiens exemptionism—we are so special, either endowed by a God or as the humanists might put it, by evolution—that the laws of nature that apply to other creatures—we're exempt from them...Yes, we're capable of some marvelous things, yes Malthus is wrong to date, but ultimately he's gonna be proven right—at least in some ways.

Simon wrote extensively on economics, immigration, population, natural resources, and the environment. He generally concluded that immigration quotas should be raised, natural resources were not finite "in any economic sense," and population growth would likely have a "long-run beneficial impact on the natural resource situation" (1996).

Restrictionists not only criticize Simon's positive-sum views, but imply that expansionists are captive to their emotions or subscribe to a groundless faith. Referring to the multiple motives of expansionists, one activist condenses the opinions of other restrictionists with one single thought:

A lot of it's tied up in American exceptionalism...that natural laws don't operate in the United States: "We are a better people," "God...put together...the new man here"...The idea that we could do something other people couldn't—in terms of mixing all kinds of different cultures, and all of that...All of this is things that help people feel good about being an American, so it's an emotional thing—"If we cuts this off, we've taken away something really special about our identity..."

American exceptionalism not only snubs natural laws, but according to one restrictionist, underrates the importance of culture:

> Americans are...so ethnocentric, so unworldly, that we really think that everybody deep down is just like us..."They just speak a different language." But they're not—they're from very different cultures. They're playing under a very different set of rules...The more people you bring in who are playing by a different set of rules...the harder the game is to play—the less stable the game is...That is what we stand to lose—America itself. We seem to think that culture is something that seeps out of the ground like worms when it rains. It's not—it's us...Our culture is what is responsible for our success. Change too dramatically who we are, change our culture too dramatically...change that success...The idea that...America is somehow magic is naïve.

Beliefs in American "magic" and "exceptionalism" are impediments to change. Restrictionists find declarations of inexhaustible resources and human exemptionism incomprehensible. This "anti-scientific, anti-logical, anti-reality strain" promotes a ho-hum utopian posture radically at odds with the views of Thomas Malthus, a man practically revered by some restrictionists. In 1798 his *Essay on the Principle of Population* was first published anonymously, but later underwent a series of revisions and editions bearing his name (McCleary 1952). Restrictionists esteem Malthus in much the same way that Marxists regard Marx—generally correct and shamefully disregarded.

Malthus argued that the human power to reproduce is greater than the human ability to produce subsistence. Misery and vice spring from this disparity (McCleary 1952). One restrictionist explains:

> ...that was a startling discovery that Malthus made 200 years ago—that there's excess reproduction in every species of plant and animal in the biological kingdom. And the people who you were referring to [expansionists who examine fiscal impacts and cultural issues]...they'll talk economics, they'll talk culture, language, and this and that, but they never deal with people and resources. They just can't see us in this test

tube of nutrients, where the nutrients are being depleted. That's beyond the realm of their comprehension...

Malthus stressed that the exponential growth of the human population exceeds the human capacity to produce subsistence. This tendency, when unchecked by "moral restraint," leads to human misery and vice (Rhoe 1997). Malthus' projections, however, did not materialize because, as one restrictionist explains, population pressures were relieved by the migration of sixty million Europeans between 1840 and 1930: "So it took the pressure off. And in fact, picking up and moving on was a solution to a lot of human problems then, but there's basically no place left to move now."

Criticisms of American exceptionalism are sometimes accompanied by words like "emotion" and "sentimentalist." Restrictionists describe their perspective as "rational" or "logical," or as one put it, "Spockesque," referring to the always-logical Captain Spock of Star Trek®. These perceptions are not uncommon. In many ways, restrictionists see America's immigrant past as an obstacle to present and future reforms:

> ...one of the common trite sayings in the immigration debate is that we are a nation of immigrants. Well, so is every other nation a nation of immigrants. We're maybe a bit more recent in ours, but there's no nation that wasn't populated by people who came from elsewhere at some point in history, so that's not a distinctive thing...I don't think that admitting immigrants is key to the future of the United States any more than it is to any other nation. I would say what's more key to our future is recognizing when the time for a certain course of public policy is passed and revising it to fit the new realities and trying to get a moral fix on the whole thing so that we don't damage other countries, say by admitting their brightest and best, and further accentuating the economic and social and political gap between the United Sates and less developed countries, which in turn comes back to bite us as increased pressure for illegal immigration.

I go with logic and what makes sense and what I can physically see...Folks who look at the facts, I think, usually end up on our side of the issue. You'll hear a lot of things...our immigrant tradition—we were all once immigrants—and I mean, that's good rhetoric, but...everyone in London...were all once immigrants too...The United States was a nation of immigrants. I think now more today...we are a nation of citizens, and I think that's something that needs to have a little higher respect...

Restrictionists think expansionists cannot objectively examine immigration because "they're emotionally tied" to the "nation of immigrants" conception. The United States, they argue, needs to focus on the present if it's going to counteract the ruinous consequences of overpopulation. People must recognize the limits of humans and nature.

Humans, they insist, are not exempt from natural laws. Technology cannot "fix" the population problem, and even if it could potentially solve it, why risk it? Why not live within nature's limits and experience its dividends rather than wager it all at the technology table? For restrictionists, the resource base is finite. The United States, just like every other country in the world, sits on top of a fixed resource base. Every additional person born in, or admitted to, the United States represents a subtraction of some kind, and in the absence of a technical solution, the situation will not change. The population problem is, to use Garrett Hardin's term, a "no-technical-solution problem." A technical solution only requires a change "in the techniques of the natural sciences, demanding little or nothing in the way of change in human values or ideas of morality" (1995: 13). The game of tick-tack-toe is impossible to win if both players understand the game perfectly and obey the rules. Similarly, the population problem is impervious to technical solutions (1995: 13-14).

Hardin's writings on abortion, population, and immigration are well-known, particularly among natural scientists and restrictionists (e.g., see Hardin 1959; 1974; 1993; Hardin and Baden 1977). His essays, reprinted by FAIR and *The Social Contract*, are familiar to some expansionists working at the national level. A genetically trained biologist, Hardin is perhaps best known for two essays—the "Tragedy of the Commons" and "Lifeboat Ethics." Both metaphors, and their connected logic, exert a profound influence on the worldviews of restrictionists.

The "Tragedy of the Commons" depicts an unmanaged economy in a crowded world. This design becomes tragic in that the logic of the system compels people to maximize their gains in a world of finite resources. The system, and the logic it encourages, ultimately destroys the belongings held in common. "Tragedy" is not sadness, but "resides in the solemnity of the remorseless working of things" (Harding 1995: 17).

Hardin describes the commons as a pasture "open to all" in which each rancher is allowed to manage and maximize his herd. This arrangement works fine until the number of cattle eventually exceeds the carrying capacity of the pasture. "At this point, the inherent logic of the commons remorselessly generates tragedy" (Hardin 1995: 18). Each rancher, acting rationally, decides that is in his best interest to add to his herd:

> Explicitly, or implicitly, more or less consciously, he asks, "What is the utility *to me* of adding one more animal to my herd?" This utility has one negative and one positive component. (1) The positive component is a function of the increment of one animal. Since the herdsman receives all the proceeds from the sale of the additional animal, the positive utility is nearly +1. (2) The negative component is a function of the additional overgrazing created by one more animal. Since, however, the effects of overgrazing are shared by all the herdsmen, the negative utility for any particular decision-making herdsmen is only a fraction of –1. Adding together the component partial utilities, the rational herdsmen concludes that the only sensible course for him to pursue is to add another animal to his herd...But this is the conclusion reached by each and every rational herdsmen sharing a commons. Therein is the tragedy. Each man is locked into a system that compels him to increase his herd without limit—in a world that is limited. Ruin is the destination toward which all men rush, each pursuing his own best interest in a society that believes in the freedom of the commons. Freedom in a

commons brings ruin to all (Hardin 1995: 18; italics in original).

Hardin also applies the meaning of his metaphor to human reproduction by arguing that the "freedom to breed is intolerable" in a crowded commons. "To couple the concept of freedom to breed with the belief that everyone born has an equal right to the commons is to lock the world into a tragic course of action" (1995: 23)

Because the costs of overbreeding are not borne solely by the responsible family (i.e., the children of "improvident parents" are not allowed to starve), but instead are distributed among society's members (e.g., via the welfare state or foreign aid), it is in the public interest to manage the breeding of families. The human freedom to reproduce must be relinquished because no technical solution will remove the pains of overpopulation. "A finite world can support only a finite population; therefore, population growth must equal zero" (Hardin 1995: 13-15; 23, 30).

An affected majority needs to develop some system of mutual coercion in order to curtail this freedom. Appeals to conscience are ineffective. Rather, responsibility must be produced by "definite social arrangements" which recognize the "necessity of abandoning the commons in breeding" (1995: 22-30). As discussed below, notions of responsibility and coercion are integral to lifeboat ethics.

Public Image

Many restrictionists share Hardin's view of the world to the extent that they believe overpopulation, both here and abroad, threatens to destroy the American environment and diminish the quality of people's lives. It is difficult, however, to determine the extent to which restrictionists accept his analysis because some restrictionists, particularly cultural restrictionists, worry that Hardin and his ideas are a political handicap. They contend that the case for lower immigration levels is being hampered, in part, by population restrictionists.

One prominent restrictionist suggests that their effectiveness as a political coalition is impeded by restrictionists primarily interested in

population control. Their focus on population growth sometimes gets in
the way of political strategy:

> Spencer Abraham [R-Mich., chair of the Senate immigration
> subcommittee] had a hearing earlier this week which was, you
> know, six immigrants saying, "Well, you know, I just love
> America and I started a business when I gŏt here" and all this
> stuff. And I think, you know, that's really good, more power
> to you, but what does that have to do with immigration policy,
> what does this tell us about getting rid of the fourth
> preference...? Nothing, zero, it's just absurd playing of heart
> strings. The problem is on our side...many of the people...are
> not moved by that kind of story. You have to be moved by
> that kind of story...in order to be able to communicate with
> people...If you're not moved by it, you're not speaking the
> same language as the public at large...Too many people on
> our side don't like the Statue of Liberty..."It's been
> appropriated by the other side so let's not talk about it," and
> what they don't understand is that the Statue of Liberty is a
> central icon of American national identity. You don't
> badmouth it, you don't downplay it. If we're gonna win, and
> if there's an element of this war that is a battle over symbols,
> we need to reappropriate the Statue of Liberty, not disparage
> it. And that in a sense, to me, sort of sums up the real
> shortcomings of the low immigration side, and that is that
> simply—so much of it derives from liberal concerns about
> population growth. That's [who] really started [this
> movement]...These people are not...patriotic...not in the
> sense that they're enemies of America, they just don't see this
> as a patriotic movement, and what they end up doing is
> conceding, in a sense, the issue of patriotism to the high
> immigration side...They see pro-abortionism and reductions
> in immigration as the same issue. You cannot legitimately be
> pro-life and be for low immigration—if you are, you must be a
> racist...In other words, you're somebody they don't want to
> deal with...That is where this whole movement comes
> from—is liberal, population control...Garrett Hardin is on the
> board [of FAIR]...He exemplifies the worst fears of people on

the Right—you know, pro-abortion, anti-human...and in fact, if you read this guy's stuff...the impression really is that he really doesn't like people...

Another restrictionist makes a similar observation, but connects the interest in population growth to the expansionist suspicion that some restrictionists are "anti-Catholic."

If I were in your shoes, doing this study...the thing that would strike me is how cold a lot of the immigration reform people [i.e., restrictionists] are, how cold, how into biology, sociobiology—not enough of the warmth of human kindness...in general...The reason is because the people who first got into this were more environmentalists and population people, especially population people. Their major concern was just how many people are here. They don't care who it is. They don't really care if they come from the outside or whether they're born here—they just don't want any more. And that's not a illegitimate view, but the people who believe that tend to be hostile to religion—they aren't always that way, but they tend to be...They only think one thing with Catholicism—anti-family planning—that is their one thought. They typically despise the Roman Catholic Church...So there's a kind of enmity there, and because there's such sentimentalism on the other side, there is...a contempt for those who are just sentimentalist, instead of compassion...

Two former Peace Corps volunteers returned to the United States fearful of population growth and frustrated with the Catholic Church. One of them, a former Catholic, concluded that the Church's position on birth control degraded people's lives and were fundamentally at odds with the Golden Rule: "...after having been in the Philippines for a few years, and seeing how the Vatican's policies affected the quality of life there, I mean, I have to tell you, there's no way I could ethically remain—my allegiance to the Catholic Church just vanished." While some restrictionists are critical of the Church's positions on abortion, birth control, and immigration, I did not interview any one who "despised" the Church.

Another restrictionist, an American born and raised in Africa, entered the debate through the population gate, but is very critical of the way some population restrictionists approach the debate:

> Reality is that if you have lived overseas, you know that there are billions...of real—all of these are real people. They're people who you can love, who I have loved. People who's only crime is they were born poor, whose only crime was they were born into a country that had no resources, or government that was corrupt...The environmental movement, I think is—at some level—fundamentally broken in its thinking...If you go back to the environmental movement, and you look at the great thinkers in this, the people like Paul Erlich, a butterfly biologist, Garrett Hardin...probably had a greater impact on my thinking than anyone that I've ever read, but Garrett's basic work is in yeast, okay? Edward O. Wilson on sociobiology—where a lot of the nativists start building their little weird empire of thought...Well, he...[studied] ants. Bugs, yeast, and butterflies are not human beings, and you can't treat population dynamics as if they're bugs. These are real...people, and if you miss that, you miss the debate.

Criticisms like these are often sandwiched between sympathetic explanations. Restrictionists explain that their colleagues are interested in population control because they care about the quality of people's lives: "Some of them sound "anti-people" because they're so population control, but a lot of them, you gotta understand, they see that as pro-people, not anti-people. They want to keep women from having nine kids."

As the preceding comments indicate, population restrictionists are not only interested in reducing immigration levels. They're also interested in limiting fertility (via abortion, birth control, and family planning) and curbing the consumptive appetites of Americans. In *How Many Americans?*, Leon Bouvier and Lindsey Grant summarize what many restrictionists say: "Just as some Americans are "pro-children" but value quality over quantity, so too some are "pro-immigrant and prefer quality over quantity...It makes no sense to discuss birth control without considering immigration...Both contribute to population growth..." (1994: 113).

The *Tenth Anniversary Oral History Project* of the Federation for American Immigration Reform (interviews with five of the Federation's original board members and executives) is replete with references to International Planned Parenthood and Planned Parenthood. According to John Tanton, the founder of the Federation for American Immigration Reform (FAIR), the first five board members and executive director all "came out of the population and environmental movements" (FAIR Oral History Project, Tanton: 34). For example, Sidney Swensrud, former chair of Gulf Oil, was asked to join the board because another board member knew of his work at the Association for Voluntary Sterilization and International Planned Parenthood (FAIR Oral History Project, Tanton: 30).

The assumption of a zero-sum resource base (where losses equal winnings) requires that the United States curb its population growth by lowering immigration and fertility levels. To some, these options may seem unattractive or immoral, but nevertheless, restrictionists argue, hard choices have to be made even if one's heart and mind tug in opposite directions:

> ...because immigration accounts for up to 60% of our...annual growth...we just can't be a population organization and not address this issue...Our particular motive is that we just can't continue to accommodate this many people in our country, and it doesn't matter where they're from...I didn't start working here because I wanted to reduce immigration. I started working here because I was interested in the environment...To be honest, there are some things in life that sort of your head can agree with it, but it takes a lot of your heart to get into it...Our country has a finite resource base, and eventually...if we continue to grow and grow and grow...we're just not gonna be able to accommodate it...

Restrictionists see expansionists as unwilling to confront the difficult choices offered by nature. Increasing immigration levels evades a problem for which there is no technical solution and aggravates the situation by allowing high-fertility countries to funnel their "surplus populations" to the United States instead of dealing with their excess populations (Garling 1970: 70). The U.S. has no choice but to lower immigration levels and reduce the flow of illegal immigration if it is to curb population growth, both at home and abroad.

Nationalism: Drawing Lines

In a world of limits, lines have to be drawn—not the kind synonymous with isolationism, but the kind that clarify and advance national interests. The United States must assert its sovereignty in the face of stark inequalities, international policy frameworks, and migrations. The United States cannot serve as the world's soup kitchen or population safety valve, but can assist sending countries by holding them responsible for their own domestic futures. Siphoning off their dissidents, professionals, and excess populations only circumvents self-sufficiency and responsibility. By providing them with foreign aid (either directly or indirectly), the U.S. unwittingly contributes to the very problems it seeks to relieve.

National Sovereignty

The United States cannot welcome every aspiring immigrant or admit all of the world's dispossessed if it hopes to avoid the tragedy of the commons. Drawing lines is not a cruel exercise, but necessary and compassionate. One restrictionist explains that being kind—his number one value—is congruent with immigration restriction:

> The most important value I have is a very general thing...The one at the top is, as much as possible, "Be kind."...

> Brian: So you see immigration policy as being kind in some ways...the kind of immigration you would like to see?

> Yeah, now see that's an interesting problem because you run into the idea there that "Well, if you're gonna restrict immigration, aren't you being unkind to other people?" *But life is a series of drawing lines and you have to draw lines with respect to whom you want to be kind.* And with respect

to whom I want to be kind, it starts with the family, and then of course, concentric circles outward. And so my most important area is my family, friends, community here, and then extending outward...and I think the way to protect that is limit population growth [italics added].

Restrictionists often stress that national borders represent, in some sense, the outskirts of one's obligations. They are not indifferent to the needs and desires of foreigners, but generally maintain that their sense of responsibility generally ends at the U.S. border. As one lobbyist put it, in a world of limits "you've got to demark what your responsibility is to the group." Some restrictionists argue that foreign governments must assume responsibility for their own environmental and economic futures. Until they learn to stabilize their populations, they cannot become self-sufficient. A restrictionist explains:

They're unwilling to cut down their own population growth, or recognize the need to stabilize population...so they expect the U.S. to serve as their safety valve and expect us to take their "surplus population" who they can't provide land or jobs for...This is not right...However much the United States has meddled in Central American politics or dominates these so-called banana republics of Central America, they've gotta take some responsibility for their own demographic, population, environmental, economic, and social future. And they're not doing it. Rather, they're using it as an opportunity to bad-mouth...this country, rather than exercising some responsibility or restraint on their own part...I don't mean to imply that all of Latin America or all the Third World is like that...Mexico is one country that has done a lot better, and in a sense, that's because of a long-standing break between the Catholic church hierarchy in Mexico and the politicians. In a lot of Latin American countries, the two are much more wedded together...I think...trying to step back and look at things from a logical or kind of a carrying capacity perspective—population policies are the sort of very sensitive policies that can only be established nation by nation. You can't have a United Nations dictating to every nation what its population should be...If a country is unwilling to recognize its problem and the reality that the land and resources aren't growing, jobs aren't being created fast enough for a growing population...with the ultimate goal of going toward a stable population—because ultimately that's the only thing that is sustainable economically and environmentally forever if we want to stay around that long as a people—if a country is unwilling to do that, then I don't think it helps either that country or the U.S. over the long-term to be providing that escape hatch and that safety valve for them.

Brian: A lesson not being taught?

Yeah, they don't feel that kind of back pressure to deal with their demographic and population problem and to get more serious about...population stabilization...So that...at the most basic, fundamental, hypothetical, and theoretical level shows why you gotta have some control on movements of people between different countries if one is concerned about population growth as a causative factor in environmental decline and declining quality of life...

This decision may seem unkind, but trying to evenly distribute the world's resources is not the answer. Accepting "surplus" populations and intervening in a country's affairs (e.g., by sending them foreign aid) will not solve the population problem. These well-intentioned responses, in fact, usually exacerbate the situation.

Foreign Aid

In *Living on a Lifeboat*, Garrett Hardin contends that "sharing ethics lead to the tragedy of the commons" and, for the foreseeable future, "survival demands that we govern our actions by the ethics of a lifeboat" (1995: 39, 56). The world's rich and poor reside in comparatively rich and poor countries—about one-third and two-thirds, respectively. Metaphorically, each rich nation is a full lifeboat and each poor nation an overcrowded one. The poor continuously fall out of their lifeboats, swim to the rich lifeboats, and ask for "admission" (i.e., the right to immigrate) or "handouts" (i.e., foreign aid).

Hardin asks the reader to imagine that the U.S. lifeboat contains fifty people, but that the carrying capacity of the lifeboat, just to be generous, is sixty. This leaves little room for natural disasters or new plant diseases, but for the sake of argument, the carrying capacity of the American lifeboat is set at sixty. How should Americans respond to the 100 people treading water outside of the lifeboat? Hardin offers three options (1995: 37-38):

> *One*. We may be tempted to live by the Christian ideal of being "our brothers keeper," or by the Marxian ideal (Marx 1875) of "from each according to his abilities, to each according to his needs." Since the needs of all are the same, we take all the needy into our boat, making a total of 150 in a boat with a carrying capacity of 60. The boat is swamped, and everyone drowns. Complete justice, complete catastrophe.

> *Two*. Since the boat has an unused excess capacity of 10, we admit just 10 more to it. This has the disadvantage of getting rid of the safety factor, for which action we will sooner or later pay dearly. Moreover, *which* 10 do we let in? "First come, first, served?" The best 10? The neediest 10? How do we *discriminate*? And what do we say to the 90 who are excluded?

> *Three*. Admit no more to the boat and preserve the small safety factor. Survival of the people in the lifeboat is then possible (though we shall have to be on our guard against boarding parties).

More room cannot be created on the lifeboat because it only takes a few people to spoil the commons. A voluntary system in which people restrain their consumptive and reproductive habits in order to admit a few others is hardly possible in a world of imperfect human beings. More room cannot be made, and exceeding the carrying capacity of each nation will only lead to ruin.

Foreign aid in the form of a world food bank and "unrestricted immigration" will not improve the situation. "World food banks move food to people, thus facilitating the exhaustion of the environment of the poor. By contrast, unrestricted immigration moves people to the food, thus speeding up the destruction of the environment in rich countries" (1995: 51). The corrective feedback of starvation is "normal to any independent country with inadequate population control" and is cut short by well-intentioned efforts to alleviate starvation. *"Every life saved this year in a poor country diminishes the quality of life for subsequent generations"* (1995: 44, 49, italics in original).

Anticipating the assertion that "justice is fairness" (e.g., see Weiner 1997: 174), Hardin argues that Americans of non-Indian ancestry are "all the descendants of thieves," but contends that pure justice—the return of the land to descendants of the victimized—is rejected because massive disorder would likely result. Statutes of limitations were created for this very purpose. This situation is analogous to the inequitable distribution of wealth: "We cannot safely divide the wealth equitably among all present peoples, so long as people reproduce at different rates, because to do so would guarantee that our grandchildren—everyone's grandchildren—would only have a ruined world to inhabit" (1995: 53-54).

Hardin's outlook is shared by a number of restrictionists in that foreign intervention is seen as counterproductive, and immigration as a threat to the American lifeboat. William Paddock, one of the founding board members of FAIR, and later chair of what is now Population-Environment Balance, argues that the world food problem cannot be solved by agricultural research, but only by controlling population. Foreign aid will not solve the problem and immigration makes it harder to conserve the U.S. resource base:

> While I was working at the National Academy of Sciences, I became fully aware of the fact that there really was little interest in population…The United States is a most unique country. It is not unique because of the kind of people it has. It is unique because of its resources. I've already mentioned that half of the Grade A land in the world is in the United States…To me it is impossible to visualize the kind of civilization that you and I know without the world having the

benefit of these enormous resources, which means we must carefully husband them—not for the use of we Americans but for the very future of our civilization...This country is overpopulated. There is no two ways about it. With every new person that comes in, we must...divide up our resources still more—which brings me back to immigrants being a threat...to...the survival of our civilization...I've come to believe, the reason we've made so little progress on the population issue in the world is due to a group of "do-gooders" in the world who really want to help everyone, but unintentionally, cause more harm than good. To back up their point of view, the scientific community which lives on public money for its research here and outside of the United States...have used the population issue as an argument for more money. The argument they give has some validity. More agricultural research means more production, more food. Who wants to see the world starve? But something has to be done to shake the world into recognizing that there is a need for a Draconian Action on the population issue. We also need it at home. We've spent a trillion dollars in foreign aid. In thirty years, not one of the developing countries has gotten off our backs...In the 1990s, one-third of the entire world's population enters its reproductive years. That means another billion people by 2000. By 2020 there will be seven billion. The world can't support today's five billion so how are seven billion going to live? As many as possible will wrangle some means——legal or illegal—to come here. They would be fools not to. In contrast, we're the fools who let Congress enact weak or ineffective immigration laws which are easily circumvented, we are the fools who permit more and more to share our basic wealth, we are the fools who believe our resources are inexhaustible. Lack of control of our borders results in frittering away our resources, agricultural soils, minerals, hydrocarbons, etc. Its not much different than the hundreds of billions of dollars we've frittered away in foreign aid. Our laws should have the fundamental goal of protecting and conserving U.S. resources for if the civilization we know is to continue, it must have, I repeat, must have those resources on which to build its future (FAIR Oral History Project, Paddock: 9, 19-21).

Virginia Abernethy (1997) suggests that a "sense of limits" is not acquired by other countries because U.S. policies encourage foreign governments to rely on emigration for the easement of their population pressures. The prospect of migrating to a more prosperous territory "appears to be one factor supporting large family size. Psychologically, the contrasting state is a sense of limits (being bottled up; crowding and no expectation of relief)" (1997: 136). For restrictionists, a recognition of limits is imperative if one is to properly diagnose and treat the problem of overpopulation.

Restrictionists generally maintain that the world's resources cannot sustain the world's current population. The problem is more than a resource shortage or distribution problem. The real problem is overpopulation. One restrictionist, referring to his work as a Peace Corps volunteer in the Philippines, put it this way: "...shortly after getting there you realize they really don't have much of a food shortage as they do—in Garrett Hardin's terms—a people longage." Because the equal distribution of resources is either impractical or impossible, people must acquire a sense of limits with respect to the environment and economic opportunities.

An ethical system sensitive to this reality is needed. Criteria must be established, lines have to be drawn. For population restrictionists, the lines are an inescapable fact of life. One emphasizes that the Golden Rule (doing unto others as you would have done unto you) needs to contextualized:

> In thinking about the Golden Rule...how does it work in a global village?...If you could tear your cloak in half, and both the beggar and you could derive a level of comfort and warmth, well, then, that's obviously the right thing to do. But if you have to tear your cloak in a million worthless fragments, or a billion worthless fragments, then, you know, just how do you evaluate that? How do we responsibly think through that? We all want to do the right thing, and...you come down to trying to figure out, well, just who is it that has a claim on your conscience? Who is that? Is it everybody in

the world, is it everyone in the universe? Or is it the family, is it your city, is it the people in your town, is it the people in your country...how far does that go? And I got a hunch that we will find that we'll respond to that in different grades. In other words, we do have some responsibility to people in foreign countries and all over the world and we will discharge that responsibility with some level of care, but I have a greater sense of responsibility to my son, for example...I have a personal sense that the single biggest and most prominent issue confronting...our successors is our relationship to the resources that are here...

This greater sense of responsibility requires one to think about the present and future. Preferences are natural in the sense that we love some people more than others.

People unwilling to accept this reality frustrate some restrictionists. One explains that hard choices need to be made and that they flow from normal attachments:

Someone who says "I love all mankind equally" is a person who really can't love anyone or anything because if you love everyone, or if you claim you love everyone, you really end up loving no one. Love is something that's directed towards specific people and specific groups of people. That's not to say you can't love people outside of those groups...Theodore Roosevelt said "A man who loves all nations as much as his own is like a man who loves all women as much as his own wife."...I love my wife more than I love other women, which doesn't mean that I hate other women, but I love her more than I love them...But these people who talk about borderless worlds and loving all humanity...they really are saying the same thing. And what they are saying, really, is [that] they're incapable of loving anyone or anything—they're above such attachments. And that's the mentality of these people...

Brian: Why do you think they think that way?

Pride...Of being above normal human attachments...The
other side tries to give you the idea that if you have these
natural preferences, that you are a Nazi or a Fascist or
whatever words they throw at you...

These hard choices, however, are not only in the United States' best
interest, but in the self-interest of other countries as well.

The emigration of highly skilled individuals from poor countries to
rich countries widens the gap between rich and poor. Affluent
countries benefit at the expense of poor countries. Some expansionists
question the ethics of "brain drain" migration, but most of the
reservations are voiced by restrictionists. The United States, they
argue, not only attracts the "best and brightest," but also "robs"
countries of their "change agents." Excerpts from three population
restrictionists typify this outlook:

I also believe that it's [immigration] a terrible thing to do to these
other countries...I think it robs the brains of people who, if they
didn't have this outlet, would have channeled their brain power
into making things better for their own countrymen...It robs the
change agents...People in a lot of these other countries think,
"Well, why put this effort into making this community better? I
may be able to get to America one day."

There's also what Roy Beck talks about is the "change
drain"...The people who are looking to better themselves—if
they didn't have that outlet they would look around
and...might, you know, make some revolution. In fact, Castro
is the best example of that. The dissidents—he was happy to
get rid of...They're all in Miami yelling at him...Those are
futile gestures, but if they were home, they might actually
have been able to organize some change.

Is it really legitimate that we take the brightest and the best
and the change agents away from these less developed
countries?...I don't think that admitting immigrants is key to

the future of the United States any more than it is to any other nation. I'd say what's more key to our future is recognizing when the time for a certain course of public policy has passed and revising it to fit the new realities and trying to get a moral fix on the whole thing so that we don't damage other countries, say by admitting their brightest and best and further accentuating the economic and social and political gap between the United Sates and less developed countries, which in turn comes back to bite us as increased pressure for illegal immigration...My contention is that the single most effective...form of foreign aid is to help the best and brightest stay home rather than bail out...The point has been made that by, for instance, accepting "refugees" from Cuba, we take the pressure off the Castro regime...So I think the model for the future is Lech Walessa and Nelson Mandela—people who stood and fought for the future of their countries and their fellow countrymen, rather than just cut and ran for their own personal, short term, materialistic, sole interest. I think it's a moral and ethical question.

By characterizing immigrants and countries as self-seeking, restrictionists acknowledge the value of some immigrants, but indirectly dispute expansionist depictions of immigrants as "survivors." Migrating to a more advantageous locale is a rational decision, but that doesn't mean the choice is honorable or in the sending country's best interest.

Conclusion

To restrictionists, immigration is more of a national question than a human one. The health of the American culture, economy, environment, and polity supercedes the desires of immigrants to enter the United States. Immigration is not a solution to the world's problems of overpopulation, government corruption, and asthmatic economies, but in fact, contributes to each of these problems. The notion that the U.S. is somehow exceptional or exempt from natural laws must be debunked, restrictionists argue, if the government is ever going to establish immigration policies in harmony with human nature and the environment. Until then, the country can expect higher levels of illegal immigration, interethnic tension, and environmental degradation. In short, restrictionists argue that the time has come to temporarily end the "American experiment."

CHAPTER 6

Expansionist Worldviews

From the expansionist point of view, there are many reasons why the United States should expand, or at least maintain, current immigration levels. Some expansionists believe the American experience with immigration has benefited the country in countless ways and will provide future dividends if properly managed. Other expansionists think emigration *and* immigration are human rights, or at the very least, prerogatives worthy of accommodation. Because "human beings are human beings," people are entitled to certain freedoms regardless of where they live or where they were born. The expansionist worldview collides with the restrictionist worldview in many areas. Expansionists consider human *nurture*, not human nature, decisive in matters of human ability and self-sacrifice. Instead of "drawing lines" around the country, the United States should start erasing the "lines" that impede the circulation of human and financial capital. By engaging globalism, the nation-state can stimulate economic productivity and provide citizens and immigrants with virtually unmatched opportunities and freedoms.

Entry Points

Expansionists enter the immigration debate through a number of corridors, although two passageways see more traffic than others. Many accentuate the *current* advantages of immigration by defining immigrants as capital. In their minds, immigrants are a resource to procure and manage. Other expansionists fix their eyes on American history and highlight the *historical* benefits of immigration. Taken together, expansionists believe the American experiment with immigration has been—and will continue to be—a key to the country's success. Although separated for ease of analysis, past and present contributions of immigrants are usually intertwined in the minds of expansionists.

Immigrant Contributions

Expansionists normally see immigration in terms of augmentation (e.g., immigrants contribute to the economy and enhance American culture), whereas restrictionists usually view it in terms of depletion (e.g., immigrants deplete natural resources and strain race relations). Immigrants represent a medley of resources to expansionists. By strengthening the economy, enriching American culture, stimulating innovation, and revitalizing traditional American values, immigrants satisfy national needs and stimulate beneficial change.

Expansionists regularly emphasize such benefits, but libertarian expansionists are particularly attentive to the economic advantages of immigration. They ask, why should the United States only accept some kinds of capital and not others? Two self-described libertarians put it this way:

> ...the point I always make is that immigration is really a great opportunity for the United States because we're the one nation in the world—in this race for capital, human and investment capital—we're the one nation in the world that can import both...See, one of the reasons I think immigration has been such a benefit to the United States is the whole cultural melting pot phenomenon...In my opinion, what happens is you get...almost a kind of cultural Darwinism where essentially...we assimilate the best features of immigrant culture and they assimilate the best features of ours. And so that you get this ever-evolving culture that is very positive...For example...why are Americans so much more inventive than people in Europe or Asia?...You know, a lot of those inventions [over the last 200 years] have been made by immigrants...The bringing together of people, all looking at problems different ways—because they come from different cultures—I think really expands the innovation process. And again, you can't measure that in any way...And innovation is what really drives economic growth and productivity...Like, if

you look at this National Science Foundation report that just came out—I'm very skeptical of these various kinds of economic models, you know, that say immigrants...increase the economy by 10 billion dollars or something like that. Well, it's impossible to measure the most important benefit of immigration, which is the impact that they have on the whole process of innovation and invention, and I really believe...if you could properly take that into account, then they're off by orders of magnitude...Immigrants are not just more people, they're people that are self-selected that bring in skills and talents that we don't have, and yet these models just treat the immigrants as additional people.

I view labor as a commodity, like any other, and just as I believe in free trade of television sets and cars and anything else, I believe in free trade of labor...I would take the *Wall Street Journal* view of open borders...which is not to say that I couldn't see problems...I may change my mind if a lot of problems develop, but at this point, I would advocate a position of...open borders...

With the exception of favoring open borders, these sentiments are fairly representative of libertarian expansionists. Contrary to the arguments of some restrictionists, expansionists—including libertarians—rarely support open borders. Some argue for a *more* open border, but few subscribe to the editorial position of the *Wall Street Journal*: "Our view is, borders should be open" (cited in Isbister 1996: 5). This issue is later raised under the rubric of globalization.

Expansionists are generally satisfied with the economic contributions of immigrants. Some, however, question the ethics of "brain drain" migration. The director of a foster care program for unaccompanied refugee minors describes her misgivings: "...we have an immigration policy that tends to drain off all the educated and successful and intelligent of other nations...and if you're real liberal, you have a lot of concerns about doing that." Similar misgivings are sometimes aired, but most expansionists are basically content with the arrangement: "...some people...say it's skimming the cream and so forth, but...if we want the United States...to be the global superpower, then we ought to exploit this opportunity we have with immigration."

Immigration not only promotes national interests in a global economy, but can also mend national problems and renew traditional American values. One expansionist thinks immigration is "*the* key to the future of race relations in the United States." By building bridges to local civil rights coalitions, women's coalitions, churches, conservatives, and labor unions, local immigration coalitions have the capacity to rejuvenate communities and nurture interracial cooperation. Other expansionists believe immigration restores values once characteristic of native-born Americans.

Unlike many Americans, immigrants capitalize on available opportunities and appreciate their newfound freedom. One congressional staffer put it this way:

> I think that immigrants kind of perpetuate and revitalize traditional American values. I think immigrants come here because they respect freedom and they want opportunities. And I think that natives tend to take some of those things for granted very much and I think it's good for the country and for the culture to have a significant body of people who genuinely appreciate the freedom and opportunity and equality under the law. And I think that rubs off on the rest of us and helps to perpetuate those values...It helps preserve the values that the country is founded on.

> Brian: Like what?

> Hard work, appreciating an opportunity, the opportunity to succeed...appreciating freedom, understanding that freedom only comes at a high price and that it's a precious thing and that it's not to be taken for granted—that we have to be willing to sacrifice for it. Many of these people come from places where you don't have freedom and people are dying trying to get it. And I think it is important for us to be reminded of that...And I think they have good values beyond that. They tend to be religious people, their families tend to be

more intact than American families, and they tend to work harder.

Some expansionists especially admire the strength, perseverance, and work ethic of refugees. Unlike Americans, refugees are willing to start at the bottom and seize opportunities. Observations from three administrators, the first by a 1979 Vietnamese refugee, extol the efforts of refugees and (directly or indirectly) chide natives for their complacency:

> ...people say the refugee come here to take their jobs from them. The refugee come here—they have no English. They was reborn again, they start all over...how can they take the job away from Americans who born here, fluent in the language...? Why don't they get the job? And I think that...they don't have the job that the refugee have now because they don't try hard, I think. I think they learn to take things for granted too much and the opportunity is here and why the refugee can have the job they want?...They have to have somebody to blame—that's what I think.

> Refugees come here with absolutely nothing, they are stronger than most Americans and they have a lot more perseverance.

> The handicap of the refugee—with culture and language—is accommodated, gladly, by an employer, for the kind of support that that refugee is given in his employment...They're interested in figuring out the American system and they're willing to start at the bottom of an entry-level job...It's quite remarkable...

Expansionist observations sometimes portray America as a leaky bucket and immigrants as stoppers. Immigrants arrest the seepage of values and ultimately become a part of the bucket, reinforcing its strengths and moderating it deficiencies. More than beneficial, their values and perspectives are almost vital. If the American work ethic cannot be restored from within then an external solution must be sought.

Business and libertarian expansionists regularly advance such arguments. Discerning a deflating work ethic, they commend immigrants for their willingness to work hard and reproach Americans for their ingratitude and complacency:

> You know, anyone who is willing to hop on some leaky boat and cross ninety miles of shark-infested water just to come here and work—I'd say that makes you an American...I don't care if you don't speak English...that alone...makes you more of an American than anybody who was born here and has no appreciation for the country.

> I think there are certain low immigration groups, and I think, talking about the skilled side now—the mathematicians and the computer workers—there are certain people who have been displaced in the current economy and are blaming that on immigration. In talking with [company representatives]—these workers who have been displaced—either they can't be trained because you can't just move a computer person from one computer language to another...without years of retraining, and also there are people who, you know, when the opportunities were presented to them to take advantage of the billions of dollars companies spend on retraining their own workers, they don't take advantage of it...And so people don't take the initiative to keep up their skills and then they're displaced. Well, there's not a lot you can do about that.

For expansionists, the very act of migration can signify a bright future. Immigrants, they say, are "self-selected" in that they already possess characteristics indicative of future success—risk taking, motivation, and a willingness to work hard. This, along with the propensity to exert more effort than natives (Simon 1989: 97-100), enhances the overall attractiveness of immigrants. This is especially true of highly skilled immigrants, who solidify America's technological edge and (among other things) keep Silicon Valley on the San Francisco peninsula. Spencer Abraham (R-Mich.), chair of the Senate immigration subcommittee, explains: "If we can't hire these talented people and bring them here now, foreign competitors can and will. If American companies can't bring the talent here to fill their needs...they'll move some of their operations overseas" (Wilgoren 1998).

This line of thinking is typical of libertarian and business expansionists. The American experience with immigration has been, and is, mutually beneficial. So why, they ask, should the United States reduce its current intake of immigrants? Ending the symbiotic relationship between Americans and future Americans impedes the progress of both populations. Equipped with history and empirical research, expansionists argue that America's experiment with immigration will—if properly managed—generally serve the interests of Americans and Americans in the making.

The American Experiment

Repeated investments in immigration have generated valuable returns. Like a mutual fund brochure, expansionists caution that historical performance does not guarantee future results, but emphasize the strengths of the prospectus. Unlike most countries, the United States transforms diversity into a strength and enjoys an almost unrivaled level of prosperity and political stability. True, immigration is an experiment, but it's also one backed by a reassuring history of overall success. Throughout its short history the United States has benefited greatly from immigration—why discontinue a successful tradition?

Expansionists generally see past achievements as indicative of future success. The status of "experiment" should not dissuade Americans from venturing a small risk. Two prominent expansionists explain:

> A lot of what drives me is a faith that immigrants, by and large, are gonna turn out to be great Americans, good solid Americans...There's a faith...You know, it is an experiment after all—so there's some faith involved that it's gonna work out...Generosity, tolerance...they're manmade, they're not divinely given from my perspective, so you have to acquire them, you have to practice them. So we immigration enthusiasts [expansionists] take very sincerely this notion that if you cut off immigration, we would stop practicing and giving

life to those values in the same way, that if we let the pessimists [restrictionists] win, that we as a society will lose some of our spirit, and it's that spirit which infuses what we do …We acquire it as a nation by being generous, in our self-interest…I see the restrictionist impulse in this country, which has a strong tradition, to be a very self-referential, you know, "I'm first." I mean, their code is "Let's take care of our own and let's take care of me first." And…if that is what this country is about, we will be a poorer country in every sense of the word. Whereas when we don't, when we say "Wait a minute, we're bigger than just ourselves—maybe we're better off by extending ourselves out and by allowing and engaging and struggling." And I just think that…is the genius of America, that dynamism, and that flexibility, and that diversity. To me, I look at the United States as a classic example of a society built on those values and immigration being so central, such a defining element, of who we are as a nation and that American exceptionalism is built on. I mean, diversity is a threat in most places in the world, and here it's an asset because the bonds of unity are strong enough to tolerate and to actually transform the diversity into a source of creativity that allows more and better solutions than would have been had we all been from the same place and we lived in a more closed-off society…

…Let's be real romantic about this. I think it's a great American tradition and I think immigrants coming to America and trying to pursue the American dream…provides us with a constant reminder of what it means to be American. In some ways, the most American people are those who are born abroad and come here and really believe in this country deeply—in ways that people born here can't or don't understand…I worry that if there were no immigrants, we would lose a sense of who we are as a people…And what links us as a people is a set of political beliefs, a set of principles, and a commitment to an idea, a dedication to a proposition, and I think a constant infusion of new blood reminds us of that, because if we didn't have it, I think we might actually drift towards being more of an ethnic kind of nation...For a debate that's filled with numbers and fiscal impact statements and this and that, I think this speaks way beyond any of it, and is the most absolute, most compelling reason. Now, that doesn't tell us we need to have a million immigrants a year or two hundred thousand immigrants a year—it says we need to have immigration, so it doesn't speak to numbers, but it does speak to a flow.

Immigration carries a degree of risk, but so does postponing or ending it. Why discontinue immigration when it has in fact been—as one expansionist put it—"a godsend"? Restrictionist arguments for a temporary moratorium or replacement-level policy strike expansionists as risky, unnecessary, selfish, or simply unrealistic.

Restrictionists criticize expansionists for their faith in the American experiment. Their beliefs, they contend, are emotional and irrational. But for expansionists, critiques like these symbolize the indecency of restrictionist arguments. Variations of the phrase "human beings are human beings" are regularly repeated. Treating human beings like numbers is inhumane. Quotas and the national interest are legitimate topics, but other considerations need to be considered. As the executive director of one organization put it: "Henry Kissinger once said that countries have interests, not friends, and I think that's a very sad way of looking at the world...if we all functioned just as having interests and not friends, what kind of human beings would we be?"

An expansionist critical of both restrictionists and expansionists (and incidentally, the one who suggested the terms "expansionist" and "restrictionist") criticizes restrictionists for their calculator-like approach to immigration. To him, their calls for a moratorium (e.g., by Peter Brimelow, Carrying Capacity Network, and Negative Population Growth) breathe an air of absurdity:

> ...every time anyone has ever advocated a moratorium on immigration...that is to say...none, zero, I've always said "Well, what about Klinger?" Do you remember Klinger?

Brian: From M*A*S*H?

Yes...What happened to Klinger at the end of the show?...He married Soon-Lee...It's important to understand just how typical this is. In the first place, the government did not choose that this Korean woman was going to go live in Toledo, Ohio. An American soldier did. Those who argue a moratorium, and attempt to mean it—the word means "zero," "none," "stop immigration"—what that means in practical terms is a soldier like Klinger who falls in love with a foreigner like Soon-Lee, could not bring her to live in his hometown of Toledo, Ohio. By falling in love with a foreigner, in order for him to obey his marriage vows, he's going to have to live in exile from the United States. Never go to another Mudhen's game. Immediately, when I say this, people say, "Well, of course not, that's not what I meant." I said, "Okay, you're not talking about zero now, you're talking about 200,000 a year.

Brian: Why 200,000?

Because that's...the number of spouses and minor children of U.S. citizens coming in as immigrants...In other words, you can have an abstract discussion about it and it will make no sense. If you're gonna have a real discussion about it, that's how to do it.

Removing emotion and faith from the policy process is not only impractical, but can potentially weaken the American "spirit" responsible for much of the United States' success. Expansionists ask, where would the U.S. be economically and culturally if it were not for immigration?

Expansionists indirectly answer this question by asserting that immigrants expand the country's strength and creativity. It is one of the keys to American success.

I think people who oppose further restrictions do that on the basis of real life experiences in communities where immigration is an important part of family dynamics or in the high tech industry...or people committed to...the concept that we're a nation of immigrants, and you know, it's part of what has made America strong and vibrant is the energy, and creativity, and risk taking that comes from...newcomers coming in and bringing their talents.

Another expansionist elaborates on this potential:

I fundamentally am very hard-nosed American...The anti-immigrant side has got it wrong. The most pro-American thing you could possibly do would be to have immigration better managed, better formulas...because ultimately that is the secret.

Brian: Secret?

That American success is indeed immigration. That is a value, that's an ideal, that's a, you know, call it...internationalist, but it's not religion. It is not political party allegiance ...This is where all of your experience, all of your intelligence, all of your studying, all of your interviews, all of your interactions with people on this debate—all of it gives you that essential optimism.

A joint study by the Alexis De Tocqueville Institute, American Immigration Institute, and Hudson Institute questioned 38 distinguished U.S. economists in 1990 about the impact of legal and illegal immigrants on the American economy. Asked "What is the major economic effect of immigration to the United States?," the reply of world-renowned economist John Kenneth Galbraith captures the essence of expansionist arguments: "We all look back with favor on our past immigration policies and what they have done for us. It is deeply inconsistent that we think the future to be different...*Why is it that what contributed so much in the past should be questioned in the present?*" (Cato *Handbook for Congress*: 1997, italics added).

From the perspective of expansionists, the American experiment with immigration benefits immigrants and the United States. Immigrants are afforded unparalleled opportunities and the country receives a return that is, in many respects, immeasurable. One expansionist put it simply: "I am beginning to see...more and more the beauty of it. This country would not be the same without immigration." Compared to the risks of discontinuing the tradition, the risks of continuing immigration are negligible.

However, financial metaphors cannot capture the entire expansionist worldview. The implied comparisons describe their views on immigrant resources, but the idea of "human nurture" better represents their perceptions of refugees and natural resources. For some expansionists, natural resources and national economies are not bound by the rules of a zero-sum game, where losses equal winnings. Technological progress, *nurtured* by human intelligence and ingenuity, creates positive-sum (win-win) situations. In the case of refugees, the metaphor of human nurture is more straightforward—desperate humans merit human nurture, irrespective of cost.

Human Nurture

Expansionists tend to see more "nurture" than "nature" in human potential. Because there is a clear, positive-sum element to natural resources, humans can exceed natural "limits" by nurturing inventiveness—by empowering people to tap the "ultimate resource"—the human mind. Over time, and in terms of decreasing prices and increasing substitutability (of resources), humans have been *expanding* the world's resource base (Simon 1996). Humans also enhance humanity by nurturing it directly. Expansionists insist "human beings are human beings" and believe that refugees, in particular, deserve special attention.

Human Ingenuity

Expansionists generally hold positive-sum views of the world with respect to natural resources, employment, and immigration quotas. Unlike the zero-sum views of restrictionists, where losses equal winnings, expansionists see win-win scenarios. Immigrants entering the U.S. economy do not necessarily displace native-born workers, but in fact, often expand the opportunities of native-born workers.

For example, a review of industry-specific case studies by Fix and Passel (1994) demonstrates that immigrants, even in highly skilled occupations, rarely displace native workers. Specific jobs in low-wage industries are "segmented in a manner that assigns different positions to differing ethnic groups, immigrant groups, or both, *thus mitigating displacement*" (1994: 51, italics added). Additionally, some domestic industries have remained in the United States precisely because there is an abundance of immigrant workers. By keeping their operations in the U.S., immigrants preserve jobs for some low-skilled native-workers in various regions (1994: 52). Furthermore, even when immigrant hiring networks do exclude native-born workers, these recruitment procedures tend to concentrate immigrants in certain industries, thereby "reducing the extent of competition with natives and potentially expanding natives' opportunities in other sectors" (1994: 52).

Whereas restrictionists primarily see humans in reductive terms (e.g., additional humans reduce the quality of life for future generations), expansionists (particularly libertarian expansionists) see human beings in additive terms. Here is how three expansionists interpret the relationship between humans and natural resources:

> I'm more a Julian Simon person. I value human ingenuity. I think we can get ourselves out of tight fixes. I wouldn't like to consider myself overly-optimistic, but I think people are remarkably quite clever and I think Julian Simon is right—you know, the ultimate resource is up here in our heads. And I certainly don't think we will always have cars that run on gas, you know, something better will come along. I don't know what it will be, but someone will figure it out. I think the kinds of natural resource controversies we have fifty years from now are gonna be completely different from what they are today. They're gonna be completely unexpected. We don't know what they're gonna be and when we get to them, we'll figure it out.

> ...this Donald Huddle research...is...just total junk science...It's so flawed and it's...this kind of zero-sum—you know, "That every immigrant who comes in takes a job from a native and then the native goes on welfare"—and all these ridiculous assumptions that are, you know, preposterous...It sounds cliché, but we're in a kind of globalized economy right

now where the whole notion of scarcity of resources is
nonsense. I mean, we're not running out of food or energy or
oil—the things that people use to worry about. In high
technology...the idea of limits to growth are kind of outmoded,
but the two things that really are scarce as we move into the
twenty-first century economy are investment capital and human
capital. And investment capital is something that flows across
borders instantaneously and it flows to wherever it's treated
most kindly. And the same thing is now happening with human
capital—that human capital also tends to migrate where it has
the highest rate of return.

[Restrictionist] organizations mostly...believe in the whole
thing of "fixed pie" theory—that we have limited resources,
we only have so many square miles of land in this country,
you know...you can only fit so many cars on the roads...that
we need time to expand our infrastructure before we can
accommodate, comfortably, more people...the position that
more people are not necessary for economic growth, that
having more people in the country doesn't necessarily benefit
the country...that's the attitude...The position of the high
immigration groups would be...that [immigrants] are a
resource, that they contribute to an economy...If someone
were giving you gold, you wouldn't turn it away because you
say, "Well, I have too much"—there's no such thing as too
much wealth...Human beings are essentially wealth, they are a
resource, and they shouldn't be looked upon as a burden...The
United States is not, by any means, overcrowded...We have
more room in this country than we will ever use...and...the
whole debate over national resources is really false because
new technologies emerge, different resources are discovered...

To restrictionists, banking on human ingenuity is an unnecessary risk.
Instead of relying on the human ability to get "out of tight fixes," they
ask: why not accept the scientific truism that growth cannot occur
forever on a finite resource base?

But some expansionists, particularly libertarian expansionists, are not convinced. Their skepticism of finiteness is largely based on the data and logic submitted by Julian Simon. The late economist maintained that "natural resources are not finite in any economic sense" (1996: 6). According to Simon, finiteness cannot be determined because the cosmos cannot be measured. The hypothesis of finiteness cannot be proved or disproved because the theory is not amenable to scientific inquiry, but only to metaphysical speculation. In the absence of such data, shortages must be gauged in other ways (1986: 184-215; 1990: 67-77). "The appropriate measures of scarcity (the costs of natural resources in human labor, and their prices relative to wages and to other goods) all suggest that natural resources have been becoming less scarce over the long run, right up to the present" (1996: 3). Contrary to the arguments of some restrictionists, Simon never argued that "infinite substitutability" is possible—now or in the future. Rather, he maintained that substitutability has been *increasing* over time. There "have been more and cheaper substitutes for each raw material with the passage of time" (1996: 596-97).

But how can this be? Simon admitted that his analysis is not commonsensical, but repeatedly demonstrated the plausibility of his perspective with historical data. Simon summarized his seven hundred plus page book, *The Ultimate Resource 2*, this way:

> In the short run, all resources are limited...The longer run, however, is a different story. The standard of living has risen along with the size of the world's population since the beginning of recorded time. There is no convincing reason why these trends toward a better life should not continue indefinitely. Many people find it difficult to accept this economic argument. Dwindling resources, increasing population, starvation and misery—all this seems inevitable unless we curb population growth or otherwise cut back consumption of natural resources...The new theory that is the key idea of the book—and is consistent with current evidence—is this: Greater consumption due to an increase in population and growth of income heightens scarcity and induces price run-ups. A higher price represents an opportunity that leads investors and business people to seek new ways to satisfy the shortages. Some fail, at cost to themselves. A

few succeed, and the final result is that we end up better off than if the original shortage problems had never arisen. That is, we need our problems, though this does not imply that we should purposely create additional problems for ourselves. The most important benefit of population size and growth is the increase it brings to the useful stock of knowledge. Minds matter economically as much as, or more than, hands or mouths. Progress is limited largely by the availability of trained workers. In the long run the basic forces influencing the state of humanity and its progress are...the number of people who are alive to consume, but also to *produce* goods and knowledge... and...the level of wealth. Those are the great variables which control the advance of civilization (1996: 12-13, italics in original).

The human mind, then, is the "ultimate resource." Through supply and demand mechanisms, a larger population creates a short term demand for more resources, which in turn, raises prices. A larger population (in a free society) will eventually hit upon a solution because, all things being equal, a larger population produces a larger amount of knowledge. In many cases, humans have apparently filled their niche (i.e., seemingly reached the limit of obtainable resources), only to expand it. "There are limits at any moment, but the limits continually expand, and constrain us less with each passing generation. In this we are quite unlike all other animals" (1996: 382-83).

Simon agrees with Garrett Hardin (and other population restrictionists) that population growth does cause some problems. However, the agreement ends here. Hardin sees population growth as a problem in and of itself because (1) there is a fixed resource base and (2) the relationship between humans and natural resources cannot be solved technically. Simon, on the other hand, sees population growth as a *temporary* problem. Population-induced problems encourage new developments which, in the end, "leave us *better off than if the problems had not arisen*" (1996: 383, italics in original). Population growth contributes, directly and indirectly, to progress.

Not surprisingly, Simon saw immigration in additive terms. Immigrants stimulate demand and innovation because improvements in productivity spring from human ingenuity and because immigrants enlarge the U.S. population (via migration and fertility). They create cultural variety, "a key ingredient of invention," and transport innovative ideas (1989: 166, 174-182). Without ever mentioning Julian Simon, one expansionist refers to the transference of *political* ideas:

> ...one of the things I understood twelve years ago...was that people from other countries no longer just send money back home—they send ideas back home—political remittances. Hey, you want to build democracy and freedom abroad? Work with immigrants here, family to family, friend to friend, colleague to colleague—it's not just about governments...And it's not just economics, not just trade. It also has to do with values and politics and human rights movements, etcetera.

Natives are not the only ones who benefit from immigration. So do immigrants and their relatives. Even democracy benefits. "The migration of people from poor to rich countries is as close to an everybody-wins government policy as can be" (Simon 1996: 7). Recognizing that human progress ultimately hinges on the output of human nurture, and not the initial input (or regenerative capacity) of nature, why tamper with this win-win scenario?

Many expansionists see a comparable world—even if they are unfamiliar with Simon's work. To the extent they consider population growth relatively harmless or believe human ingenuity can regularly overcome nature's "limits," their views generally synchronize with his ideas. Unlike restrictionists, expansionists are, at the most, only mildly concerned about population size. There has to be limits, but stringent guidelines are not the answer. Asked about annual immigration quotas, two expansionists emphasize the need for flexibility:

> I think it would float, kind of like the dollar floats against the yen. I think it would float depending on circumstances...So, in terms of quotas, there does need to be a cap on the number of people we can absorb per year, but within that cap we need to show some flexibility...Circumstances change. The world isn't the same tomorrow...

...I wouldn't set a number. There's nothing magical anywhere in the immigration formula. It has to develop in an understanding of what the category is...Fundamentally, the system is okay. I'd like to see, again, less reliance on categories and more reliance on people that nobody else wants. In the end, nobody wants refugees. We're the only people, who at some level, still think that we would want refugees.

Predominantly concerned with the economic and social impacts of immigrants, expansionists enjoy the benefits of flexibility. Unrestrained by notions of carrying capacity and replacement, expansionists are able to convert this pliancy into political leverage.

Where restrictionists find it difficult to compromise, expansionists are able to make trade-offs. Flexibility is the not a byproduct of relativism, but an intentional strategy to capitalize on the perceived inflexibility of restrictionists:

On any issue you can find members who don't agree with other members...and because immigration does attract odd bedfellows, we try to be flexible so that if conservatives like legal immigration, but they don't like welfare, we'll work with them on legal immigration and we won't work with them on welfare. We'll work with liberal groups who want to defend benefits for legal immigrants...From our point of view, the goal is to be successful in action, and given the strange dynamics of this issue and then all of the sub-issues that attract different supporters and opponents, if we're not flexible, then we're ineffective... They [restrictionists] have, I think, a taller mountain to climb than we do. On the other hand, that's in terms of their objectives...They overreached [in 1996] in terms of what they wanted. They went for it all...They're so set on, say a moratorium or something very significant like that, that the idea of whittling away, little by little, doesn't appeal to them...They're not willing to work in increments. At least, they haven't shown a willingness. As a result, they're marginalizing themselves as the pendulum swings back. See, we made a lot of concessions...and we ended up being more effective and now we're whittling away at what they got...The things you feel most strongly about—those are the things that are most likely for you to get involved in some advocacy. So, the people who are drawn to work on these issues feel very strongly and very righteous. But the thing that draws them to the cause can be a liability if you can't override it somewhat. You gotta maintain the motivation, and at the same time…lift your gaze from your own righteous box and be able to see a bigger picture…That's the dilemma…you need the righteousness to get you to fight for the cause…and the flexibility to…not be so dogmatic that in a democratic system you lose your effectiveness and are outside looking in…And for the restrictionists to be effective, that's what it requires—that's what I think it requires for them. I am thrilled that they're more interested in being right than being effective, that they're so convinced that they have the prescription that they are not taking advantage of what they could take advantage of, given the context we're operating in.

Expansionist dismissals of population warnings, and optimistic predictions, make pliability, in a sense, more workable. Unlike restrictionists, who find small reductions in immigration unacceptable, expansionists are more willing to make concessions. Some expansionists "tolerate" the plasticity and turn it into a political strategy. These same expansionists, however, also confront unyielding limits. For example, their flexibility with immigrant-related issues is generally not extended to refugee-related matters.

Refugees

Among expansionists there exists a firm commitment to admitting and assisting needy refugees. For some, this conviction doubles as an entry point, but for others, it simply belongs to a wider web of beliefs about human rights and responsibilities. Experiences and/or some set of religious beliefs usually forge their sense of duty toward refugees.

Some expansionists accentuate the survival and aspirations of refugees. Real-life observations and refugee accounts provide compelling images. Volunteering at a refugee camp for Vietnamese refugees in the late 1970s, a prominent expansionist recounts his first impression:

And I was more captivated by the Vietnamese, not from an immigration point of view, but more, you know, it was just so compelling that people were risking their life...And when I started working with refugees it...really impacted my thinking to see people risking their lives (a) to leave a country that they grew up in, and (b) wanting so desperately to go to America...

Some expansionists recite stories of refugee survival. When deserving refugees are denied admittance or legitimate asylum claims are rejected, one social worker "sees faces." Relaying a story provided by one of her clients, she explains:

We have a Bosnian girl whose both parents were murdered—her mother was raped to death, and her father was a surgeon and just died in a bomb attack, but then that made mom and the two daughters very vulnerable to attack by the Serb military. They came regularly to rape the girls and mom, and finally mom just died from injuries of being beaten and raped and the girls were held captive almost a year and used as a concubine for the military, basically. And she's says on one occasion they took her to a house where...a...girl [had] gotten pregnant. And so in front of her, the military killed the girl and removed the fetus and killed it in front of them and said "If you get pregnant, this is what'll happen to you." As if though her getting pregnant or not was within her control with repeated rapes...And this is a fifteen year old girl. And like I said...how can people?...

Unable to finish without crying, a prior comment will have to suffice: "I don't care what our standard of living would be, we will always have problems." For she and other expansionists, people fleeing these realities deserve help regardless of cost.

While many are moved more by empathy and emotion, some cite religious reasons for assisting refugees. A Christian, Jew, and Muslim emphasize the principles and perspectives of their faiths:

I know Christ was a refugee, and what would have happened if when his family fled with him as an infant, if he was pushed back across the border, to be massacred with all the other children under one?...I think you can apply a lot of refugee work to...basic Christian principles about feeding the hungry...

As a religious community, we have religious values. The Bible says...you were a stranger in Egypt...We have this whole religious imperative. I don't think about it on my day to day work, but it definitely underlies the work that's there. As a Jewish community, we've always taken care of our own...I think there's definitely a religious and moral imperative for us to help the downtrodden...and I think that underlies probably every single piece of work that we do...There's a real value to treating the stranger in Judaism...

I don't think that...God makes any distinction. In Islam it is very clear—human beings are human beings. If someone is in a difficult situation we try to help them...Yeah we're trying to help a group of people that we share an affinity with. Our motivation isn't so much just to help these people for any self-serving reason aside from [having] God pleased with us...

Although most expansionists are not "religious" in terms of beliefs and affiliations, their views on refugee assistance seem almost sacred. While immigration extracts strong opinions, refugee admissions evokes undiluted beliefs, and in some cases, even dissension.

Some expansionists scrutinize the practices of their colleagues in the same way that some cultural restrictionists criticize the views and tactics of population restrictionists. Already displeased with U.S. refugee policy, some expansionists worry that the already stingy system will be trimmed on account of imprudent behavior. One prominent expansionist put it bluntly:

I believe our side is too dominated by special interests. That's a charge that FAIR makes. I think there's truth to it—I don't think it's true as they make it, but I think there's some truth to it, and the primary example of that is in the refugee area—not the only example, but the primary example of that where you've had—particularly in the last six or seven years—Jewish communities dominating the refugee policy arena. In my view, absolutely, totally irresponsible in the last 3 or 4 years. Ironically, the Jews are destroying the U.S. refugee program and they're destroying it through selfishness. And the selfishness epitomized by HIAS, the Hebrew Immigrant Aid Society, the leading Jewish refugee organization, which is using the power of the Jewish community to sustain what's called the Lautenberg Amendment—which means if you're a Soviet Jew—this was enacted first in '89—I thought it was justified in '89 for probably 3 or 4 years—you don't have to prove that you have a well-founded fear of persecution. You simply have to prove that you are a Jew, and there's a presumption you're entitled to refugee status to admission to the United States. Well, what we have now is a refugee program that is dominated by the Jewish flow, the remnants of the Indo-Chinese flow...maybe 40% of the refugees...in the last five or six years have been Soviet Jews...Well, the problem is they have Israel. That's problem number one. They're not in danger the way other people are in danger—like Africans. Second, you always have Israel as a place of safe haven for Jews. Doesn't mean Jews shouldn't come to the United States, it just means there is a safety option that other refugees don't enjoy. You can't come here as a Jewish refugee unless you got relatives in the United States—that's how the community self-selects...So, it's a back door family immigration program for family relatives that couldn't get in because the relationship's too distant under the current family visa program. And the government is subsidizing it dramatically because if you're a refugee you're eligible for welfare...Now, Lautenberg is about to be extended again. This is now 1997. Excuse me, we're sending foreign aid to Russia. Sure, there's still anti-Semitism in Russia. Sure, there's still racism in Los Angeles too. And I'm not saying Soviet Jews who really are facing serious problems shouldn't be able to get out and a fair proportion coming to the United States—but that's not what the deal is...You've got thousands of people who've been granted refugee travel documents coming to the United States who aren't leaving Russia—who are staying there—and this is just like their ticket to safety in case they need it in the future...But that's an African whose spot has been taken, who's dying in the Rwandan jungle...

While more candid than most expansionists, others allude to similar concerns. References to "powerful constituencies," "African refugees," and "real refugees" are standard. Criticisms of current practices are primarily directed at refugee mismanagement, not Jewish misuse. A concern for threatened lives is so important to expansionists that they are willing to criticize (directly or indirectly) their own colleagues—a rarity.

Lives, and accurate information, are both at stake. The public has enough trouble distinguishing legal from illegal immigration, let alone refugees:

> ...I have always been a very, very harsh person on refugees. I believe in saving people who need saving, not in saving people by designating entire categories, entire nationalities, as needing saving. Not everybody who wants to leave Cuba needs saving. Not everybody who wants to leave the former Soviet Union, or any of the republics, needs saving. I mean, this is an extraordinary grant...That's why you have all this confusion about immigration.

For a group proud of its ability to overlook differences and converge on shared interests, this small fissure demonstrates just how important refugee admission are to expansionists. More than a catchphrase, "human beings are human beings" is a core value.

Expansionists regularly contend that the application of refugee policy is largely bereft of generosity and fairness. The annual number of refugees admitted to the United States is miserly, and of those permitted to enter, only a few are "real refugees." The United States, does a "paltry amount given the worldwide demand" and ought to "start bringing real refugees" into the country. The "real refugees" are largely concentrated in Africa, but few will ever be accommodated by the U.S. because of racism and constituency-based politics. This, according to expansionists, makes the United States look like a "very prejudiced nation" and tarnishes the image of expansionists. Most important of all, it does not effectively save the lives of people who truly need saving.

Among expansionists there exists a general dissatisfaction with U.S. refugee policy. While some are disturbed by recent changes in immigrant policies (e.g., further restricting noncitizen rights and entitlements), the mismanagement of refugee policy is especially troublesome. Considerations brought to bear on immigrants (e.g., family reunification, employment opportunities, diversity, etc.) shrink in significance when compared to the life and death realities encountered by real refugees.

Globalism: Erasing Lines

In a very general sense, globalism signifies the countless streams of information, people, resources, and goods crossing national boundaries on a regular basis. Tough to define, yet easy to spot, expansionists see it as an inevitable force in national and international affairs. From their perspective, the activities comprising globalism are basically benign and governable if international agreements and immigration policies are adjusted to its inner workings and varied impacts. To expansionists, globalism is something to engage—as much as possible—on one's own terms. Their views on border enforcement and various immigration policies demonstrate a desire to manage immigration, not with "open borders," but with fair and flexible policies.

Engaging the Globe

On the expansionist porch, the welcome mat for globalization is king-size. According to expansionists, the cross-border circulation of people and products should be accommodated, not resisted. Besides, fighting the inevitable makes no sense. Immigration is a fact of life so why not manage it with better policies and programs instead of bemoaning the new world order? As the world's drawstrings are pulled tighter by international linkages, immigration becomes increasingly important to the health of the American economy:

...I'm not an economist, but I'm fairly persuaded that, in the aggregate, immigration is good for America, economically...When a man like George Gilder says that our technology industry would be 40% behind where it is right now if it weren't for foreign-born brain power, you know, I kind of nod and think, "That may be right."...I think immigrants create opportunities for everybody...I'm basically a [supporter of] free trade, tear down barriers to economic activity—both here and abroad. I want an America that can prosper by engaging with the world economically.

The idea of "engaging" is central to the expansionist perspective on globalism. Almost every policy decision—in some way—radiates from this midpoint.

If the U.S. is to engage the world, its policy makers must recognize that severing immigration policy from other policies is not only imprudent, but also impractical. The historical and economic links welcoming capital also invite people (Sassen 1996). One expansionist explains: "There's a very, very small difference between closing the doors on immigration and closing the doors to international trade because they both respond to the same impulse..."

According to one lobbyist, the United States needs to align its policies with the realities of globalization:

...the companies I deal with—a lot of them don't even consider themselves U.S. companies anymore. They consider themselves global companies that happen to be located in the United States...so the realities of the market today are that we have to accommodate these flows of people because if we don't, other countries will and, frankly, companies—especially in the services industry—can pick up and move...operations pretty quickly....And so that's why I think businesses get into it. You know, I don't know that they're all in favor of...open borders, but they know they need the people...In my view you can't stop the globalization of the economy. Whether it's good to have a McDonalds in every country, you know, I don't know. But the fact is that's what's happening.

The U.S. has to *manage* immigration. The option of cutting it off doesn't exist: "...I just believe that we are moving towards a world economy where national boundaries are gonna make less difference...Whether you're pro-immigration or anti-immigration—the immigrants are coming one way or the other." This view is representative of most expansionists. One way or the other, immigrants come standard with a post-industrial economy and American foreign policy:

> I continue to believe, as I always did, that the crux is the demand side...You want to control immigration...you need to reshape the size of the low wage labor market. As long as you have a kind of unregulated, low wage labor market, people are going to seek out and recruit the lowest wage workers available... I think that immigration is a fact of life—a fact of life in the United States, a fact of life globally...One of the things that I would do was to try to tell the truth...Look, immigration is here to stay...it's part of the world. We have a large immigrant population [in California] and they're not going home...It's in our interest to ensure the integration of immigrants—that's what's good for everyone in the United States...Full participation is, in fact, in the interest of everyone.

> ...another component that motivates a lot of people in the pro-immigrant [camp]...is a sense that the United States somehow has a direct responsibility for the conditions that lead people to emigrate and come to the United States. Because of the international scope of our economic, political, and military activities, as a nation...we have a responsibility...to people who want to come to the United States.

Given these realities, some expansionists believe the United States should assist immigrants and refugees who are, in some way, responding to contexts created—at one time or another—by the federal government. Other expansionists recommend adapting national immigration laws to the rudiments of international agreements and norms. The Refugee Act of 1980, for example, was enacted to accomplish this very objective (Portes and Rumbaut 1996). In like manner, some argue that employment-based immigration policy requires immediate updating. If immigration law does not keep up with the ever-evolving strategies and procedures of business, the global competitiveness of U.S.-based, international firms will be undermined.

Realpolitik

Charles Keely recently interviewed human resource professionals from nine globally-oriented firms (e.g., Digital Equipment, Eastman Kodak, Ford, Intel, etc.) about the hiring and moving of international personnel. Relating their practices to immigrant and nonimmigrant visa programs, Keely and his respondents repeatedly emphasize the disjunction between immigration policy and post-industrial economies.[26] One interviewee maintains: "If you want to have a competitive company, staying alive for the future, you have to grow people with an international mindset, a breadth of understanding" (Keely 1998: 25). Keely, himself, concludes that the United States needs to "catch up" with international practices and norms (1998: 11, 33):

> The increased use of temporary visas for international personnel movement and the labor force dynamics of knowledge-based economic activities reflect the realities of the contemporary global marketplace. Changes in international personnel movement are here to stay. Immigration laws needs to emphasize the facilitation of international personnel movement consonant with the needs of international business, as well as to protect domestic labor markets. American labor self sufficiency is no longer

---

[26] Keely sometimes blurs the line between personal opinion and interview paraphrase because he seemingly agrees with many of the respondents. Funding and interview contacts were primarily supplied by the American Council on International Personnel, an expansionist organization. This does not imply a conflict of interest, but does suggest that his views are fairly congruent with international firms engaged in international hiring and personnel movement.

descriptively accurate (if it ever was) and, given the nature of knowledge-based industries, is a self-defeating norm...The world of business has changed while immigration policy thinking is hampered by outmoded models of economics, of business practices, and of the factors that help and harm job growth as well as the health of firms and the U.S. economy.

This suggestion is fairly congruent with the expansionist tendency to see positive-sum solutions to immigration problems, and the propensity to ignore restrictionist warnings of overpopulation and environmental degradation. Keely concludes there is a degree of friction between protecting domestic labor and facilitating the international movement of personnel, but that "it makes little sense to contend that international personnel movement does not contribute to the health of the U.S. economy and the national interest" (1998: 61). Not a pure win-win situation, nor a strict zero-sum scenario, both labor and business stand to benefit from a robust economy.

In addition to developing alternative visa strategies, some expansionists suggest that instead of treating employment- and family-based admissions as competing goals, why not consider them complementary:

>...our political strategy all along...basically...has always been founded on the premise that the support for immigration, politically, is very fragile. And that support has stuck together. And the reason we've generally prevailed, is that you have two groups that are out there fighting for immigration: sort of the family groups and the ethnic groups that fight for family-based immigration and then the business community which fights for the employer-based immigration. And we've always felt like we don't want to pit the two sides against each other because divided they'll fall. And so we've always said, you know, "More of one doesn't mean less of another."

Other expansionists, however, recommend that certain policies and practices be amended or discontinued. The fourth preference (category for adult siblings of citizens), "diversity visa" lottery system (where visas are allocated to countries "adversely affected" by the 1965 amendments), and Lautenberg Amendment (described earlier) are regularly criticized as impractical and/or unjustifiable.[27]

Generally absent among restrictionists and "lower-ranking" expansionists, influential expansionists typically possess a "realpolitik" approach to immigration policy. From their perspective, there is little room for nonsensical policies:

> We have a diversity lottery, as a purely political animal—it has nothing to do with immigration. It had to do with what we needed to do in order to get the support of certain groups back in 1990...I would shed it—no compelling reason to have it. It makes absolutely no sense. It's unnecessary. It also gives people around the world the impression that somehow you need people. When a country advertises a lottery system to get visas to that country, what kind of impression do you get in Bangladesh?...I'm a firm believer we did this...in order to, in a very indirect way, satisfy proclivities that Kennedy and Morrison had and promises that they had made to the Irish...I'm offended by this very concept of diversity. You want to bring Irish in? You have balls? Push it through. Push it through, okay? Let's not really screw up the entire system in order to hide all sorts of special preferences...Fourth preference—out, done. Why? I'm not interested in how the Asians or the Hispanics or the Greeks define family. It's of no interest to me. I'm looking at the practicality of the issue.

Even "high ranking" expansionists cannot agree on what to discard, keep, or revise. However, they do agree that theoretical and ethical objectives can, at times, be traded in for political success.

For example, the bipartisan U.S. Commission on Immigration Reform was very critical of the large backlog in the category for immediate relatives. Protracted waiting periods for spouses and minor children of U.S. citizens (who are legally entitled to enter the United States) were deemed unacceptable. In their report to Congress, they

---

[27] See Appendix 1 in the *1994 Statistical Yearbook of the Immigration and Naturalization Service* for a brief description of U.S. immigration legislation.

recommended that the long waiting lines be cleared—not by expanding the numbers or relaxing regulations—but by transferring visas:

> The Commission recommends allocation of 550,000 family-based admission numbers each year until the large backlog of spouses and minor children is cleared. Numbers going to lower priority categories (e.g., adult children, siblings, and diversity immigrants), should be transferred to the nuclear family categories. Thereafter Congress should set sufficient admission numbers to permit all spouses and minor children to enter expeditiously...In 1995, the wait between application and admission of the spouses and minor children of LPRs [legal permanent residents] was approximately three years. It is now more than four and one-half years and still growing (U.S. Commission on Immigration Reform 1997: 19).

This suggestion reflects the kind of tradeoff prominent expansionists are willing to make, although it doesn't mean they would make the same recommendation. One explains:

> I think there's a tendency of the pro-immigrant sides to be dominated by ethnic politics in a way that has been positive in a sense of our political mobilizing, but gets overdone in the sense that—you know, policies that I can't justify on the merits to myself, you'll find Hispanic groups or Asian groups defending and justifying because of ethnic politics...Take fourth preference, the brothers and sisters category, I would've given it up a long time ago—not the pending cases, but the pipeline cases. We got twenty years of pipeline cases...And how can you defend brothers and sisters of U.S. citizens with a twenty year backlog when spouses and minor children of legal immigrants are waiting five years or six years—and they're immediate relatives and you got nuclear families...The Jordan Commission's report was total bullshit in this regard because they were trading only one side of the trade, but there's something to their analysis that you do have immediate relatives waiting in line—more distant relatives coming in, and that we need to do a better job of reuniting nuclear

families more quickly. So I buy that diagnosis—I don't buy their solution, which is to throw all the other categories overboard in the process.

In terms of worldview, this statement is very typical of powerful expansionists. They provide theoretical, ideological, and moral reasons for their actions, but unlike restrictionists, find it hard to step outside of the political arena—even for a short while.

When asked to describe an "ideal" immigration policy, prominent expansionists regard the question as irrelevant or, in some cases, take it as an opportunity to draft a short wish list. One veteran expansionist combined both sets of remarks:

> Brian: If it was up to you, and you didn't have to worry about what's politically expedient...what would U.S. immigration policy look like?...

That's a question I really haven't given much thought to...I try to stay so focused on what's realistic...I just see this as a very dynamic and contingent process—that there's no right policy...And I'm not even sure if it's worth me thinking about what would I really want. I want the policies, given the current political context and climate, to be as favorable and generous as possible. I do not support open borders. I don't think those are realistic...That might make my heart sing for a few minutes, but I just know it would lead to such a backlash that probably the doors would slam shut. So, it's hard for me to get out of the kind of pragmatic point of view that I think from. So, you know, I think I'd like to see legal immigration perhaps a little higher, refugees a little higher, asylum a little more generous, like to see more investment in immigrants and the other folks that live in their communities where they settle, I would like a better refugee protection regime internationally...I'd love to see a new amnesty program for undocumented immigrants in the United States. But I don't mind tougher deportation and stronger border controls and more effective enforcement as long as its intelligent and not done in such a heavy-handed way that it intrudes on other values and rights that we hold dear…There's no single truth. The truth is whatever it is in the moment and you know, if we do our job better, we'll have a more generous and open policy…So, what's the price of a house, what's the right price of a house? Well, it's what the market determines. You know, what's the right immigration policy is what the political market determines, and we're players in that marketplace, and I think we're doing much better than we've been doing in recent years and that we're gonna probably…gain ground over the next five years.

For many expansionists, the overall system is fine. They would like to see better people "minding the store" (i.e., overseeing immigration policy) and some new programs, but overall, if they had their way, the system would basically remain the same. American immigration policies are "full of problems…but fundamentally…when you look at what we call the fundamental architecture of the law…there's nothing wrong with the system."

Perhaps because current estimates of net illegal immigration vary between two and three hundred thousand per year (National Research Council 1997: 50), the above statements are viewed by some restrictionists as an endorsement of illegal immigration. A reluctance to endorse current illegal immigration controls might be interpreted as favoring open borders. Whatever the reasons may be, one influential expansionist explains that this is not the case: "…I don't believe in open borders…I believe in good public policy…I believe in a very, very regulated and tightly managed border, but that doesn't make me a supporter of whatever we're doing at the border…"

A prominent expansionist who regularly interacts with other influential colleagues explains that the ones who "don't believe in enforcement" prevent them from being proactive in the debate:

The pro-immigrant side has gotta have a set of answers on enforcement. We don't believe, I don't believe, in open borders. I've never believed in open borders. A hundred years from now I might believe in open borders. Well, I don't today…I do believe in a kind of community of the Americas, like the European community, over a couple of generations. I think it's gonna happen anyhow so we might as well try to shape it, but I've always believed that my side of this debate had to have a serious attitude toward enforcement...But the left of the pro-immigrant debate doesn't believe in enforcement and doesn't believe it's our job to tackle enforcement issues...Well, we had a big internal debate in '93-'94. A number of us developed an enforcement agenda...[Our organization] was stopped from pursuing that agenda by its left-wing, who engineered a real crisis...Bottom line—nobody on the pro-immigrant side had anything to say about enforcement these last two years except, "No, we don't like it. We don't like this, we don't like that, we don't like that, we don't like this." We had no affirmative agenda, so it [the 1996 Illegal Immigration and Immigrant Responsibility Act] was like a default. We just gave it away, just gave it away...So, it's a big political lesson to so-called good guys that if you don't grapple with tough issues then somebody else will and you'll be shut out of the debate...So, that's one of my perspectives on my side of the debate that we've been, with the exception of myself and a few others, woefully irresponsible over years in not acknowledging...the legitimacy in public concerns about illegal immigration, the legitimacy of trying to make enforcement work...

Only two expansionists interviewed for this study unequivocally support open borders, although neither comes from the "left" side of the pro-immigration debate. The above statement, however, is difficult to substantiate. Only two interviews were conducted with representatives from left-of-center ethnic lobbies like La Raza and MALDEF (e.g., see Figure 3 in Chapter 4).

Without being put to the question, most expansionists regularly assert their commitment to a regulated border. Another expansionist emphasized: "I don't think you'll find barely a person who opposes some kind of orderly, systematic... limitation on immigration...You may find an open border person somewhere or another, but pretty much not in most of the groups who are working on this issue." The idea of a *more* open border, however, does appeal to some expansionists.

As intimated earlier, why should outmoded, fatiguing INS regulations slow the flow of human capital when investment capital is allowed to cross without inspection? Some expansionists point to mountainous backlogs in family- and skills-based admissions as cause for less restrictions: "I think we do need to stop illegal immigration. I would just go about it a different way. I wouldn't close the borders to stop it, but I would actually make it easier for more people to come in and not have to wait in line so long to do that."

Ideas like this are regularly interwoven with a realpolitik. Reassured by a comforting past, and confident of their assessments, expansionists work together so they can win: "The rewarding [part of my job] is doing coalition work...and learning that we're all in this together, and together, trying to figure out how...to form a flank that is unbeatable."

Conclusion

To expansionists, immigration is more of a humanitarian and economic question than a national one. The national interest is significant, but other aspirations also deserve special consideration, such the rights of refugees, desires of immigrants, and needs of business. In the expansionist vision these objectives are interconnected and complementary. For example, the United States acquires generosity by giving it away and American businesses profit from immigrant proficiencies just as immigrants gain from American deficiencies. The list could go on, but the point is this—by and large, immigration benefits the United States and the people it accommodates. The national interest is achieved by expanding immigration, not by reducing it. The American experiment with immigration is not an empty tradition, but part of a broad, imprecise strategy to synchronize the extension of democracy with the unceasing march of capital.

CHAPTER 7

Summary and Conclusions

The findings of this investigation are reviewed and integrated into a more comprehensive analysis of immigration reform. The intensity and scope of immigration politics fluctuates with perceptions of immigrant phenomena, which in turn, are shaped by domestic interest groups, international relations, national contexts and legal categories. The confluence of these contingencies is briefly examined, as well as the worldviews of activists, which are organized into a typology of expansionist and restrictionist motives. The chapter closes with two suggestions for future research.

Review

The definition of nativism offered in Chapter 2 consists of shifting categories and perceptions. "Native" and "alien" are socially constructed, relationally defined *categories*. Natives define themselves vis-à-vis aliens by converting their *perceptions* of aliens into contrastive identities. In other words, natives know who they are by knowing who they are not (e.g., see Blumer 1958; Sartre 1946). "Proprietary claim" and "encroachment" are *perceptions* of entitlement and infringement. The assertion that immigrants are taking American jobs, for example, assumes that certain jobs are the property of Americans.

Restrictionists and expansionists regularly demonstrate the congruence between their interests and the national interest by promoting their perceptions of immigration. They manage the impression that they are "living up to the many standards by which they and their products are judged" so they will appear credible and legitimate (Goffman 1959: 251). This observation, along with the categories and perceptions noted above, are integrated below. By way

207

of review, these categories and perceptions are broken down into three sections: (1) perceptions and context, (2) categories and context, and (3) legitimacy and context. All three "components" owe their significance, in large measure, to the social and legal contexts from which they originate.

Perceptions and Context

The immigration debate is overflowing with empirical and moral arguments shipped from different warehouses of values and interpretations. The worldviews of expansionists and restrictionists frame immigration in contrastive ways and assign different meanings to immigrants and the changes they generate. These meanings are constructed and handled within a range of contexts variously connected to immigration reform.

For example, the most egregious examples of American nativism have historically transpired during wartime (see Table 1 in Chapter 3). During these eras, the *social meanings assigned* to immigrant populations primarily converge on matters of *national security*.[28] In the early stages of World War I, the German-American Alliance and German-American press supported Germany. These actions were *considered* a threat to national security because the United States was at war with Germany. Had they supported their homeland in a different setting (e.g., during peacetime or in a war of little consequence to the U.S.), the ensuing arrests and internments would most likely have never occurred. Their actions would have been interpreted as an exercise in free speech, ethnic pride, or an unwillingness to assimilate, but not as a threat to national security. War is an intense political act for any state (Panayi 1990), and its emergence can transform "normal" immigrant behaviors into national security issues. Immigrant actions are not intrinsically anything—their meanings arise within the context of social interaction. Interpretation is not an "automatic application of established meanings," but "a formative process in which meanings are

---

[28] This observation extends Finnemore's (1996) analysis of state interests and state behavior to the exigencies of immigration reform (see section three in this chapter).

used and revised for the guidance and formation of action" (Blumer 1986: 5).

This process is also observable in the interview data. The restrictionist agenda is principally advanced by environmentalists (see Chapters 4 and 5), but researchers usually associate restrictionist motives with economic conditions, demographic considerations, and racial proclivities (e.g., see Calavita 1996; Feagin 1997; Muller 1997). Assumptions like these are often accurate (e.g., see Chapters 5 and 7; Abernethy 1993; Brimelow 1996), but inferring motives from these contexts reduces the restrictionist agenda to a potpourri of Pavlovian responses.[29]

For example, restrictionists can be indifferent to a given set of circumstances, yet still manipulate them for political ends. Prominent expansionists acknowledge the importance of population stabilization to their restrictionist counterparts, but distinguish between their personal motivations and political opportunities:

> ...I think if you trace the last 5 years...you can give credit to the anti-immigration groups for effectively getting their arguments out and creating the climate that they did. There was a context called "recession," "disaffection with the Federal Government," some notorious incidents, and they rode the wave beautifully.

Population restrictionists rode the wave of public opinion even though their objectives, and the contexts they were operating in, were not a perfect match. The public may not have associated their problems with immigration (or population growth), but restrictionists "made" the connection for them. In return, expansionists tried to "blunt their momentum" by associating immigration with history and the "American dream." The above expansionist continues:

---

[29] The same, of course, could also be said about the expansionist agenda. It is advanced during "good" and "bad" times, although its political objectives are (like the restrictionist agenda) tempered by contextual considerations.

Meanwhile, we didn't respond effectively. We were on the sidelines, "Oh, it's scapegoating, oh it's racism," and we never figured out how to engage the debate until, really I think, the last two years. In the last two years, we've figured out how to blunt their momentum: "There's a difference between legal and illegal immigration;" "We're a nation of immigrants—don't throw the tradition out the window;" "Immigrants work hard, revitalize the American dream." Some of those arguments started to catch.

As emphasized above, meanings arise within the context of social interaction. While some settings seemingly have a profound impact on human interpretation (e.g., war), some contexts are only incidental in their influence. That is, their occurrence has little impact on the way people see, or think about, immigrants. For example, nativist initiatives regularly occur during boom and bust cycles because it is the interpretation of an event—not the event itself—that ultimately influences mass behavior (see Table 1 in Chapter 3). Public opinions are, of course, also influenced by the presentation of, and interactions between, interest groups (Blumer 1966; 1986: 198).

These interactions (between interest groups) are primarily guided—not by knee-jerk reactionaries—but by principle-driven, true believers. Expansionists and restrictionists already know what they believe. In most cases, "new findings" will not change their minds because their beliefs and values principally rest on metaphysical, not empirical, assumptions. For example, expansionists generally believe the economy is comprised of positive-sum possibilities and restrictionists generally think it is composed of zero-sum limits. Or, here's another example: many restrictionists think natural resources are finite, but some expansionists believe they are infinite (at least in an economic sense).

Scientists cannot conclusively "prove" or "disprove" these assumptions because they are metaphysical claims. Garrett Hardin (1995) and Julian Simon (1996) both concede that their arguments are built, respectively, on assumptions of finiteness and infiniteness. Scientists simply cannot measure all of the world's natural resources. Nor can they "test" the metaphors of positive and zero-sum economies. They can amass piles of studies to *demonstrate the plausibility* of each perspective, but they cannot "prove" the existence of either. A seemingly zero-sum situation (immigrants displacing native-born workers) might have positive-sum results (additional jobs are created, therefore expanding opportunities for native-born workers). Or, a positive-sum event (immigrant entrepreneurs creating additional jobs) might only be a passing development in an otherwise zero-sum scenario (the creation of additional jobs is achieved at the expense of competitors who must then downsize their workforces in order to stay in business).

The point is this—activists amend their arguments and goals in light of various conditions (economic downturns, etc.), but their beliefs remain basically unchanged. I asked a libertarian expansionist if he would change his mind about immigration if the economic contributions of immigrants were "in the red." His answer indicates that his position, while not waterproof, is certainly water resistant: "It would lessen my enthusiasm, but I don't think I'd therefore say, 'Well, we should close the borders.'" This comment, I argue, is typical of expansionists and restrictionists (see population and environment section in Chapter 5 and refugee section in Chapter 6). Their beliefs are not impervious to new conditions and facts, but are largely unaffected by them.

A typology of their motivations can be advanced from this investigation. The *primary* perceptions of expansionists and restrictionists are listed alphabetically in Table 2. Compiled from interview data and published documents, their perspectives are also described as "motives" because their interpretations rationalize their worldviews and ensuing behaviors (see Chapter 4). "As a word, *a motive tends to be one which to the actor and the other members of a situation an unquestioned answer to questions concerning social and lingual conduct*" (Mills 1940: 907, italics in original). In one sense, the motives are "types" of expansionists and restrictionists, although many activists enter the debate through multiple "entry points" (see Chapters 4-6).

Table 3 Expansionist and Restrictionist Motives

Expansionists	Restrictionists
Business	Assimilation (perceived lack thereof)
Cultural (assimilation or multiculturalism)	Cultural
Family Reunification	Demographic (ethnic politics, fertility)
Humanitarian (asylees and refugees)	Environmental
Libertarian	Labor
Religious	Population
Traditional (immigration history)	Racial

It must be emphasized (again) that these motives, or worldviews, are primarily derived from interviews with immigration activists operating at the national level. As one restrictionist put it, "...the driver for [restrictionists]—there are two: one is population, the other is culture...Culture is much more important when you get out of Washington." I suspect this is accurate, but their perceptions, whether they are formulated in the nation's capitol or in Miami, are also influenced (to varying degrees) by the legal and social categories "used" in the immigration debate.

Categories and Context

Membership in a polity is predicated on social and legal distinctions. The word "alien" is, in fact, used by the INS to refer to any person who is "not a citizen or national of the United States" (INS 1994). The separation between citizens and noncitizens is recognized by national and international laws, although human rights law limits the scope and significance of these distinctions. For example, the regulation of immigration is a national right, but this right is largely dependent on the incorporation of customary laws into national laws by U.S. courts (Malone 1995: 43, 56, 118-128).

Socially defined categories like citizen/noncitizen and native/alien are used by public officials, government agencies, immigration activists, and everyday citizens to "solve pressing organizational problems by means of categorical distinction" (Tilly 1998: 8). That is, people who have the right to distribute or protect collective resources (e.g., American citizens, "natives," Representative Lamar Smith, FAIR, etc.) manage these boundaries in order to resolve "pressing" national problems. For example, Senator Abraham (R-Mich.) is attempting to bridge the gap between the needs of global, U.S.-based firms and the presumed shortage of highly-skilled Americans by proposing an increase in the number of H1-B visas (nonimmigrant visas for specialty occupations). His proposal would monitor the movement of immigrants across certain boundaries (e.g., the border and INS categories) without changing the basic distinction between citizens and noncitizens. However, the *Wall Street Journal's* editorial position (which advocates a constitutional amendment to establish open borders) would blur the line between natives and aliens (at least on one front) if it were implemented. The distinction between citizens and noncitizens might stay intact, but removing national borders (if only for immigration purposes) would redefine the meaning of national sovereignty because the very idea of sovereignty assumes the existence of a national territory (Malone 1995).

For restrictionists, boundaries between natives and aliens are unavoidable: "...life is a series of drawing lines and you have to draw lines with respect to whom you want to be kind." The paired categories of citizen/noncitizen and national/international are fundamental to their mindset. This is especially true of environmental and population restrictionists. Their "solutions" for minimizing population growth and environmental degradation rely heavily on such distinctions. As one restrictionist put it: "...population policies are the sort of very sensitive policies that can only be established nation by nation." In a stratified and "overpopulated" world, sovereignty is—in their minds—a precondition for drafting efficacious policies. As Tilly explains: "People who create or sustain categorical inequality...rarely set out to manufacture inequality...Instead they solve other organizational problems by establishing categorically unequal access to valued outcomes" (1998: 11). The nation-state is used by restrictionists to mitigate the presumed problems of overpopulation and environmental decline. In their minds, the U.S. can only stabilize its population by maintaining replacement-level fertility (births = deaths) and migration (immigration = emigration) ratios. These goals are national-level goals, and their success hinges in large measure on the reformulation of national immigration laws.

Legitimacy and Context

Of course, immigration polices are not only shaped by domestic politics, but also by international relations (Finnemore 1996; Mitchell 1992; Sassen 1996). State interests and behaviors are modified by international organizations, relations, and norms. The objectives, values, and *perceptions* of nation-states are affected by the demands of domestic interest groups *and* an ever-changing context of international norms and values:

> We cannot understand what states want without understanding the international social structure of which they are a part. States are embedded in dense networks of transnational and international social relations that shape their perceptions of the world and their role in that world. States are *socialized* to want certain things by the international society in which they and the people in them live...Interests are not just "out there" waiting to be discovered; they are constructed through social interaction...State interests are defined in the context of internationally held norms and understandings about what is good and appropriate. That normative context influences the behavior of decisionmakers and of mass publics who may choose and constrain those decisionmakers. The normative context also changes over time, and as internationally held norms and values change, they create coordinated shifts in state interests and behavior across the system (Finnemore 1996: 2, italics in original).

At first sight, this observation—that states are socialized by the international community—seems trite. But it is not. Scholars typically use a language of constraint to explain interactions between states and international organizations, but Finnemore argues that international organizations actually *change* state interests. The international system influences state action, "not by constraining states with a given set of preferences from acting, but by changing their preferences" (1996: 6). Finnemore does not examine immigration policy structures, but her analysis does shed light on the politics of immigration reform. The preferences of immigration activists are, to varying degrees, influenced by international norms and organizations. Provisional support is found in cross-national comparisons of immigration policies (e.g., see Papademetriou and Hamilton 1996; Teitelbaum and Winter 1998), and the responses of restrictionists and expansionists to international phenomena. Restrictionists and expansionists are generally familiar with, or at least sense, the impact of international conceptions and practices (see nationalism section in Chapter 5 and globalism section in Chapter 6). In terms of international organization, their perceptions are most likely influenced by human rights law (e.g., see Malone 1995; Sassen 1996), world population conferences (e.g., see Hays 1989), global economic and environmental summits (e.g., see Rothman 1998; Simon 1996), and attempts by the European Union to develop continent-wide policy frameworks (Papademetriou and Hamilton 1996; Papademetriou 1996).

Of course, there are other influential discourses—grounded in various institutions and embodied in different institutional practices—that can be explored as sites of meaning (e.g., see McCall and Becker 1990: 13; McCall and Wittner 1990: 56-59). The typology of motives arranged in Table 3, for instance, resembles the range of "racial projects" envisioned by Omi and Winant (1994) and Winant (1994; 1997). Racial projects try to explain racial dynamics and organize outcomes and opportunities along racial lines (e.g., the distribution of resources). Each project represents "race" in a unique way, but at the center of each articulation lies a political agenda (Winant 1994: 30, 139). For example, the "neoconservative" racial project tries to *preserve* white advantages by denying racial differences, while the "neoliberal" racial project tries to *limit* white advantages by denying racial differences (Winant 1997; Winant 1994: 31). The overlap of racial and native discourses in some of the immigration reform discourses may explain why the debate is often rife with identity politics, moral divisiveness, and motive imputation. Promoters of these projects seek different arrangements, yet embrace some of the very same "rationalizing formulas" (Winant 1997).

Similarly, expansionists and restrictionists contend for public approval and governmental policies congruent with their perspectives, yet both are *nationalistic* in that the national interest is ostensibly at the center of their reforms. That is, the discourse of nationalism is used to represent the national interest and legitimize their claims (Light 1996). There is a significant difference, however, between racial projects and "native projects." In both endeavors, the racialization of "others" and their ensuing subordination has played, and continues to play, a significant role in determining questions of membership (see Chapter 3 for examples). Native systems of exclusion and privilege intersect with other hierarchies to protect native advantages, but unlike racial projects, often enjoy a modicum of legitimacy and legality. In the United States, gradations of membership are largely acceptable if they are based on the status of citizenship, as opposed to, say, race or gender (e.g., see Brubaker 1989).

Much has already been said about legitimacy (see Chapters 2 and 4), but its historical variability and political importance are worth reiterating. Restrictionists and expansionists devote considerable time and energy to developing arguments that appeal to the public's opinions of what is right and wrong. The normative context surrounding immigration reform has changed, and will continue to change. The international context is only one influence among many, but I suspect its influence will only grow with time.

Suggestions for Future Research

This investigation examines the historical roots (Chapter 3) and contemporary branches (Chapters 4-6) of American immigration reform. Nativism scholars generally use history, contemporary conditions, and popular restrictionist writings to define nativism and explain its occurrence (see Chapters 1-2). This study travels each of these paths—then clears a new one. Examining the historical contexts associated with nativist outbreaks *and the worldviews of restrictionists and expansionists* exhibits some of the material conditions, ideas, and norms influencing the *interpretation* of immigrant-related phenomena.

The meanings of these experiences develop within various contexts (normative, material, etc.) and are used by interest groups to influence public opinion and mass behavior (Blumer 1958; 1966; 1986). Unlike most studies of American immigration reform, this one investigates the beliefs systems of immigration activists. Their worldviews are not only formed by the winds of economic change, but are hammered in the fires of belief systems and diverse contexts (of which the national economy is only one). While some social scientists are guilty of reducing immigration beliefs to economic, demographic, and social contexts, others rely on identity politics to do their thinking for them. The assumption that restrictionists are patently racist or that expansionists are only concerned about cheap labor is regularly aired, but how many of them have bothered to ask restrictionists and expansionists about their worldviews and involvement? Very few. Clearly, there are some racist restrictionists and some greedy expansionists, but I strongly suspect that they are in the minority. Most expansionists and restrictionists are principled people pursuing an immigration reality they see as reasonable and just.

This research does not replace existing analyses, but complements their forms of inquiry. It scrutinizes untested assumptions about motives and context and lays the groundwork for future investigations, and like its predecessors, also stands to benefit from supplementary studies. Specifically, better public opinion polls and in-depth interviews with local (as opposed to national) activists would be especially valuable.

Do Americans think the U.S. allows too many, too few, or just the right amount of immigrants into the country each year? Variations of this "Goldilocks and the Three Bears" question have been regularly asked since 1946 and most Americans, unlike Goldilocks, rarely conclude that current levels are "just right" (e.g., see Espenshade and Hempstead 1996; Simon 1993). Instead, the majority of Americans say they would like a decrease in immigration. But as Teitelbaum and Winter point out, "American views on immigration are not so uniformly negative as such data suggest" (1998: 145). Public opinion questions on whether specific categories of immigrants should be let in (like family members and refugees) "elicit more favorable responses than do questions on aggregate numbers" (1998: 145).

The only reliable and valid way to gauge American (or resident) attitudes toward U.S. immigration is to collect and analyze national survey data. This study unfolds the worldviews of immigration activists, but does not represent the typical American or U.S. resident (although their opinions are probably shaped by the efforts of expansionists and restrictionists). Constructing an "immigration receptivity" scale might resolve the problem of wording effects, but such an instrument would probably require a number of open-ended questions to identify (and understand) American attitudes toward immigrants. For instance, when Americans say they want to increase, decrease, or maintain current immigration levels, what are they assuming about present levels? When they talk about immigrants, what types of immigrants do they have in mind (e.g., labor migrants, professional immigrants, etc.)? Questions like these would complicate coding and statistical procedures (e.g., by comparing *similar* responses instead of *identical* answers), and necessitate in-depth interviews, but they would permit unanticipated responses and reveal the respondents' frames of reference (Neuman 1994: 232-34).

The second and related suggestion addresses the purposive sample used for this research study. As mentioned in Chapter 4, the exploratory nature of this research project, absence of a precise sampling frame, and focus on national activists, makes it difficult to answer questions of representation. While representativeness was not the objective per se, the sample seems fairly representative of national activists, given the extensive overlap in themes and interview referrals (see Chapter 4 for details). However, studying regional and local immigration reform initiatives would probably refine some of the pictures developed in Chapters 4-6.

Conducting interviews with local activists would not only diversify the responses, but the respondent pool as well. Hellwig (1982) examines historical patterns of "black nativism, and Walby (1996) suggests that the political activities of women are generally "less nationalist" and more local than those of men, but no researcher, to my knowledge, has examined the specific involvement of women and African Americans in contemporary efforts to reform immigration. There are gendered and racialized places for women and men in national initiatives (Dill, Zinn and Patton 1998; Nagel 1998; Winant 1994), and studying the participation of women and nonwhites in immigration politics may reveal different interests and perceptions (e.g., see Fitzpatrick 1997; Hondagneu-Sotelo 1995; Roberts 1997; Zavella 1997). There are, of course more than two ways to build upon and improve this study. The preceding analysis demonstrates that the politics of immigration reform are not reducible to simple contexts and perceptions, but are also moved by domestic power struggles and newly emerging values and norms. As in previous eras, its appearance on the national agenda emanates from a presumption that the national interest somehow conflicts with the dynamics of immigration. If history is any indication, the accuracy of this assumption will only become clear when the intentions and outcomes of today's policies are faced by tomorrow's policymakers.

Appendices

APPENDIX 1: Consent Form

Dear

I am currently working on my dissertation as a doctoral student in the Department of Sociology at Michigan State University. My research examines, in part, the controversy over current immigration and immigrant policies. I am curious why people become involved in efforts to maintain or change current immigration/immigrant policies, and I'm also interested in the ideas and opinions of people who work in organizations associated with immigrants. The goal of my research is to better understand why people become involved in work dealing with immigration and immigrants, and to learn what they think about their jobs and the current controversy over immigration.

As someone who has knowledge of these issues, I hope that you will share your views on these matters. Understanding your perspective, and the viewpoints of other individuals who are interested in immigration, will help me to understand why some people become involved in organizations that influence, directly or indirectly, public policy and opinion with respect to immigrants. The interview questions should take about 45 to 60 minutes and will be recorded onto an audio cassette. Your participation is completely voluntary. Please ask me about any question that is not clear, and if we should come to a question that you do not wish to answer, just let me know and I'll go on to the next one. Also, you are free to withdraw from the interview at any time.

Anything you say in the interview will be kept strictly confidential, that is, your responses will not be associated with you in any way. I will do everything in my power to ensure confidentiality. There may be some cases where persons may be identifiable because they hold a prominent or public position. Even in these cases, I will be careful not to mention anything that would reveal your identity.

Your help and cooperation would be greatly appreciated. If you have any questions before or after the interview, please feel free to call me at (517) 394-1171 or send me an e-mail (frybrian@pilot.msu.edu). My mailing address is: 316 Berkey Hall, MSU, East Lansing, MI 48824-1111.

I would be grateful if you would check the box below and sign this form to show that you have read its contents:

☐ I agree to be interviewed as described above.

_____ (signed)

_____ (printed)

_____ (dated)

Please send me a report on the results of this research project (check one):
_____ Yes _____ No

If "yes," please send to:

_____
_____
_____
_____

Interviewer: keep signed copy; leave unsigned copy with respondent.

APPENDIX 2: Interview Schedule

Respondent's name:
Date:
Time:
Place:
DOB:
POB:
Education:
Political Persuasion:

I. Primary duties/responsibilities

1. How long have you been with [name of organization/office/department]?
2. What are your primary responsibilities, or duties, at [name of organization/office/department]?
3. How did you become involved in this line of work?
4. What are some of the most rewarding aspects of your work?
5. What are some of the most frustrating aspects of your work?

II. Immigration and Immigrants

[Note: If necessary, begin by discussing the difference between *immigration* and *immigrant* policy]

1. Do you remember the first time you thought about immigration? When? Why?
2. Would you like to see the current level of immigration changed? Why? In what ways?
3. How do you feel immigrants are received by the public? Why? In what ways?
4. Is there anything that would make you change your mind about immigration?
5. Are your opinions tied to religious beliefs or a set of values that you hold?
6. Some people might say that you have other "motives" for wanting to [mention some of the opinions they offered in response to questions 2

and 3]. What do you think some of those motives might be? How would you respond to these kind of accusations?

7. Do you have a personal interest in seeing the current situation [immigration/immigrants] changing? Staying the same?

8. Why is immigration important to you?

9. What do you think of Proposition 187? Of the new welfare legislation in regard to legal immigrants?

10. Why do you think immigrants come to the United States?

III. Personal History

1. Who in your family were the original immigrants? When did they come here? Why did they come to the United States?

2. If native-born: Do you remember you first encounter with immigrants or your first relationship with someone who was foreign-born? When? What kind of relationship/encounter was it?

2a. Were there immigrants in your neighborhood where you grew up?

2b. In the schools you attended?

2c. Where you've worked?

2d. At the present time, are any of your "good" friends foreign-born?

3. If foreign-born: Do you remember your first encounter with Americans? When? What kind of encounter/relationship was it?

3a. Were there native-born Americans in your neighborhood where you grew up?

3b. In the schools you attended?

3c. Where you've worked?

3d. At the present time, are any of your "good" friends native-born?

References

Abernethy, Virginia D. 1993. *Population Politics: The Choices that Shape Our Future*. New York: Plenum Press.

Adorno, T.W., Else Frenkel-Brunswik, Daniel J. Levinson, and R. Stanford. 1950. *The Authoritarian Personality*. New York: Harper.

Aguirre Jr., Adalberto. 1997. "Nativism, Mexican Immigrant Workers, and Proposition 187 in California." Pp. 142-153 in *California's Social Problems*, edited by Charles F. Hohm. New York: Longman.

Aguirre Jr., Adalberto, and Jonathan H. Turner. 1995. *American Ethnicity: The Dynamics and Consequences of Discrimination*. New York: McGraw-Hill.

Alba, Richard. 1990. *Ethnic Identity: The Transformation of White America*. New Haven: Yale University Press.

Alba, Richard. 1996. "Italian Americans: A Century of Ethnic Change." Pp. 172-181 in *Origins and Destinies: Immigration, Race, and Ethnicity in America*, edited by Silvia Pedraza and Rubén G. Rumbaut. Belmont, CA: Wadsworth.

Albrow, Martin. 1990. *Max Weber's Construction of Social Theory*. New York: St. Martin's Press.

Aleinikoff, T. Alexander. 1997. "The Tightening Circle of Membership." Pp. 324-332 in *Immigrants Out! The New Nativism and the Anti-Immigrant Impulse in the United States*, edited by Juan F. Perea. New York: New York University Press.

Almaguer, Tomás. 1994. *Racial Fault Lines: The Historical Origins of White Supremacy in California*. Berkeley: University of California Press.

Anbinder, Tyler. 1992. *Nativism and Slavery: The Northern Know Nothings and the Politics of the 1850s*. New York: Oxford University Press.

Anderson, Benedict. 1991. *Imagined Communities: Reflections on the Origin and Spread of Nationalism*. London: Verso.

Appadurai, Arjun. 1996. *Modernity at Large: Cultural Dimensions of Globalization*. Minneapolis: University of Minnesota Press.

Auster, Lawrence. 1997. *Huddled Clichés: Exposing the Fraudulent Arguments That Have Opened America's Borders to the World*. Monterey, VA: American Immigration Control Foundation.

Banton, Michael. 1995. "Rational Choice Theories." *American Behavioral Scientist* 38: 478-497.

Barber, Benjamin R. 1996. *Jihad vs. McWorld: How Globalism and Tribalism are Reshaping the World*. New York: Ballantine Books.

Barkan, Elliot Robert. 1996. *And Still They Come: Immigrants and American Society: 1920 to the 1990s*. Wheeling, IL: Harlan Davidson.

Barkan, Elliott R. 1995. "Race, Religion, and Nationality in American Society: A Model of Ethnicity—From Contact to Assimilation." *Journal of American Ethnic History* 19:1995.

Barry, Colman J. 1958. "Some Roots of American Nativism." *The Catholic Historical Review* 44:137-146.

Barth, Fredrick. 1969. "Introduction." Pp. 9-38 in *Ethnic Groups and Boundaries: The Social Organization of Culture Difference*, edited by Fredrick Barth. London: Allen & Unwin.

Basch, Linda, Nina Glick Schiller, and Cristina Szanton Blanc. 1995. *Nations Unbound: Transnational Projects, Postcolonial Predicaments, and*

Deterritorialized Nation-States. Switzerland: Gordon & Breach Science Publications.

Bayor, Ronald. 1986. "Klans, Coughlinites and Aryan Nations: Patterns of American Anti-Semitism in the Twentieth Century." *American Jewish History* 76:181-196.

Beck, Roy. 1992. "'Xenophobia': Scrabble Winner, Debate Stopper." *The Social Contract* 2:144-149.

Beck, Roy. 1994. *Re-Charting America's Future.* Petoskey, MI: The Social Contract Press.

Beck, Roy. 1996. *The Case Against Immigration: The moral, economic, social, and environmental reasons for reducing U.S. immigration back to traditional levels.* New York: W.W. Norton & Company.

Bendix, Reinhard. 1960. *Max Weber: An Intellectual Portrait.* Garden City, NY: Doubleday.

Bennett, David H. 1995. *The Party of Fear: From Nativist Movements to the Far Right in American History.* New York: Vintage Books.

Berger, Peter. 1997. "Four Faces of Global Culture." *The National Interest* 49:23-29.

Bergquist, James M. 1986. "The Concept of Nativism in Historical Study Since *Strangers in the Land.*" *American Jewish History* 76:125-141.

Billington, Ray Allen. 1963. *The Protestant Crusade 1800-1860: A Study of the Origins of American Nativism.* Gloucester, MA: Peter Smith.

Blau, Peter M. 1963. "Critical Remarks on Weber's Theory of Authority." *American Political Science Review* 57:305-316.

Blauner, Robert. 1972. *Racial Oppression in America.* New York: Harper & Row.

Blumer, Herbert. 1958. "Race Prejudice as a Sense of Group Position." *Pacific Sociological Review* 1:3-7.

Blumer, Herbert. 1966. "The Mass, the Public, and Public Opinion." in *Reader in Public Opinion and Communication*, edited by Bernard Berelson and Morris Janowitz. New York: The Free Press.

Blumer, Herbert. 1971. "Social Problems as Collective Behavior." *Social Problems* 18:298-306.

Blumer, Herbert. 1986. *Symbolic Interactionism: Perspective and Method.* Berkeley: University of California Press.

Bobo, Lawrence, and Vincent L. Hutchings. 1996. "Perceptions of Racial Group Competition: Extending Blumer's Theory of Group Position to a Multiracial Social Context." *American Sociological Review* 61:951-972.

Bobo, Lawrence, and Camille L. Zubrinsky. 1996. "Attitudes toward Residential Integration: Perceived Status Differences, Mere In-Group Preference, or Racial Prejudice?" *Social Forces* 74:883-909.

Bonacich, Edna. 1980. "Class Approaches to Ethnicity and Race." *The Insurgent Sociologist* 10:9-23.

Booth, William. 1996. "In a Rush, New Citizens Register Their Political Interest As More Immigrants Become Naturalized, First Tendency is Toward Democratic Party." in *The Washington Post.*

Borjas, George J. 1994. "The New Economics of Immigration: Affluent Americans gain; poor Americans lose." Pp. 1-6 in *The Atlantic Monthly.*

Bosniak, Linda S. 1997. ""Nativism" the Concept: Some Reflections." Pp. 279-299 in *Immigrants Out! The New Nativism and the Anti-Immigrant Impulse in the United States*, edited by Juan F. Perea. New York: New York University Press.

Bouvier, Leon F., and Lindsey Grant. 1994. *How Many Americans? Population, Immigration and the Environment.* San Francisco: Sierra Club Books.

Brigham, C.C. 1923. *A study of American intelligence.* Princeton, NJ: Princeton University Press.

Brimelow, Peter. 1996. *Alien Nation: Common Sense About America's Immigration Disaster.* New York: Random House.

Brimelow, Peter. 1997. "Un-American Activities." Pp. 44-45 in *National Review.*

Brown, Rupert. 1995. *Prejudice: Its Social Psychology.* Oxford: Blackwell Publishers.

Brownstone, David M. 1994. *Timelines of War.* Boston: Little, Brown.

Brubaker, Rogers. 1989. "Citizenship and Naturalization: Policies and Politics." Pp. 99-127 in *Immigration and the Politics of Citizenship in Europe and North America,* edited by William Rogers Brubaker. Lanham, MD: University Press of North America.

Brubaker, Rogers. 1989. "Introduction." Pp. 1-27 in *Immigration and the Politics of Citizenship in Europe and North America,* edited by William Rogers Brubaker. Lanham, MD: University Press of America.

Brubaker, Rogers. 1992. *Citizenship and nationhood in France and Germany.* Cambridge, MA: Harvard University Press.

Brubaker, Rogers. 1996. *Nationalism Reframed: Nationhood and the national question in the New Europe.* Cambridge: Cambridge University Press.

Burawoy, Michael, Alice Burton, Ann Arnett Ferguson, Kathryn J. Fox, Joshua Gamson, Nadine Gartrell, Leslie Hurst, Charles Kurzman, Leslie Salzinger, Josepha Schiffman, and Shiori Ui. 1991. *Ethnography Unbound: Power and Resistance in the Modern Metropolis.* Berkeley: University of California Press.

Cahill, Gilbert A. 1958. "Comments." *The Catholic Historical Review* 44:159-164.

Calavita, Kitty. 1996. "The New Politics of Immigration: "Balanced-Budget Conservatism" and the Symbolism of Proposition 187." *Social Problems* 43:284-305.

Calhoun, Craig. 1993. "Nationalism and Ethnicity." *Annual Review of Sociology* 19:11-39.

Calhoun, Craig. 1994. "Nationalism and Civil Society: Democracy, Diversity, and Self-Determination." Pp. 304-335 in *Social Theory and the Politics of Identity*, edited by Craig Calhoun. Cambridge, MA: Blackwell.

Campbell, Colin. 1996. "On the Concept of Motive in Sociology." *Sociology* 30:101-114.

Carens, Joseph H. 1996. "Realistic and Idealistic Approaches to the Ethics of Migration." *International Migration Review* 30:156-170.

Carrasco, Gilbert Paul. 1996. "Latinos in the United States: Invitation and Exile." in *Immigrants Out! The New Nativism and the Anti-Immigrant Impulse in the United States*, edited by Juan F. Perea. New York: New York University Press.

Castles, Stephen, and Mark J. Miller. 1993. *The Age of Migration: International Population Movements in the Modern World*. New York: The Guilford Press.

Cato Institute. 1997. Cato Handbook for Congress: 105th Congress. Washington, DC: Cato Institute.

Chang, Robert S. 1997. "A Meditation on Borders." in *Immigrants Out! The New Nativism and the Anti-Immigrant Impulse in the United States*, edited by Juan F. Perea. New York: New York University Press.

Chavez, Leo R. 1997. "Immigration Reform and Nativism: The Nationalist Response to the Transnationalist Challenge." in *Immigrants Out! The New*

Nativism and the Anti-Immigrant Impulse in the United States, edited by Juan F. Perea. New York: New York University Press.

Child, Clifton. 1939. *The German-Americans in Politics 1914-1917*. Madison: University of Wisconsin Press.

Conner, Walker. 1986. "The Impact of Homelands Upon Diasporas." Pp. 16-46 in *Modern Diasporas in International Politics*, edited by Gabriel Sheffer. New York: St. Martin's Press.

Cornell, Stephen. 1996. "The variable ties that bind: content and circumstance in ethnic processes." *Ethnic and Racial Studies* 19:265-289.

Coser, Lewis. 1956. *The Functions of Social Conflict*. New York: The Free Press.

Crawford, James. 1992. *Hold Your Tongue: Bilingualism and the Politics of "English Only"*. Reading, MA: Addison-Wesley Publishing Company.

Daniels, Roger. 1986. "Changes in Immigration Law since 1924." *American Jewish History* 76:159-180.

Daniels, Roger. 1988. *Asian America: Chinese and Japanese in the United States Since 1850*. Seattle: University of Washington Press.

Daniels, Roger. 1990. *Coming to America: A History of Immigration and Ethnicity in American Life*. New York: Harper Perennial.

Daniels, Roger. 1993. *Prisoners Without Trial: Japanese Americans in World War II*. New York: Hill and Wang.

Delgado, Richard. 1997. "Citizenship." Pp. 318-323 in *Immigrants Out! The New Nativism and the Anti-Immigrant Impulse in the United States*, edited by Juan F. Perea. New York: New York University Press.

Dill, Bonnie Thornton, Maxine Baca Zinn, and Sandra Patton. 1998. "Valuing Families Differently: Race, Poverty and Welfare Reform." *Sage Race Relations Abstracts* 23:4-31.

Dinnerstein, Leonard, and David Reimers. 1986. "Strangers in the Land: Then and Now." *American Jewish History* 76:107-116.

Durham, David F. 1997. "Fatal Challenges: Prospects for Real Solutions." *Focus* 7:10-13.

Edmonds, Patricia. 1991. "FBI is accused of 'hunting' Arab Americans." Pp. 8A in *Detroit Free Press*.

Edmonds, Patricia. 1991. "Hate crimes grow: Arab Americans say the rate has jumped since war began." Pp. 3A in *Detroit Free Press*.

Ehrenreich, Barbara. 1990. *Fear of Falling: The Inner Life of the Middle Class*. New York: Harper Perennial.

Ehrlich, Paul R., and Anne H. Ehrlich. 1990. *The Population Explosion*. New York: Simon and Schuster.

Ellis, Mark, and Panikos Panayi. 1994. "German Minorities in World War I: a comparative study of Britain and the USA." *Ethnic and Racial Studies* 17:238-259.

Espenshade, Thomas J., and Katherine Hempstead. 1996. "Contemporary American Attitudes Toward U.S. Immigration." *International Migration Review* 30:535-570.

Espiritu, Yen Le. 1992. *Asian American Panethnicity: Bridging Institutions and Identities*. Philadelphia: Temple University Press.

Feagin, Joe R. 1997. "Old Poison in New Bottles: The Deep Roots of Modern Nativism." in *Immigrants Out! The New Nativism and the Anti-Immigrant Impulse in the United States*, edited by Juan F. Perea. New York: New York University Press.

Federation for American Immigration Reform. 1993. "Tenth Anniversary Oral History Project of the Federation for American Immigration Reform." Washington, DC: Federation for American Immigration Reform.

Finnemore, Martha. 1996. *National Interests in International Society*. Ithaca, NY: Cornell.

Fitzpatrick, Joan. 1997. "The Gender Dimension of U.S. Immigration Policy." *Yale Journal of Law and Feminism* 9:23-49.

Fix, Michael, and Jeffrey S. Passel. 1994. *Immigration and Immigrants: Setting the Record Straight*. Washington, D.C.: The Urban Institute.

Fox, Stephen. 1988. "General John DeWitt and the Proposed Internment of German and Italian Aliens during World War II." *Pacific Historical Review* 57:407-438.

Fox, Stephen. 1990. *The Unknown Internment: An Oral History of the Relocation of Italian Americans during World War II*. Boston: Twayne Publishers.

Frankenberg, Ruth. 1993. *White Women, Race Matters: The Social Construction of Whiteness*. Minneapolis: University of Minnesota Press.

Fredrickson, George M., and Dale T. Knobel. 1981. "Prejudice and Discrimination of." Pp. 829-847 in *Harvard Encyclopedia of American Ethnic Groups*, edited by Stephan Thernstrom. Cambridge: Harvard University Press.

Frey, William H. 1995. "Immigration and Internal Migration 'Flight' from US Metropolitan Areas: Toward a New Demographic Balkanisation." *Urban Studies* 32:733-757.

Frey, William H. 1996. "Immigration, Domestic Migration, and Demographic Balkanization in America: New Evidence for the 1990s." *Population and Development Review* 22:741-763.

Frey, William H., and Jonathan Tilove. 1995. "Immigrants In, Native Whites Out." Pp. 44-45 in *New York Times Magazine*.

Friedman, Kathi V. 1981. *Legitimation of Social Rights and the Western Welfare State*. Chapel Hill: University of North Carolina Press.

Friedman, Norman L. 1967. "Nativism." *Phylon* 28:408-415.

Fuchs, Lawrence. 1990. *The American Kaleidoscope: Race, Ethnicity, and the Civic Culture.* Hanover, CT: Wesleyan University Press.

Gans, Herbert J. 1979. "Symbolic Ethnicity: The Future of Ethnic Groups and Cultures in America." *Ethnic and Racial Studies* 2:1-20.

Gans, Herbert J. 1992. "Second generation decline: scenarios for the economic and ethnic futures of the post-1965 American immigrants." *Ethnic and Racial Studies* 15:173-192.

Garling, Scipio. 1997. *How to Win the Immigration Debate.* Washington, DC: Federation for American Immigration Reform.

Gibney, Mark. 1996. "A Response to Carens and Weiner." *International Migration Review* 30:198-202.

Glenn, Evelyn Nakano. 1986. *Issei, Nisei, War Bride: Three Generations of Japanese American Women in Domestic Service.* Philadelphia: Temple University Press.

Glenn, Evelyn Nakano, and Rhacel Salazar Parreñas. 1996. "The Other Issei: Japanese Immigrant Women in the Pre-World War II Period." Pp. 125-140 in *Origins and Destinies: Immigration, Race, and Ethnicity in America*, edited by Silvia Pedraza and Rubén G. Rumbaut. Belmont, CA: Wadsworth.

Goffman, Erving. 1959. *The Presentation of Self in Everyday Life.* New York: Anchor Books.

Gold, Steven J. 1992. *Refugee Communities: A Comparative Field Study.* Newbury Park, CA: Sage.

Gold, Steven J. 1997. "Religious Agencies, Immigrant Settlement, and Social Justice." *Research in Social Policy* 5:47065.

Gold, Steven J. 1997. "Transnationalism and Vocabularies of Motive in International Migration: The Case of Israelis in the United States." *Sociological Perspectives* 40:409-427.

Gould, Stephen Jay. 1981. *The Mismeasure of Man*. New York: W.W. Norton & Company.

Grant, Lindsey. 1996. *Juggernaut: Growth on a Finite Planet*. Santa Anna, CA: Seven Locks Press.

Grodzins, Morton. 1949. *Americans Betrayed: Politics and the Japanese Evacuation*. Chicago: University of Chicago Press.

Habermas, Jurgen. 1975. *Legitimation Crisis*. Boston: Beacon Press.

Hailbronner, Kay. 1989. "Citizenship and Nationhood in Germany." Pp. 67-79 in *Immigration and the Politics of Citizenship in Europe and North America*, edited by William Rogers Brubaker. Lanham, MD: University Press of America.

Hall, Stuart. 1991. "Ethnicity: Identity and Difference." *Radical America* 23:9-20.

Hardin, Garrett. 1959. *Nature and Man's Fate*. New York: Rinehart & Company.

Hardin, Garrett. 1974. *Mandatory Motherhood: The True Meaning of "Right to Life"*. Boston: Beacon Press.

Hardin, Garrett. 1993. *Living Within Limits: Ecology, Economics, and Population Taboos*. New York: Oxford University Press.

Hardin, Garrett. 1995. *The Immigration Dilemma: Avoiding the Tragedy of the Commons*. Washington, DC: Federation for American Immigration Reform.

Hardin, Garrett, and John Baden. 1977. "Managing the Commons." San Francisco: W. H. Freeman and Company.

Harrington, Mona. 1981. "Loyalties: Dual and Divided." Pp. 676-686 in *Harvard Encyclopedia of American Ethnic Groups*, edited by Stephan Thernstrom. Cambridge: Harvard University Press.

Hays, Samuel P. 1989. *Beauty, Health, and Permanence: Environmental Politics in the United States, 1955-1985*. Cambridge: Cambridge University Press.

Heilemann, John. 1996 (August). "Do You Know the Way to Ban Jose?" Pp. 45-48, 176-181 in *Wired*.

Hellwig, David J. 1982. "Strangers in Their Own Land: Patterns of Black Nativism, 1830-1930." *American Studies* 23:85-98.

Hernández-Truyol, Berta Esperanza. 1997. "Reconciling Rights in Collision: An International Human Rights Strategy." in *Immigrants Out! The New Nativism and the Anti-Immigrant Impulse in the United States*, edited by Juan F. Perea. New York: New York University Press.

Higham, John. 1958. "Another Look at Nativism." *Catholic Historical Review* 46:147-158.

Higham, John. 1984. *Send These to Me: Immigrants in Urban America*. Baltimore: Johns Hopkins University Press.

Higham, John. 1992. *Strangers in the Land*. New Brunswick, NJ: Rutgers University Press.

Higham, John. 1996. "In Place of a Sequel: A History of Nativism for Today." Pp. 1-12 in *Social Science Research Council on "Becoming America/America Becoming*. Sanibel Island, FL.

Hinckley, Ted C. 1962. "American Anti-Catholicism during the Mexican War." *Pacific Historical Review* 31:121-137.

Hing, Bill Ong. 1993. *Making and Remaking Asian America Through Immigration Policy 1850-1990*. Stanford, CA: Stanford University Press.

Hofstadter, Richard. 1996. *The Paranoid Style in American Politics and Other Essays*. Cambridge: Harvard University Press.

Hollinger, David A. 1995. *Postethnic America: Beyond Multiculturalism*. New York: Basic Books.

Holt, Michael F. 1973. "The Politics of Impatience: The Origins of Know Nothingism." *Journal of American History* 60:309-331.

Hondagneu-Sotelo, Pierrette. 1994. *Gendered Transitions: Mexican Experiences of Immigration*. Berkeley: University of California Press.

Hondagneu-Sotelo, Pierrette. 1995. "Women and Children First: new directions in anti-immigrant politics." *Socialist Review* 25:169-190.

Horowitz, Donald L. 1992. "Immigration and Group Relations in France and America." *The American Academy of Arts and Sciences Bulletin* 45:9-30.

Hosokawa, Bill. 1969. *Nisei: The Quiet Americans*. New York: William Morrow and Company.

Huber, Gregory A. 1997. "Neo-Isolationism, Balanced-Budget Conservatism, and the Fiscal Impacts of Immigrants." *International Migration Review* 31:1031-1054.

Hughey, Michael W. 1992. "Americanism and Its Discontents: Protestantism, Nativism, and Political Heresy in America." *International Journal of Politics, Culture and Society* 5:533-553.

Ignatiev, Noel. 1995. *How the Irish Became White*. New York: Routledge.

Inniss, Lolita K. Buckner. 1996. "California's Proposition 187—Does it Mean What it Says? Does it Say What it Means? A Textual and Constitutional Analysis." *Georgetown Immigration Law Journal* :577-622.

Isbister, John. 1996. *The Immigration Debate: Remaking America*. West Hartford, CT: Kumarian Press.

Jiobu, Robert M. 1990. *Ethnicity and Inequality*. Albany, NY: State University of New York Press.

Johnson, Kevin R. 1995. "Public Benefits and Immigration: The Intersection of Immigration Status, Ethnicity, Gender, and Class." *UCLA Law Review* 42:1509-1563.

Johnson, Kevin R. 1997. "The New Nativism: Something Old, Something New, Something Borrowed, Something Blue." Pp. 165--189 in *Immigrants Out! The New Nativism and the Anti-Immigrant Impulse in the United States*, edited by Juan F. Perea. New York: New York University Press.

Jones, Maldwyn Allen. 1992. *American Immigration*. Chicago: University of Chicago Press.

Kadetsky, Elizabeth. 1994. "Bashing Illegals in California." Pp. 416-422 in *The Nation*.

Kanstroom, Daniel. 1997. "Dangerous Undertones of the New Nativism: Peter Brimelow and the Decline of the West." Pp. 300-317 in *Immigrants Out! The New Nativism and the Anti-Immigrant Impulse in the United States*, edited by Juan F. Perea. New York: New York University Press.

Karst, Kenneth L. 1989. *Belonging to America: Equal Citizenship and the Constitution*. New Haven, CT: Yale University Press.

Kawanabe, Kenzo S. 1996. "American Anti-Immigrant Rhetoric Against Asian Pacific Immigrants: The Present Repeats the Past." *Georgetown Immigration Law Journal* 10:681-706.

Keely, Charles B. 1998. *Globalization and Human Resource Management: Nonimmigrant Visa Strategies and Behavior of U.S. Firms*. New York: Center for Migration Studies.

Kitano, Harry H.L. 1981. "Japanese." Pp. 561-571 in *Harvard Encyclopedia of American Ethnic Groups*, edited by Stephan Thernstrom. Cambridge, MA: Harvard University Press.

Knapp, Kiyoko Kamio. 1996. "The Rhetoric of Exclusion: The Art of Drawing a Line Between Aliens and Citizens." *Georgetown Immigration Law Journal* 10:401-440.

Knobel, Dale T. 1996. *"America for the Americans": The Nativist Movement in the United States*. London: Twayne Publishers.

Kraut, Alan M. 1986. "Silent Strangers: Germs, Genes and Nativism in John Higham's *Strangers in the Land*." *American Jewish History* 76:142-158.

Krikorian, Mark. 1995. "A Flawed Jewel." *Immigration Review* 22:14-16.

Lafitte, Francois. 1988. *The Internment of Aliens*. London: Libris.

Lal, Barbara Ballis. 1995. "Symbolic Interaction Theories." *American Behavioral Scientist* 38:421-441.

Lane, A.T. 1987. *Solidarity or Survival? American Labor and European Immigrants, 1830-1924*. New York: Greenwood Press.

Lee, Sharon M. 1989. "Asian immigration and American race-relations: from exclusion to acceptance?" *Ethnic and Racial Studies* 12:368-390.

LeMay, Michael C. 1994. *Anatomy of a Public Policy: The Reform of Contemporary Immigration Law*. Westport, CT: Praeger.

Leonard, Ira M., and Robert D. Parmet. 1971. *American Nativism, 1830-1860*. New York: Van Nostrand Reinhold Company.

Light, Ivan. 1996. "Nationalism and Anti-Immigrant Movements." Pp. 58-63 in *Society*.

Lipset, Seymour Martin, and Earl Raab. 1978. *The Politics of Unreason: Right-Wing Extremism in America, 1790-1977*. Chicago: University of Chicago Press.

Lopez, David, and Yen Espiritu. 1990. "Panethnicity in the United States: a theoretical framework." *Ethnic and Racial Studies* 13:198-224.

Ludmerer, Kenneth M. 1972. "Genetics, Eugenics, and the Immigration Restriction Act of 1924." Pp. 367-389 in *Nativism, Discrimination, and Images of Immigrants*, edited by George E. Pozzetta. New York: Garland Publishing.

Luebke, Fredrick. 1974. *Bonds of Loyalty: German Americans and World War I*. De Kalb, IL: Northern Illinois Press.

Luebke, Fredrick. 1987. *Germans in Brazil: A Comparative History of Cultural Conflict During World War I*. Baton Rouge, LA: Louisiana State University Press.

Luker, Kristin. 1985. *Abortion and the Politics of Motherhood*. Berkeley: University of California Press.

Lutton, Wayne, and John Tanton. 1994. *The Immigration Invasion*. Petoskey, MI: The Social Contract Press.

Malone, Linda A. 1995. *International Law*. Larchmont, NY: Emanuel.

Malthus, T. R. 1992. *An Essay on the Principle of Population; or A View of its past and present Effects on Human Happiness; With an Inquiry into our Prospects respecting the future Removal or Mitigation of the Evils which it occasions*. Cambridge: Cambridge University Press.

Martin, Philip. 1995. "Proposition 187 in California." *International Migration Review* 29:255-263.

Marshall, Catherine, and Gretchen B. Rossman. 1994. *Designing Qualitative Research*. Newbury Park, CA: Sage Publications.

Massey, Douglas S. 1993. "Latinos, Poverty, and the Underclass: A New Agenda for Research." *Hispanic Journal of Behavioral Sciences* 15:449-475.

Massey, Douglas S. 1995. "The New Immigration and Ethnicity in the United States." *Population and Development Review* 21:631-652.

Massey, Douglas S. 1998. "March of Folly: U.S. Immigration Policy After NAFTA." Pp. 22-33 in *The American Prospect.*

Massey, Douglas S., Joaqín Arango, Graeme Hugo, Ali Kouaouci, Adela Pellegrino, and J. Edward Taylor. 1993. "Theories of International Migration: A Review and Appraisal." *Population and Development Review* 19:431-466.

Massey, Douglas S., Joaqín Arango, Graeme Hugo, Ali Kouaouci, Adela Pellegrino, and J. Edward Taylor. 1994. "An Evaluation of International Migration Theory: The North American Case." *Population and Development Review* 20:699-751.

McCall, Michal M., and Howard S. Becker. 1990. "Introduction." in *Symbolic Interaction and Cultural Studies*, edited by Howard S. Becker and Michal M. McCall. Chicago: University of Chicago Press.

McCall, Michal M., and Judith Wittner. 1990. "The Good News About Life History." Pp. 46-89 in *Symbolic Interaction and Cultural Studies*, edited by Howard S. Becker and Michal M. McCall. Chicago: University of Chicago Press.

McCarthy, Thomas. 1994. *The Critical Theory of Jurgen Habermas.* Cambridge, MA: MIT Press.

McCauley, Timothy. 1990. "Nativism and Social Closure: A Comparison of Four Social Movements." *International Journal of Comparative Sociology* 31:86-93.

McCleary, G.F. 1968. *The Malthusian Population Theory.* London: Faber & Faber Limited.

McCracken, Grant. 1988. *The Long Interview.* Newbury Park, CA: Sage.

McDonnell, Patrick J. 1996. "New Citizens From Latin America Back Clinton, Poll Finds." in *Los Angeles Times.*

Merton, Robert K. 1949. "Discrimination and the American Creed." Pp. 99-126 in *Discrimination and the National Welfare*, edited by Robert M. MacIver. New York: Harper & Row.

Miller, Randall M. 1985. "The Enemy Within: Some Effects of Foreign Immigrants on Antebellum Southern Cities." Pp. 390-413 in *Nativism, Discrimination, and Images of Immigrants*, edited by George E. Pozzetta. New York: Garland Publishing.

Mills, C. Wright. 1940. "Situated Actions and Vocabularies of Motive." *American Sociological Review* 5:904-913.

Mills, Nicolaus. 1996. "Lifeboat Ethics and Immigration Fears." *Dissent* 43:37-44.

Mitchell, Christopher. 1992. "Western Hemisphere Immigration and the United States Foreign Policy." University Park, PA: Pennsylvania State University Press.

Morgan, Scott M. 1987. "Regressivism in the Progressive Era: Immigrants, Eugenists, and Ethnic Displacement." Pp. 197-228 in *People in Upheaval*, edited by Scott Morgan and Elizabeth Colson. New York: Sage.

Muller, Thomas. 1997. "Nativism in the Mid-1990s." Pp. 105-118 in *Immigrants Out! The New Nativism and the Anti-Immigrant Impulse in the United States*, edited by Juan F. Perea. New York: New York University Press.

Murphy, Paul L. 1964. "Sources and Nature of Intolerance in the 1920s." *Journal of American History* 51:60-76.

Nagel, Joane. 1995. "Resource Competition Theories." *American Behavioral Scientist* 38:442-458.

Nagel, Joane. 1998. "Masculinity and nationalism: gender and sexuality in the making of nations." *Ethnic and Racial Studies* 21:242-269.

Neuman, Gerald L. 1996. *Strangers to the Constitution: Immigrants, Borders, and Fundamental Law*. Princeton, NJ: Princeton University Press.

Neuman, W. Lawrence. 1994. *Social Research Methods: Qualitative and Quantitative Approaches*. Boston: Allyn and Bacon.

Noel, Donald I. 1968. "A Theory of the Origin of Ethnic Stratification." *Social Problems* 16:157-172.

Noiriel, Gérard. 1996. *The French Melting Pot: Immigration, Citizenship, and National Identity*. Minneapolis: University of Minnesota Press.

Oakmura, Raymond. 1982. "The American Concentration Camps: A Cover-Up Through Euphemistic Terminology." *The Journal of Ethnic Studies* 10:95-108.

Olzak, Susan. 1992. *The Dynamics of Ethnic Competition and Conflict*. Stanford: Stanford University Press.

Omi, Michael, and Howard Winant. 1994. *Racial Formation in the United States: From the 1960s to the 1990s*. New York: Routledge.

Palmer, Howard. 1982. "Ethnic Relations in Wartime: Nationalism and European Minorities in Alberta during the Second World War." *Canadian Ethnic Studies* 14:1-23.

Palmer, Howard. 1986. "Strangers in the Land: A Canadian Perspective." *American Jewish History* 76:117-124.

Panayi, Panikos. 1990. "National and Racial Minorities in Total War." *Immigrants and Minorities* 9:178-194.

Papademetriou, Demetrios G. 1996. *The Faltering of European Integration: Migration and Related Issues*. Washington, DC: Carnegie Endowment for International Peace.

Papademetriou, Demetrios G., and Kimberly A. Hamilton. 1996. *Converging Paths to Restriction: French, Italian, and British Responses to*

Immigration. Washington, DC: Carnegie Endowment for International Peace.

Passel, Jeffrey S., and Barry Edmonston. 1994. "Immigration and Race: Recent Trends in Immigration to the United States." Pp. 31-71 in *Immigration and Ethnicity: The Integration of America's Newest Arrivals*, edited by Jeffrey S. Passel and Barry Edmonston. Washington, DC: Urban Institute Press.

Pedraza, Silvia. 1991. "Women and Migration: The Social Consequences of Gender." *Annual Review of Sociology* 17:303-325.

Pedraza, Silvia, and Rubén Rumbaut. 1995. *Origins and Destinies: Immigration, Race, and Ethnicity in America*. Belmont, CA: Wadsworth.

Perea, Juan F. 1992. "Demography and Distrust." *Minnesota Law Review* 77:269-373.

Perea, Juan F. 1997. "Introduction." Pp. 1-10 in *Immigrants Out! The New Nativism and the Anti-Immigrant Impulse in the United States*, edited by Juan F. Perea. New York: New York University Press.

Perea, Juan F. (Ed.). 1997. *Immigrants Out! The New Nativism and the Anti-Immigrant Impulse in the United States*. New York: New York University Press.

Peterson, Wallace C., and Paul S. Estenson. 1992. *Income, Employment, and Economic Growth*. New York: W.W. Norton & Company.

Phillips, Michael M. 1996. "Scholars Facing Joblessness Seek Curbs on Immigration." in *The Wall Street Journal*.

Pitt, Leonard. 1961. "The Beginnings of Nativism in California." *Pacific Historical Review* 30.

Portes, Alejandro, and Rubén G. Rumbaut. 1996. *Immigrant America: A Portrait*. Berkeley: University of California Press.

Portes, Alejandro, and Alex Stepick. 1993. *City on the Edge: A Transformation of Miami*. Berkeley: University of California Press.

Portes, Alejandro, and Min Zhou. 1993. "The New Second Generation: Segmented Assimilation and Its Variants." *Annals of the American Academy of Political and Social Science* 530:74-96.

Quillian, Lincoln. 1995. "Prejudice as a Response to Perceived Group Threat: Population Composition and Anti-Immigrant and Racial Prejudice in Europe." *American Sociological Review* 60:586-611.

Raphael, Marc Lee (Ed.). 1986. "A Reexamination of a Classic Work in American Jewish History: John Higham's *Strangers in the Land* [special issue]." *American Jewish History* 76:107-226.

Roberts, Dorothy E. 1997. "Who May Give Birth to Citizens? Reproduction, Eugenics, and Immigration." in *Immigrants Out! The New Nativism and the Anti-Immigrant Impulse in the United States*, edited by Juan F. Perea. New York: New York University Press.

Rodríguez, Néstor P. 1997. "The Social Construction of the U.S.-Mexico Border." in *Immigrants Out! The New Nativism and the Anti-Immigrant Impulse in the United States*, edited by Juan F. Perea. New York: New York University Press.

Roediger, David R. 1993. *The Wages of Whiteness: Race and the Making of the American Working Class*. London: Verso.

Roosens, Eugeen E. 1989. *Creating Ethnicity: The Process of Ethnogenesis*. Newbury Park, CA: Sage.

Rose, Peter I. 1993. "Tempest-Tost: Exile, Ethnicity, and the Politics of Rescue." *Sociological Forum* 8:5-24.

Rosenthal, Harry F. 1994. "Panel wants to stop illegal immigrants." Pp. 5A in *Detroit Free Press*.

Ross, William G. 1994. *Forging New Freedoms: Nativism, Education, and the Constitution, 1917-1927*. Lincoln: University of Nebraska Press.

Rothman, Hal K. 1998. *The Greening of a Nation? Environmentalism in the United States Since 1945*. Fort Worth, TX: Harcourt Brace College Publishers.

Rubin, Jay. 1978. "Black Nativism: The European Immigrant in Negro Thought, 1830-1860." *Phylon* 39:193-202.

Ruefle, William, William H. Ross, and Diane Mandell. 1993. "Attitudes Toward Southeast Asian Immigrants in a Wisconsin Community." *International Migration Review* 27:877-898.

Rumbaut, Rubén G. 1994. "The Crucible Within: Ethnic Identity, Self-Esteem, and Segmented Assimilation Among Children of Immigrants." *International Migration Review* 28:748-794.

Rumbaut, Rubén G. 1994. "Origins and Destinies: Immigration to the United States Since World War II." *Sociological Forum* 9:583-621.

Rumbaut, Rubén G. 1997. "Ties That Bind: Immigration and Immigrant Families in the United States." Pp. 3-46 in *Immigration and the Family*, edited by Alan Booth, Ann C. Crouter, and Nancy Landale. Mahwah, NJ: Lawrence Erlbaum Associates.

Samora, Julian. 1971. *Los Mojados: The Wetback Story*. Notre Dame: University of Notre Dame Press.

Sánchez, George J. 1997. "Face the Nation: Race, Immigration, and Rise of Nativism in Late Twentieth Century America." *International Migration Review* 31:1009-1030.

Sánchez, George J. 1993. *Becoming Mexican American: Ethnicity, Culture, and Identity in Chicano Los Angeles, 1900-1945*. New York: Oxford University Press.

Sartre, Jean-Paul. 1946. "Portrait of the Antisemite." *Partisan Review* 13:163-178.

Sassen, Saskia. 1996. *Losing Control? Sovereignty in an Age of Globalization.* New York: Columbia University Press.

Scheff, Thomas J. 1994. "Emotions and Identity: A Theory of Ethnic Nationalism." Pp. 277-303 in *Social Theory and the Politics of Identity,* edited by Craig Calhoun. Cambridge, MA: Blackwell.

Schutte, Gerhard. 1995. *What Racists Believe: Race Relations in South Africa and the United States.* Thousand Oaks, CA: Sage.

Immigration and Naturalization Service (INS), U.S. Department of Justice. 1996. *1994 Statistical Yearbook of the Immigration and Naturalization Service.* Washington, DC: U.S. Government Printing Office.

Shibutani, Tamotsu, and Kian M. Kwan. 1965. *Ethnic Stratification: A Comparative Approach.* New York: MacMillan Company.

Simon, Julian L. 1986. *Theory of Population and Economic Growth.* Oxford: Basil Blackwell.

Simon, Julian L. 1989. *The Economic Consequences of Immigration.* Oxford: Basil Blackwell (in association with the Cato Institute).

Simon, Julian L. 1990. *Population Matters: People, Resources, Environment, and Immigration.* New Brunswick: Transaction Publishers.

Simon, Julian L. 1996. *The Ultimate Resource 2.* Princeton: Princeton University Press.

Simon, Rita J. 1993. "Old Minorities, New Immigrants: Aspirations, Hopes, and Fears." *Annals of the American Academy of Political and Social Science* 530:61-73.

Simon, Rita J., and Susan H. Alexander. 1993. *The Ambivalent Welcome: Print Media, Public Opinion and Immigration.* Westport, CT: Praeger.

Smelser, Neil J. 1965. *Theory of Collective Behavior.* New York: The Free Press.

Smith, Anthony D. 1972. "Ethnocentrism, Nationalism, and Social Change." *International Journal of Comparative Sociology* 13:1-20.

Smith, James P., and Barry Edmonston. 1997. "The New Americans: Economic, Demographic, and Fiscal Effects of Immigration.". Washington, DC: National Academy Press.

Smith, Rogers M. 1988. "The "American Creed" and American Identity: The Limits of Liberal Citizenship in the United States." *Western Political Quarterly* 41:225-251.

Smith, Rogers M. 1997. *Civic Ideals: Conflicting Visions of Citizenship in U.S. History.* New Haven, CT: Yale University Press.

Smith, Susan J. 1993. "Immigration and nation-building in Canada and the United Kingdom." Pp. 50-77 in *Constructions of Race, Place, and Nation,* edited by Peter Jackson and Jan Penrose. Minneapolis: University of Minnesota Press.

Smith, Wade A. 1981. "Racial Tolerance as a Function of Group Position." *American Sociological Review* 46:558-573.

Snow, C.P. 1964. *The Two Cultures: and a Second Look.* Cambridge: Cambridge University Press.

Song, Miri, and David Parker. 1995. "Commonality, Difference and the Dynamics of Disclosure in In-Depth Interviewing." *Sociology* 29:241-256.

Sowell, Thomas. 1980. *Ethnic America: A History.* New York: Basic Books.

Sowell, Thomas. 1987. *A Conflict of Visions.* New York: William Morrow and Company.

Sowell, Thomas. 1994. *Race and Culture: A World View.* New York: Basic Books.

Soysal, Yasemin Nuhoglu. 1994. *Limits of Citizenship: Migrants and Postnational Membership in Europe*. Chicago: University of Chicago.

Star, Alexander. 1997. "Don't Look Back: A proposal for our roots-obsessed culture." Pp. 81-83 in *The New Yorker*.

State Ballot Measures. [Online] Available http://Primary98.ss.ca.gov/Returns/prop/, July 10, 1998.

Stefancic, Jean. 1997. "Funding the Nativist Agenda." Pp. 119-135 in *Immigrants Out! The New Nativism and the Anti-Immigrant Impulse in the United States*, edited by Juan F. Perea. New York: New York University Press.

Steinberg, Stephen. 1989. *The Ethnic Myth: Race, Ethnicity, and Class in America*. Boston: Beacon Press.

Stone, John. 1995. "Race, Ethnicity, and the Weberian Legacy." *American Behavioral Scientist* 38:391-406.

Strauss, Anselm L. 1991. *Qualitative Analysis For Social Scientists*. Cambridge: Cambridge University Press.

Streisand, Betsy. Is it hasta la vista for bilingual ed? [Online] Available http:www.usnews.com/usnews/ news/enghigh.htm, November 18, 1997.

Takaki, Ronald. 1990. *Iron Cages: Race and Culture in 19th-Century America*. New York: Oxford University Press.

Takaki, Ronald. 1994. "Introduction." Pp. 3-8 in *From Different Shores: Perspectives on Race and Ethnicity in America*, edited by Ronald Takaki. New York: Oxford University Press.

Takaki, Ronald. 1994. "Reflections on Racial Patterns in America." Pp. 24-35 in *From Different Shores: Perspectives on Race and Ethnicity in America*, edited by Ronald Takaki. New York: Oxford University Press.

Tatalovich, Raymond. 1993. "Who Sponsors Official Language Legislation? A Comparative Analysis of Fourteen States." *Southeastern Political Review* 21:721-735.

Tatalovich, Raymond. 1997. "Official English as Nativist Backlash." Pp. 78-102 in *Immigrants Out! The New Nativism and the Anti-Immigrant Impulse in the United States*, edited by Juan F. Perea. New York: New York University Press.

Teitelbaum, Michael S., and Jay Winter. 1998. *A Question of Numbers: High Immigration, Low Fertility, and the Politics of National Identity*. New York: Hill & Wang.

Thomas, W. I., and Dorothy Swayne Thomas. 1928. *The Child in America*. New York: Knopf.

Thurow, Lester C. 1980. *The Zero-Sum Society: Distribution and the Possibilities of Economic Change*. New York: Penguin Books.

Tilly, Charles. 1998. *Durable Inequality*. Berkeley: University of California Press.

Torres, Luis A. 1993. "The National English Only Movement, Past and Future." Pp. 251-264 in *American Mosaic: Selected Readings on America's Multicultural Heritage*, edited by Young I. Song and Eugene C. Kim. Englewood Cliffs, NJ: Prentice Hall.

Turner, Jonathan H. 1991. *The Structure of Sociological Theory*. Belmont, CA: Wadsworth Publishing.

Turner, Jonathan H. 1994. *Sociology: Concepts and Uses*. New York: McGraw-Hill.

Ueda, Reed. 1981. "Naturalization and Citizenship." Pp. 734-748 in *Harvard Encyclopedia of American Ethnic Groups*, edited by Stephan Thernstrom. Cambridge, MA: Harvard University Press.

U.S. Commission on Immigration Reform. 1997. "Becoming an American: Immigration and Immigrant Policy." Washington, DC: U.S. Commission on Immigration Reform.

Walby, Sylvia. 1996. "Woman and Nation." in *Mapping the Nation*, edited by Gopal Balakrishnan. London: Verso.

Waldinger, Roger. 1996. "Who Makes the Beds? Who washes the dishes?: Black/Immigrant Competition Reassessed." Pp. 265-288 in *Immigrants and Immigration Policy: Individual Skills, Family Ties, and Group Identities*, edited by H.O. Duleep and Phanindr V. Wunnava: JAI Press.

Waldinger, Roger. 1996a. *Still the Promised City? African Americans and New Immigrants in Post-Industrial New York*. Cambridge, MA: Harvard University Press.

Waters, Mary. 1990. *Ethnic Options: Choosing Identities in America*. Berkeley: University of California Press.

Weber, Max. 1968. *Economy and Society*. New York: Bedminster Press.

Webster, Yehudi O. 1992. *The Racialization of America*. New York: St. Martin's Press.

Weiner, Myron. 1995. *The Global Migration Crisis*. New York: Harper Collins College Publishers.

Weiner, Myron. 1996. "Ethics, National Sovereignty and the Controls of Immigration." *International Migration Review* 30:171-197.

Wellman, David T. 1994. *Portraits of White Racism*. Cambridge: Cambridge University Press.

Wimmer, Andreas. 1997. "Explaining xenophobia and racism: a critical review of current research approaches." *Ethnic and Racial Studies* 20:17-41.

Winant, Howard. 1994. *Racial Conditions: Politics, Theory, Comparisons*. Minneapolis: University of Minnesota Press.

Winant, Howard. 1997. "Behind Blue Eyes: Whiteness and Contemporary U.S. Racial Politics." in *Off White*, edited by Michelle Fine, Louis Weis, Linda C. Powell, and L. Munn Wong. New York: Routledge.

Wittke, Carl. 1936. *German-Americans and the World War*. Columbus, OH: Ohio State Archaeological and Historical Society.

Woldemikael, Tekle M. 1987. "Assertion Versus Accommodation: A Comparative Approach to Intergroup Relations." *American Behavioral Scientist* 30:411-428.

Wright, Lawrence. 1994. "One Drop of Blood." Pp. 46-55 in *The New Yorker*.

Yinger, J. Milton. 1994. *Ethnicity: Source of Conflict? Source of Strength?* Albany, NY: State University of New York Press.

Zavella, Patricia. 1997. "The Tables Are Turned: Immigration, Poverty, and Social Conflict in California Communities." in *Immigrants Out! The New Nativism and the Anti-Immigrant Impulse in the United States*, edited by Juan F. Perea. New York: New York University Press.

Zimmerman, Warren. 1995. "Migrants and Refugees: A Threat to Security?" Pp. 88-116 in *Threatened Peoples, Threatened Borders: World Migration and U.S. Policy*, edited by Michael S. Teitelbaum and Myron Weiner. New York: W.W. Norton & Company.

Index